D1069070

GOD'S ANSWERS TO PERSONAL PROBLEMS

WHAT THE
BIBLE SAYS
ABOUT

GOD'S ANSWERS TO
PERSONAL PROBLEMS

By

Carl W. Pruitt

College Press Publishing Company, Joplin, Missouri

Copyright © 1982
College Press Publishing Company

Printed and bound in the
United States of America
All Rights Reserved

Library of Congress Catalog Card Number: 82-71252
International Standard Book Number: 0-89900-086-X

Dedicated

to

my Father and Mother

in their 90th year

who have stored up treasures of love

to help deal with personal problems.

Table of Contents

TABLE OF CONTENTS

Preface

This book is an outgrowth of a number of different lectures for conventions, leadership conferences, workshops in local churches, articles in religious journals, Bible School lessons, sermons I've preached and last, but certainly not least, my presentations in college psychology classes at Kentucky Christian College. Some of the psychological insights have been presented in a university classroom at Ohio University, Ironton Branch.

I have found the material to be helpful to many of the students who have presented their personal problems and to me as their counselor at the college. The clients who trusted me with their burdens in the last few years in which I have been in private practice as a marriage and family counselor have appreciated the Biblical perspective.

The wide scope of experiences from which this book took root and eventually came to fruition is indicative of its possible use for the reader. It will be useful to the minister as he prepares to deal with the vital issues facing people today; it will come in handy for the woman who is asked to speak for the Parent Teachers Association. Perhaps your Bible school class or study group would choose to deal with "What the Bible Says About God's Answers to Personal Problems." (The division into thirteen specific lessons makes it fit the Bible School quarterly system.) Since many of the chapters were first tested in a Bible college classroom in a number of different courses in psychology, the material would be helpful in Christian ministries' courses, Christian education and Bible courses where the practical value of the Bible to meet personal problems would be stressed.

Most of all this book is designed to help meet individual problems. Each chapter stands alone. It addresses a specific problem and intends to bring Scriptural insights to bear on that problem.

Introduction

THE RELATIONSHIP OF THE CHRISTIAN, THE BIBLE AND THE COUNSELOR IN MEETING PERSONAL PROBLEMS

The Christian Has Problems, Too

Everyone has problems. Few would argue with that statement. However, the way some Christians approach life, it would lead you to think that God is supposed to protect them from troubles. "What did I do to deserve this? Here I am living a Christian life and this happens to me. In fact, I've had more problems since I've become a Christian." The implication is, "If I had known what I know now, I would never have become a Christian." The conclusion is, "What has it gotten me?" To them the Christian experience isn't a relationship with the Lord that speaks to them through His Word. It is a business transaction. They bought the line, "Be a Christian and discover the road to peace and prosperity." The person and the book have not measured up to the advertisement and they want their money back. After all, isn't Christianity guaranteed? These people want the preacher to know that they tried his church and his sermons and found them wanting. They even tried the Bible and couldn't understand it.

One could argue that this approach is but a rationalization for a person who simply didn't want the Christian experience badly enough to work at it and who wasn't willing to put the effort into it to make it work. Or perhaps they entered into it like a lot of other areas of life, even marriage. They will try it. If they don't like it, they'll try something else. Consequently, it is not by accident that they have given up on Christianity.

Perhaps there is a kernel of truth in this view that must be acknowledged by the Christian worker. The kernel of truth is, of course, that the Bible does provide answers to problems and God is present in our lives. The question for the Christian worker is how to present this in a realistic and accurate way.

If in the midst of people's problems we assert that the Bible is the answer and abandon them to their own devices to understand how that Book can be effective, we have manipulated them into thinking it is a book of miracles—in the sense of a charm or a fetish. Instead of a book that must be studied systematically, worked at diligently and applied fervently, we've given the impression that somehow the Bible can skirt the whole issue of motivation completely. Even the Lord can't help a person become that which their own stubborn wills refuse to accept. Jesus' frequent encounters with the Pharisees are manifold witness to this obstacle (Matthew 23:27-28). Instead of showing how Christianity will make you happy, help your business and bring reconciliation to your marital problems of twenty-five years, just once I would like to hear someone tell it like it really is. If you pursue happiness you lose it. This comes as a by-product of the Christian life and not as a commodity that can be packaged and delivered. If you receive Christ in order to help your business, you may still go bankrupt. Family problems may be so entrenched that it is too little, too late. The seeds of years of disruption have resulted in a harvest of destruction. Honest is the minister who insists that neither he nor anyone can guarantee the act of conversion will save a marriage. (Often when it is done merely to save a marriage, it is just that—to save the marriage, not to save one's soul for eternity, not to establish a commitment but as a panacea.) Sometimes it is nothing but another smooth con job.

Jesus said of himself, "Foxes have holes and birds of the air have nests, but the Son of Man has no place to lay his head" (Luke 9:58, NIV). He dispelled the notion that his disciples were going to be benefactors of an earthly kingdom. They were instead to be servants (John 13). He espoused a realignment of priorities to disclaim the importance of material things (Matthew 6:25-34). Of course, Jesus balanced this with other claims such as the concept that his "burden was easy" (Matthew 20:12). In considering Jesus' ministry, it would be difficult to conclude that He drew a multitude with an easy Gospel. Our Lord "never promised a rose garden" or "an easy road." In fact, Jesus insisted that life in His service would be difficult and dangerous (Matthew 16:24).

The Apostle Paul's ministry demonstrates this reference to trials in II Corinthians 11:22-28. Quite significantly the Apostle to the Gentiles concludes this list with the sobering thought that "besides everything else, I face daily the pressure of my concern for all the churches" (II Cor. 11:28, NIV). The Christian may assume extra burdens and responsibilities that may lead to pressure in his King's service.

The choice to receive Christ often divides a house, as some make a positive decision while others diametrically oppose that stand. As a Bible college professor I have become increasingly aware of the considerable number of students who make decisions to enter a special vocation, such as the ministry, Christian education director, or missionary, under strong parental opposition. Sometimes even the decision to become a Christian has been opposed.

So Christians have problems. Many come about by the mere fact that they live in the same world and are confronted with the same pressures as anyone else. They must acknowledge the same principles of life as anyone else. If a Christian pushes himself beyond his limits, he can have a so-called "nervous breakdown." The Christian is not unaffected by severe problems in his background or a tragic sudden death in his family. The Christian does have more resources in the Bible, in his Christian faith and within the Christian community to work through his problems. But being a Christian does not permit us to short circuit the process. James put it succinctly:

> Consider it pure joy, my brothers, whenever you face trials of many kinds, because you know that the testing of your faith develops perseverance. Perseverance must finish its work so that you may be mature and complete, not lacking anything (James 1:2-4, NIV).

The Scriptures teach that problems provide the occasion to deal with our trials and grow from the experience. This approach is a far cry from the view of some well-meaning Christians.

Occasionally when Christians come to me with personal problems they have already been instructed by their friends and sometimes their pastor "to read their Bible and pray." Then they confide in me that when they do they feel even worse. Isn't the Bible the answer to personal problems? Isn't prayer powerful? Yes, I believe the Bible provides answers to personal problems, but I don't believe it is the answer in the sense this pastor meant. People are impatient —they want a quick fix, a panacea. In short, they are looking for magic. The Bible becomes the aspirin for the headache —quick relief or a drug to calm them down. We have a pill for everything. It is human nature to want the alleviation of symptoms without the painful process of rooting out the causes and changing the behavior that perpetuates the problem.

For the Bible to be helpful one needs to relate certain Scriptures that fit the situation. Usually some explanation is necessary to show their appropriateness. I have known people to claim that their procedure was to let the Bible fall open to any passage. I am not saying that God would not be a part of that process or that random chance might not allow a helpful passage to emerge, but why must one insist on divorcing the minds God gave us from coming to grips with Biblical insights to meet personal problems. The creator endowed us with a magnificent mental capacity. I believe He expects us to use what He has given to enhance the quality of our lives.

This Book and Personal Problems

This book addresses itself to a systematic presentation of Biblical answers to the personal problems Christians and non-Christians face in their lives and in the experience of their family and friends. No one is exempt from problems. The problems presented here are typical situations. The answers found within this book are intended to strengthen one's appreciation for how specific Scriptures do relate to a wide range of struggles. It is my conviction that personal faith holds life together even when the answers are not readily discovered. After all faith itself is defined as "being sure of what we hope for and certain of what we do not see" (Hebrews 11:1, NIV). Most personal problems defy simple solutions. If you have a mathematical problem you can come up with a solution. Personal problems are dilemmas that must be processed over time. People are so uptight or resistant that they cannot receive it all at once, if indeed the dilemma could be sorted out for them and the formula provided. I hope that as people read this book they might be open to how God's Word speaks to our personal problems and will enter into a serious process of growth in relationship to their personal problems.

The Bible and a firm personal faith, that is accompanied by the pastoral ministry of the church, undergirds each of us to endure the trials of life. Although the journey may be long and hard, growth can emerge from these painful circumstances. An understanding of how the Bible relates to our human dilemmas fosters growth. Each chapter in this book on personal problems brings Scripture to bear on a problem that most of us do or will face.

The Scope of the Book

In the first chapter, "Facing Crisis," basic knowledge is given to help provide an appreciation of what happens to a person in the midst of crisis. The role of the church, various caring people and the resources of the Word of God in coping with the trauma are presented. Special attention is upon I Corinthians 13:13 in this opening chapter.

Chapter two treats the problem usually considered to be number one on a stress scale—death. The impact of the loss of a spouse is considered life's greatest stress. The profound message of the Scripture on this inescapable theme helps to lay a foundation for dealing with death. Most people do not fully understand how the loss of a loved one affects every segment of life. Understanding of the reaction to the death helps the grief stricken to know they aren't cracking up. Grief is not pathological but a normal pattern that most people endure. In time, with God's help through His Word and His people, one can emerge stronger as he is forced to marshall his strengths when it seems he cannot go on.

Chapter three deals with the most life-threatening experience known to human mind—depression. More people commit suicide while caught in the grip of depression than for any other reason. An awareness of the various signs of depression, treatment approaches and Scriptural resources form a context for finding personal help and insight into ministering among the depressed. The experience of David as recorded in Psalm 42 and 43 provides the background for this chapter.

The factors which set the stage for anxiety in this "age of anxiety" are surveyed in chapter four. Also causes each person may bring within himself or herself are demonstrated in this chapter as well as some treatment procedures. The vital effect of Scriptural focus on a God who is in control and cares for us sums up chapter four.

The Bible indicates that the problems "Children of Broken Homes" experience, which loom as a gigantic concern today are not a new problem. Biblical references in both the Old Testament and the New suggest an ageless concern of God's people. The parents' skills in coping with the time of desertion, divorce or death strongly determine the resources the child will draw upon in the midst of this loss. What the parent can expect to endure during the adjustment period is suggested. Guidelines for helping the child and various solutions, including counseling, are discussed.

The knotty question that every psychologist and, in fact, every person must settle personally regarding the nature of man comes under discussion in chapter six. Is man basically good or evil? How one answers this question largely determines the potential he sees in someone else. "The Struggle for Meaningful Maturity" in this chapter finds certain principles of maturity in the picture of Jesus' growth in Luke 2:52.

A well-worn passage of Scripture, Proverbs 31, speaks forcefully to the current problem many couples find themselves caught up in—"The Two-Career Marriage." A life scope approach is employed in treating the adjustments that couples struggle with throughout their married lives. Personal experience, insights from developmental psychology and the undergirding of the Word are designed to strengthen couples who face career expectations and the economic pressures in today's world.

The "Empty Nest Syndrome" comes into focus in chapter eight. The impact that some experience at this point in life is discussed along with suggestions as to how to anticipate this transitional period and make the most of the changing relationships with children, the possible son or daughter-in-law and the role of grandparents. Some general guidelines are suggested from both the Old Testament and New Testament to help bring these changing roles into proper perspective.

The purpose of chapter nine, "Understanding and Ministering Among the Aging," is to contrast contemporary attitudes toward aging with a Biblical approach, enhance understanding of the aging process, and to share Scriptural resources and basic concepts of ministry that relate to older persons.

The next chapter shares one of the great sociological problems of our times—widowhood. With the life expectancy increasing and the data that reveals women usually outlive men, the magnitude of adjustment is greater for widows. Widowers—though fewer in number—also must wrestle with grief and adjustment to this life-changing event. The impact of the death of the spouse and the intricate process of the sociological factors that follow are recognized in this chapter. The role of the church and Scripture give us clues to a ministry among the widowed.

"Coping with Anger" forces us to take a long look at a recurring problem among many people. All of us would probably like to be able to handle our negative feelings better. This chapter gives us Scriptural warning against the neglect of this destructive emotion. Both Jesus and Paul and other Biblical references help us find answers to coping with anger. Insights from psychology help us better understand our personal dynamics. Assertiveness procedures in a Biblical context aid us in channelling the energy of anger into appropriate assertion that can assist our ministry.

Of all the problems discussed in this book, two seem to recur most frequently in my lectures and in my work with families. These involve depression and discipline. In chapter twelve, "Developing Discipline" is discussed. Parents often feel confused on this topic. Various approaches have been advocated; each child is different and the emotional involvement of the parents combine to make this a challenging area. This is an enormously complex theme but the Scriptures do provide some clear guidelines. Surprisingly for some, contemporary psychological approaches appear to be in agreement on basic style of parenting.

"Maximizing Marriage and Family Life" zeroes in on the account in Genesis where suggestions are found which, if utilized, can help every couple to maximize the potential of their marriage. The God who created us male and female and instituted marriage has provided helpful directions for enriching marriage and fulfilling family life.

Counselors: Secular and Christian

Many of the people that I see in my counseling practice are Christians. Some of these people are extremely skeptical of "secular counselors." They are fearful that their Christian values will not be appreciated. In some cases this is a very valid point. No one should receive that treatment from any professional; especially not from a counselor. A non-believing therapist may not intend any harm to his client. Ethical standards of his profession demand that he respect his client's views. Theoretically, one need not agree with us to help us draw on the resources available to us to promote our healing. Practically, however, values have a way of creeping into the counseling encounter. The counselor is a very special person whose views and feelings are important to most clients. But also how can one draw on the client's resources when one does not appreciate or simply does not understand those resources. A Christian counselor who has an intimate acquaintance with the Lord and a thorough preparation in Biblical studies is a tremendous advantage to the Christian client.

At times other therapists who are not Christians send me referrals. Most of the time they simply realize that my background enables me to easily identify with the person and to appreciate the resources available to him. (In some cases, say with a minister, my own background helps to unravel some possible dimensions of the problem that another therapist who is not a minister may miss.) I suspect that occasionally any talk of religion causes some secular counselors to push the panic button. Their own hangups make them uncomfortable with any talk of God. Of course, they might be fearful they would inappropriately over-react to the counselee. Quite obviously a counselor does not have to be a minister who is a "pastoral counselor," nor does he or she have to be in a Christian counseling center or attached to a local church in some way to be a capable Christian therapist. The counselor may simply be a psychotherapist who is thoroughly trained and credentialed and who is a Christian. In the same way we speak of a physician who is an excellent surgeon and a Christian. Some professionals simply prefer to be thought of as 'counselor' rather than with the title 'Christian therapist.'

Under whatever designation a particular therapist prefers to view himself or herself, it is clear within the profession that there is an interest in the integration of theology and psychology and the importance of religious issues and values. The divisions within the American Psychological Association and the American Personnel and Guidance Association evidence the growing interest in the religious perspective in the healing process. Various journals such as the *Journal of Religion and Health,* the *Journal of Pastoral Care,* the *Journal of Psychology and Theology, Pastoral Psychology* and the *Journal of Jewish Life and Thought* exemplify the concern to integrate the healing arts of man, Scripture, and the role of church and synagogue in stimulating mental health. A vast number of books in recent years speak to the use of Scripture in resolving problems. At the end of each chapter the sources that touch upon the specific topic will be listed for those who wish further reading. At the end of this introduction some general sources are given that treat the integration of personal problems and the Scriptures.

Although there appears to be a general recognition of the value of religion in healing among professionals and even in government as is witnessed by the funding of pastoral counseling centers through the Community Mental Health Act of 1963, there nevertheless are critics of religion in the area of mental health. Sigmund Freud was critical of religion as is Albert Ellis, an influential contemporary psychologist. The scathing attacks of these and others may be based to some extent on their experiences with neurotic patients. They assume that there is a cause and effect relationship between their faith and their emotional problems. Disturbed people often misinterpret their religion. Anyone can misapply the Scripture and make his own personal religion morbid, punitive, legalistic or destructive. The misapplication of some people who are emotionally troubled does not invalidate the source of the person's religion. In the case of sacred Scriptures these views certainly do not invalidate the Book.

As a pastoral counselor, I have observed that frequently people who come to me for help have misapplied the Scripture. For example, at times people will often view the Bible as legalistic and thoroughly judgmental. Grace and love are overlooked. They read the Bible through the dark glasses of their personal pathology even if it is depression from the faulty patterns that have been handed down to them from their teachers of religion. It is my hope that this book will provide some assistance to people in the church today who are wondering how the Bible really speaks to their problems.

Chapter One

FACING CRISIS

The Importance of the Church's Role

Sooner or later everyone experiences an excruciating crisis. Sooner or later most of us will have occasion to minister to another in crisis. Ministers, elders and deacons and others who take seriously their pastoral responsibilities will routinely encounter people facing crisis.

The church—the family of God—is in a most enviable position to help. The minister and other church workers are nearly always appreciated when a crisis strikes. The minister is expected to take the initiative when he hears of a sickness, death, injury and other problems. He does not have to wait—but is expected to intervene as quickly as possible.

An understanding of crisis is necessary for all helpers who would move courageously into those situations to minister. When this knowledge is lacking there is a tendency to shrink back from the church's unique opportunities for ministry. Hopefully, this chapter will help provide understanding and insight in facing crisis.

Scriptural Reference

What the church has to offer at the time of crisis finds expression in the proclamation of Scripture. Familiar Scriptures such as Psalm 23, Romans 8:28 and other favorite passages are especially helpful in times when one's capacity to reflect upon the unfamiliar is severely limited. A particular favorite Scripture would be helpful.

Over a period of 15 years in the located ministry and in the past 10 years in the ministry of pastoral counseling, I have

1

found one Scripture to be of immense comfort. It has been the focus of many funeral sermons as well as pastoral encounters in a number of crisis situations. It has been as valuable in the counseling room as the graveside or in the pulpit.

I Corinthians 13:13 provides the focal point of this chapter's Biblical reference. "Now abideth faith, hope and love —these three, but the greatest of these is love."

The thirteenth chapter stands as one of the most applauded passages in God's Word. Although the literary beauty and Biblical excellence of this familiar Scripture are widely acknowledged among Christians, the appreciation of the significance of I Corinthians 13:13 may not be as widely acclaimed as it relates to the borderline situation of human experience.

In a crisis a person feels as if his whole world has been swept away—that nothing of importance remains. Imagine, for example, the wife whose husband has died. She exclaims that "nothing is left." Paul's words from I Corinthians 13:13 challenge this sweeping generalization of the crisis-ridden individual. These words confront the troubled person with the affirmation of permanence when it seems that nothing remains.

In a chapter in *The Vital Balance* entitled "The Intangibles" the renowned psychiatrist William Menninger acclaims that this is the greatest short essay ever written and further states that the apostle Paul provides insight into the "human 'situation,' the dilemma of all people in this role."[1] He calls Paul's words in I Corinthians 13:13 the famous "social prescription." Elaborating on this he writes:

---

1. Karl Menninger, *The Vital Balance* (New York: Viking Press, 1963), p. 358.

Today, after twenty centuries, this prescription is taken very seriously in psychiatry. We would even go so far as to say that it describes the basic philosophy of the psychiatrist. Faith, hope and love are the three great intangibles in his effective functioning.[2]

Before coming again to precisely how I Corinthians 13:13 speaks to crisis, this chapter will explore the dynamics of crisis to increase awareness of the experience. Then help will be provided to better understand how a caretaker can minister at the time of crisis.

I. *Definition of Crisis*

Each individual has a personal way to deal with problems that develop. One person may have a trusted friend to talk with, another plays sports, still another takes a long walk through the woods. When a person reaches a point that the ordinary coping mechanisms no longer work—this is a crisis.

In a crisis changes occur that interfere with normal functioning. The student is unable to concentrate on his studies, the factory worker may become careless in the shop and begin to make mistakes. The ability of the executive to make important decisions is seriously impaired. Relationships with spouse and children suffer. In the midst of a crisis the secure, happy, outgoing, friendly person may become sad, withdrawn and curt in dealing with people. A crisis will usually produce dramatic changes in relationships. A person does not appear to be himself.

---

2. *Ibid.*

II. *Change as a Predictor of Crisis*

Excessive change in life is a predictor of crisis. The following stress scale indicates the effects of various life experiences on an individual.[3] Many of these situations are commonly considered to be positive: getting married, the birth of a child, receiving a promotion are usually thought of as occasions of celebration. However, each of these events represents a significant change in a person's life. An accumulation of these life-changing events tends to trigger some stress.

Unfortunately some people tend to handle stress in such a way as to accumulate additional stress. Take for example a widow. She has recently experienced the most traumatic situation that can be measured on the stress scale. If she attempts to cope with her grief by pretending it doesn't exist instead of gradually working through her painful experience, she may set herself up for problems. Let us say, for example, that she deals with the pain by denial. She is encouraged to escape, make a move from her small rural surroundings to a suburban area. She leaves family and friends to strike out on her own in an unknown environment. She has not worked for twenty years yet she enters the work force in a totally foreign and sometimes hostile environment. Having left family, friends and church she abandons her life style— her support system. She may well be creating her own crisis.

---

3. James C. Coleman, James N. Butcher, Robert C. Carson, *Abnormal Psychology and Modern Life* (6th ed) (Glenview: Scott, Foresman and Company, 1980), p. 110. The Social Readjustment Rating Scale (SRRS) along with a thorough presentation of the "Adjustive Demands and Stress" and "Reactions to Life Stress" pp. 105-126 present helpful insights regarding the impact of change on mental health.

Rank	Social Readjustment Rating Scale Life Event	Mean Value
1	Death of spouse	100
2	Divorce	73
3	Marital separation	65
4	Jail term	63
5	Death of close family member	63
6	Personal injury or illness	53
7	Marriage	50
8	Fired at work	47
9	Marital reconciliation	45
10	Retirement	45
11	Change in health of family member	44
12	Pregnancy	40
13	Sex difficulties	39
14	Gain of new family member	39
15	Business readjustment	39
16	Change in financial state	38
17	Death of close friend	37
18	Change to different line of work	36
19	Change in number of arguments with spouse	35
20	Mortgage over $10,000	31
21	Foreclosure of mortgage or loan	30
22	Change in responsibilities at work	29
23	Son or daughter leaving home	29
24	Trouble with in-laws	29
25	Outstanding personal achievement	28
26	Wife begins or stops work	26
27	Begin or end school	26
28	Change in living conditions	25
29	Revision of personal habits	24
30	Trouble with boss	23
31	Change in work hours or conditions	20
32	Change in residence	20
33	Change in schools	20
34	Change in recreation	19
35	Change in church activities	19
36	Change in social activities	18
37	Mortgage or loan less than $10,000	17
38	Change in sleeping habits	16
39	Change in number of family get-togethers	15
40	Change in eating habits	15
41	Vacation	13
42	Christmas	12
43	Minor violations of the law	11

Source: T. H. Holmes and R. H. Rahe, "The Social Readjustment Rating Scale," *Journal of Psychosomatic Research II* (1967): 213-18. Reprinted with permission. Copyright © 1967, Pergamon Press, Ltd.

Although this illustration is a bit far-fetched, some people will resort to this extreme.

A person undergoing change needs to exercise caution lest he set himself up for a crisis. Of course, each person is different. One person may view a traumatic loss as a challenge while another person may be devastated by it. However, as a general rule a person in the midst of a traumatic situation should be careful not to compound his grief by excessive changes.

III. *Crisis as a turning point*

Usually crisis is viewed as completely negative. A person in crisis stands at the crossroads. A person may either shrink backward into maladaptive patterns or plunge ahead to new growth. Switzer contends that "the very nature of crisis is that it forces change and readjustment."[4] Lydia Rapoport contends that "a crisis is a call to new action, the challenge it provokes may bring forth new coping mechanisms which serve to strengthen the individual's adaptive capacity and thereby, in general, to raise his level of mental health."[5] Present-day psychologists are aware that a crisis can actually result in a person mobilizing their resources in directions of growth. For the Bible student this concept comes as no surprise.

> Consider it all joy, my brethren, when you encounter various trials; knowing that the testing of your faith produces endurance. And let endurance have its perfect result, that

---

4. David Switzer, *The Minister As Crisis Counselor* (Nashville: Abingdon Press, 1974), p. 56.

5. Lydia Rapoport, "The State of Crisis: Some Theoretical Considerations" in *Crisis Intervention: Selected Readings,* Howard J. Parad, ed. (1965), pp. 22-31.

you may be perfect and complete, lacking in nothing (James 1:2-4 N.A.S.).[6]

The Lord never promised the Christian life would be easy. In fact, trials can provide an opportunity for growth as we are strengthened by them. Sorrows and disappointments threaten our faith. If we endure the test our faith becomes stronger. James goes as far as to insist that instead of bemoaning our fate we rejoice in the occasion that can result in our eventual growth. A good athlete looks forward to a challenge to test his strength and his skill. Without the hard training and the actual competition he can never realize his potential. So the Christian is prepared spiritually by the trials that test his strength. The trials provide the opportunity for renewed growth.

Time Limits of Crisis

A crisis does not continue indefinitely. A crisis will last on the average of from one to six weeks. A solution is sought to re-establish the previous level of balance that the person can deal with more comfortably. The person will conclude that "things are back to normal." At this juncture, it must be acknowledged that some people are apparently in crisis all the time. For some people a crisis is a part of their life style and is due to their inadequacy in social functioning. These people have multiple problems which do not fit into the scope of this chapter. This disorder is not dependent

---

6. The King James version translates the word "temptation" instead of trials. The context is not the idea of seduction into sin but purifying and testing through trials.

so much on external events but upon a continual internal tension and chronic anxiety.

Two Kinds of Crisis

Theorists in crisis intervention distinguish between situational crisis or accidental crisis and developmental crisis.[7] Accidental or situational crises are as the designation implies —the result of certain disturbing situations. An "accident" intervenes in the normal course of life. Situational or accidental crises are unpredictable. Frequently they represent a loss of something basic to an individual life-support system: the loss of a job, the death of a spouse, divorce, sickness, a move from a community where one is secure to unfamiliar and uncharted terrain—socially and vocationally.

Developmental crisis occurs as a part of an individual's normal growth process. Some of these crises include birth, entering school, adolescence, choosing a mate, entering a vocation, middle age, death of a spouse and one's own death. "These experiences are the occasions of crisis for an individual to the extent that they pose problems for which his previous coping abilities are inadequate."[8] For example, adolescence presents a crisis because so many changes are

---

7. For a discussion of these terms as they relate to a minister's role see David Switzer, *The Minister As Crisis Counselor*, pp. 43-56 and Howard Clinebell in *Basic Types of Pastoral Counseling* (Nashville, Abingdon Press, 1966), pp. 157-175. The original source of the terms "developmental" and "accidental" is psychiatrist Gerald Caplan, *Principles of Preventive Psychiatry* (New York: Basic Books, 1964), pp. 26-55. Erick Erikson provides the foundational work for the concept of developmental crisis in his chapter "Eight Ages of Man" in *Childhood and Society* (New York: W. W. Norton, 1950), pp. 247-274.

8. Clinebell, *Basic Types of Pastoral Counseling*, p. 159.

taking place physically, emotionally and spiritually for which the adolescent is unprepared. An emerging awareness of one's sexuality and attraction to the opposite sex, dating, career decisions, the personalizing of religion now that the person is able to conceptualize theological concepts for the first time—are a cluster of the issues the adolescent must face. Although adolescence provides perhaps the most dramatic illustration, one is only middle-aged once or old once. Each developmental stage presents a crisis—an occasion to pull back and regress or to meet the challenge by forging ahead in the direction of growth.

Caring for the Person in Crisis

Understanding the dynamics of crisis provides an important precept, but more specific instruction becomes necessary to help in a time of crisis. The approach of those trained in crisis intervention lends itself to use by the non-professional who simply wants to help a friend. An attempt is made to combine insights from crisis theory for the professional as well as approaches that are especially relevant when helping a friend. The outline for this approach consists of concepts based on a widely-used framework in crisis intervention procedures.

Contact. The first procedure essential in any form of counseling involves establishing a trusting relationship. The establishment and maintenance of this vital relationship— called in counseling "rapport" cannot be overemphasized. The concept of love found within the New Testament embodies the essence of the relationship between counselor and the client. If the kind of relationship is established in

9

which a person can share his deepest darkest secrets—
his bad side as well as his good side and be accepted, then
a vital element is realized. The would-be counselor would
do well to read again the account of Jesus' encounter with
the woman at the well (John 4:5-26). Jesus did not condone her life style. He did convey his love. He made it clear—
he did not condemn her but challenged her to new life.

In times of trouble a person lacks self-acceptance and
love of self. A caring, accepting relationship helps with this
fundamental problem.

To firmly establish rapport the helping person must attempt to get inside the hurting person's world. There is
something marvelously therapeutic—almost magical—about
having a chance to get a heavy burden off our chest. The
troubled individual must sense an openness and acceptance
before he will feel comfortable in letting go and spilling his
deepest concerns. A supervisor once spoke of "being in
their corner." What would it be like to be in their predicament. The Indians allegedly had a motto: "Walk a mile in
their moccasins." Reflections which accurately convey what
the counselor hears, help to convey to the person that the
helper listens and identifies with him.

Having identified with the person there may be a temptation to provide an instant cure. Caution must be exercised
in plunging ahead too quickly. The deeply troubled person
may be very reluctant to accept an instant solution. He
probably views his problem as catastrophic. Moving in quickly
with advice will usually mean rejection even when it appears
that it is wanted. The problem with most advice is that it
comes "from the giver's, not the user's, point of view." Paul
Welter distinguishes between occasions when advice may

be appropriate and when it is not. "Advice works with a problem because it has a solution that does not depend on a point of view. But a predicament is a vastly more complex situation than a problem."[9]

Whether the situation the person presents be called a problem or a predicament—one thing is for sure—it must be viewed from the presenter's perspective. What has worked for you may not work for him. Even if the situations and application apparently fit, the person may reject a pat answer to what appears to him to be a gigantic and unique problem. There is a tendency when hurting to feel that no one has ever been through anything quite like this before.

Respect his or her feelings. Recognize their uniqueness. Get an over-all picture. One of the most frequent mistakes of the lay person as well as the professional is the failure to assess what counselors call the "presenting problem."

A question such as, "What brings you here today?" is appropriate for the minister or other professional when an appointment has been made. When talking with a friend a question such as, "I have a hunch you want to talk to me about something" or "How do you see your problem?" would help get started. Another important question involves assessing the precipitating crisis. "Why did you decide to come now?" or "What's been happening with you in the last couple of weeks?" help to bring into focus whether the present distress is of recent origin or whether it is a persistent pattern. If no precipitating event can be found, it is assumed that there is no present crisis. Then the task as David Switzer

---

9. A helpful source for helping a friend is Paul Avelter's book, *How to Help a Friend*. The chapter in this book, "Crisis—A Short-Term Predicament in Huge Proportion," pp. 66-71 in *How to Help a Friend* (Wheaton: Tyndale House, 1978) is especially relevant to the discussion to helping in a time of crisis.

puts it is "to determine what type of help the person does need at this time: long-term counseling, occasional supportive counseling, referral to another professional or agency. Then the procedure should be pursued."[10]

If the origin is recent and it can be identified then a crisis intervention approach is appropriate. If the origin is recent, a continual opportunity to vent the emotions surrounding the presenting problem is appropriate. It may appear that the problem is merely logical, demanding a rational and speedy decision. Usually much more is involved and needs to be processed emotionally. A goal of crisis counseling as well as most approaches to therapy involves catharsis. An atmosphere must be provided for a free expression of strong negative emotions. There appears to be a common core of emotions that people experience in times of crisis: hate, anger and guilt will usually surface. These may be difficult for a friend to deal with especially if he or other significant people in his own life are the target. As a friend one is more personally involved. This is an advantage the more objective professional counselor who is previously unknown has. Many counselors look upon it as "transference" or anger that actually applies to other people in the counselee's background. At any rate since the therapist does not have an ongoing and personal involvement he will not be as sensitive to these angry feelings. Therapists in the course of their training learn to cope with these feelings and bring their productivity into the treatment process. The therapist has an advantage that the friend must keep in mind.

Although the professional has an advantage, the role of the friend cannot be underestimated. The friend can achieve

---

10. David Switzer, *The Minister As Crisis Counselor*, p. 79.

a relationship and stick with the person through thick and thin. When a threat to the person's safety becomes apparent, the friend can arrange for relatives or other people to provide support.

Focus. The dilemma must be brought into focus. The threat has to be explored and identified. Some definite formulation of the crisis which both the helper and the distressed person can agree is important. This formulation helps to make the crisis more tangible and available for careful security. In crisis intervention relevent information to the immediate crisis is discussed. In contrast to a "free association" approach where everything may be considered, in a crisis counseling only the crisis is brought into focus. All material is explored in relationship to the presenting problem.

Cope. An assessment of all the available resources among family and friends, community resources and especially the spiritual help of church and Scripture must be thoroughly explored.

In the midst of these external resources, the available internal strengths should be stressed. The individual's own coping mechanisms, ability to make decisions and generally to come to grips with the present crisis is absolutely indispensable. The caretaker must never take over completely for the person unless absolutely necessary. The more the distressed person is forced to draw on personal resources, the more prepared the person will be to cope with trials in the future

Scriptural Resources

To expand the Scriptural resources introduced at the outset of this chapter, it is fitting to more completely reflect upon the great trilogy of faith, hope and love found in I Corinthians 13:13.

1. *Faith.* Hebrews 11:1 sets forth the most familiar execution of faith. The author of Hebrews begins with a definition of faith. "Now faith is being sure of what we hope for and certain of what we do not see." It is this absolute certainty that speaks to the crisis-ridden person. In a crisis a situation with uncertain outcome presents itself. At times like these when we cannot see the way clear, faith adds another dimension to human existence. Faith helps to provide stability when the outcome cannot be clearly calculated by human judgment.

Faith gives assurance. Frequent phrases heard are "I guess" or "perhaps" or "maybe." Is there anything about which we can be certain? Faith provides that certainty. Here is something we can count on. Desperately man grasps this grounding for life. One thing is for sure—God is. Here is something the Christian need not guess at. As the Apostle Paul testified, "I know whom I have believed . . ." (II Tim. 1:12). The Christian does not "think" or "guess" but with the Apostle Paul insists "I know whom I have believed."

Barclay maintains that "faith is hope that is absolutely certain. . . . It is not the hope which looks forward with wistful longing; it is the hope which looks forward with utter certainty. It is the hope which is founded on a conviction."[11]

Faith is an integral part of everyone's life. Everyone has faith in something or someone. The driver has faith in his automobile—that it will not fly apart when barreling down the highway at top speed. The scientist has faith in his method, the philosopher in his philosophy, the patient in the surgeon's

11. William Barclay, The Letter to the Hebrews. *The Daily Study Bible* (Philadelphia: Westminster Press, 1955), pp. 144-145.

knife. The lover has faith in the object of his love. Everyone has faith in something or someone. The Christian is no different except his faith is in God, His Word, His promises and His purposes. Paul put it succinctly in the clarion call of the reformation, "The just shall live by faith" (Romans 1:17). The Christian lives by faith—that's what keeps him going, provides inspiration and direction and stability for life. It is good for all seasons—not merely in fair weather.

In order to stand the stress of life the house of our life must be solid. This is the point Jesus established at the conclusion of His Sermon on the Mount as presented in the parable of the two builders (Matthew 7:24-27, KJV).

> Therefore whosoever heareth these sayings of mind, and doeth them, I will liken him unto a wise man, which built his house upon a rock: And the rain descended, and the floods came, and the winds blew and beat upon that house; and it fell not: for it was founded upon a rock. And every one that heareth these sayings of mine, and doeth them not, shall be likened unto a foolish man, which built his house upon the sand: And the rain descended, and the floods came, and the winds blew and beat upon that house: and it fell: and great was the fall of it.

Jesus often referred to Himself as a rock. In this Scripture He clearly accents the importance of His words and His teachings. McGarvey contends that:

> No life can be founded upon Christ's teachings unless it be founded also upon faith and trust in His personality. For this we must dig deep, for as St. Gregory says, "God is not to be found on the surface."[12]

12. J. W. McGarvey and Philip Y. Pendleton, *The Fourfold Gospel* (Standard Publishing Foundation. n.d.), p. 269.

McGarvey further assesses the impact of this Scripture:

> The imagery of this passage would be impressive any-where, but is especially so when used before an audience accustomed to the fierceness of an Eastern tempest. Rains, floods, etc. represent collectively the trials, the temptations and persecutions which come upon us from without. There comes a time in every life when these things throng together and test the resources of our strength.[13]

2. *Hope.* Hope is also foundational to life. Faith and hope are intricately tied together. Faith is the assurance of things hoped for. A personal faith in our Lord gives us grounds for hope. When a person becomes a Christian, he is reborn to a living hope according to Peter (I Peter 1:3). This hope is based upon a resurrected Lord. Hope transcends this present earthly existence and reaches into eternity. However, hope is not merely for the next world but for the present world as well. Peter wrote to people in the midst of trials. This "living hope" of which Peter writes was for time and eternity both. Paul viewed the heathen world as being without hope (Ephesians 2:12). The Christian has forever beside him the Lord who conquered death and provides' hope to live for and hope that sustains us through eternity. The Christian, then, has a hope that nothing can destroy because it transcends earthly existence. This transcendent quality of hope lifts man above the world extending the significance and meaning of his life.

As hope nurtured the persecuted Christians in the ancient world so it has also in modern times as well. Karl Menninger cites countless situations in which hope made the difference

---

13. *Ibid.*

in lives of the hopelessly ill, both physically and mentally. He also shares experiences from those that were interned during World War II and how hope sustained them.[14] The survival potential of hope is also dramatically set forth by Frankl's prison experience.[15] Although the situations most people face are not this dramatic, others may be on the very brink of disaster.

On an occasion I worked with a person that had a serious problem with depression. She had thought about suicide many times. I asked her why she had never done it. She replied, "I am a Christian and never lost hope." Her faith in God and her hope kept her alive. These great intangibles coupled together to sustain her in her darkest hours. She went on to relate another aspect of hope—she felt God had finally sent someone to help her that she as a Christian could trust and she knew she would get better. She did get better. In clinical practice I have seen people get better, even before they arrived in my office, because they had regained hope. Hope can sustain people through the darkest and most terrible night if they believe that dawn will come. In the midst of crisis, it must never be underestimated the role caretakers provide in conveying that hope.

3. *Love*. Several years ago as a participant in a clinical pastoral education program, I entered a large state mental institution. The chaplain, sensing my uneasiness at the foreboding experience, asked how I felt about being there. After I shared my uneasiness and fears, he stated, "Well,

---

14. Karl Menninger, *The Vital Balance* (New York: Viking Press, 1963), pp. 388-393.

15. Viktor E. Frankl, *Man's Search for Meaning: An Introduction to Logotherapy* (Boston: Beacon Press, 1962), pp. 74-78.

one thing for sure—they are more afraid of you than you are of them." During my training in that facility among some deeply disturbed residents, the truth of that comment stood in bold relief. Later when asking them what one characteristic was more common than any other, they answered without hesitation, "fear—fear of relationship." The Scripture states the answer in "perfect love drives out fear" (I John 4:18, NIV).

Even a mentally healthy person may shrink back into his own shell in times of crisis. Then as never before a tender person is needed to come alongside and convey to the fearful and lonely person that he is accepted as he is. In so doing that caretaker speaks for the "God of all comfort" who is the very embodiment of love for "God is love" (I John 4:16).

In focusing on resources the vast spiritual community of the church comes into focus. The person who is "out of community" and "alienated" can find refuge in the fellowship of the church. The church that takes seriously a pastoral role to troubled individuals will discover ample support groups, caretakers and a functioning shepherd system to be the ministry of Christ (John 21:17; Acts 20:28).

Conclusion

Since crisis involves the most threatening changes of human existence, a person must be aware of that which remains. "And now these three remain: faith, hope and love. But the greatest of these is love" (I Corinthians 13:13, NIV). The greatest intangible Christian virtue in theology is anchored to the Rock of Ages. "Jesus Christ is the same yesterday and today and forever" (Hebrews 13:8, NIV).

DISCUSSION QUESTIONS: *Facing Crisis*

1. How does I Corinthians 13:13 fit into a discussion of crisis? What is the role of the church in a crisis?

2. Looking at the Social Readjustment Rating Scale, what do you learn about stress events? How do these apply to your life?

3. Everyone must deal with problems. How would you distinguish between the problems that cause stress and a crisis?

4. Define crisis. What role does change play on crisis? Explain.

5. Explain how change affects different people in different ways. What caution needs to be taken?

6. Is crisis negative? Explain your answer. What Scriptural references would you cite to defend your answer?

7. Distinguish between developmental and situational or accidental crises? How do these concepts fit your personal experience? How can the awareness of these two kinds of crises help you in counseling someone else?

8. What Scriptural reference provides a model for caring for a person—especially in making contact.

9. Why is advice inappropriate? What is meant by a "presenting problem"? Paul Welter uses the term "predicament" to describe the situation people experience in crisis. Generally, counselors employ the term "presenting problem." Are these contradictory concepts? Explain your answer.

10. What common goal does crisis intervention have along with other approaches to therapy. Explain its importance.

11. Role play a crisis situation. Have an individual in class choose some situation he is familiar with. (Remember

19

a crisis situation need not be one solitary problem. Very often it involves a series of stressful events. See the chart in this chapter for examples. The presentor may have several developmental and accidental crises). The con- selor should attempt to use the outline: Contact, Focus, Cope. Have the rest of the class assist the person by providing feedback. The counselor needs to identify whether he or she will take the role of a helping friend or a professional counselor. Employ Scriptural resources as appears appropriate. What distinction needs to be made between the role of the professional counselor and a friend who helps a friend. Discuss advantages and disadvantages of each.

Chapter Two

DEALING WITH DEATH

A Paradox in Society

Joseph Bayly claimed that "the last thing most people want to talk about is death."[1] Whether we talk about it or not, of course we are all dealing with it. Much in society suggests the denial of death. Stress is placed upon youth—vitality—"grabbing all the gusto in life" because "we only go around once." We talk about life insurance—never death insurance—which is what it really is. People "pass away" or are "deceased" but seldom are spoken of as dead. Ernest Becker has gone so far as to say that we are obsessed with the denial of death. He insists that the fear of death is the principle source of all our activities.[2]

On the other hand one could argue that there exists at the present time an obsession with the theme of death. The interest of young people in courses in death suggests a fascination and a search for ways to deal with it. Magazines and books are flooding the market. Television talk shows discuss it. Medical doctors and ministers work together in ministering to the dying in the Hospice[3] programs. People appear more willing to talk about it. So as can be observed in many areas of society, times are changing; concepts and values are in a state of flux. It appears that this openness to dealing with death can hardly be less than a positive breakthrough for the dignity of man.

---

1. Joseph Bayly, *The View From A Hearse* (Elgin: David C. Cook Publishing Company, 1969). (Back Cover)

2. Ernest Becker, *The Denial of Death* (New York: Macmillan Publishing, 1973), p. ix.

3. Sandol Stoddard, *The Hospice Movement* (New York: Vintage Books, 1978).

21

A Paradox in the Scripture

As one views common reactions to death by Christians one also confronts a paradox. On one hand Christians assume that death represents a time of victory. They approach the death as a time of rejoicing. The context is that death represents a fulfillment of hope. Death is the direction to which life moves and since the faithful are at home with God, the sense of a homecoming celebration is in order.

On the other hand Christians contend that the expression of grief is appropriate. They insist that they do mourn and they cannot deny the painful feelings. They need their faith, their fellowship of Christians and they insist that to deny their grief would be less than honest to themselves and to God.

In actuality this apparent contradiction is resolved in a truly Biblical approach to death and grief.[4]

Scriptural Focus

The Scripture that brings this alleged contradiction into focus and provides a balanced view of grief is found in I Thessalonians 4:13. Here Paul indicates that Christians are not to "grieve like the rest of men, who have no hope." This Scripture could be taken to mean that the Christian is not to grieve at all. In light of the other New Testament teaching, Paul apparently teaches that there is to be a difference between the despair of the pagan and the grief of the

---

4. R. Scott Sullender, "Saint Paul's Approach to Grief: Clarifying the Ambiguity" *Religion and Health* 20 (Spring, 1981) pp. 63-74.

Oscar Cullman, "Immortality of the Soul or Resurrection of the Dead" in *Immortality and Resurrection* ed. Krister Stendahl (New York: The Macmillan Company, 1965), pp. 9-53.

Christians who look forward to the fulfillment of hope in the resurrection.

Christ himself wept at the tomb of Lazarus. After Stephen had been stoned "devout men carried Stephen to his burial and made great lamentations over him" (Acts 8:2). (The very concept of lamentations may be traced into Hebrew history and is found most clearly in the book of the Old Testament by that name, Lamentations.) The Ephesian elders, anticipating that they would not see Paul again, wept (Acts 20:36-38).

In addition to these examples of open expression of grief in the New Testament, one may explore other passages of Paul which manifest the appropriateness of the grieving process (Romans 12:5; I Corinthians 12:26; and I Corinthians 7:29-31). The Lord Himself set forth the most specific statement on grief as a growth-oriented, positive experience when he said, "Blessed are those who mourn, for they will be comforted" (Matthew 5:4, NIV).

Paul acknowledged the naturalness of grief in times of bereavement, yet he tempers this grief as different from the non-believer's grief. The non-believer's loss is final, while the Christian's loss is temporary. So grief is reduced by the knowledge of eternal life. Paul contends that those who minister to the grieving may be comforted by this knowledge.

Paul in I Thessalonians 4:13 synchronizes the hope of reunion with the dead with an understanding of the reality of the loss that death brings. Restraint is suggested—not because the expression of feelings are wrong but because of the consolation found in the conviction that loss is temporary. The Christian is not to wallow in despair and hopelessness but to affirm hope and anticipate the eternal joys prepared by the Lord Himself (John 14).

Understanding the Grief Process

Physical Reactions. As observed, grief is a normal process. Unfortunately, some Christians expect that the process is unnecessary and inappropriate. However, the Scripture gives credence to the expression of emotion. A kind of stoicism expected by some Christians is just that—stoicism—and not Christianity.[5] Because of this misconception of the validity of this natural release of emotions, the believer may try desperately to hold the tears back—to refrain from any open display of feelings, lest they be considered unchristian. This pressure to maintain a front does little to assist one's emotional, physical and spiritual well-being.

Shock may be the first reaction. "I can't believe this is happening" is often heard. At the funeral home the bereaved may keep up a front, not because of any forced resolution but simply because the full impact of the loss has not hit. Another physical reaction is of queasiness in the stomach and a sharp pain in the abdomen. Other uncomfortable physical reactions may accompany this feeling, such as a quickening heartbeat. A loss of physical strength may be apparent. At the funeral service, especially at the time of commital, the long walk may be difficult. Strong, robust men have been known to give way under the strain of grief.

A frequent serious condition often follows the death of a loved one—that is loss of appetite and subsequent loss of weight. If the person is aged or in a weakened physical condition due to sickness at the outset, the grief can result in a serious threat to the bereaved.[6]

---

5. *Ibid.*

6. David Maddison and Viola Agnes. "The Health in the Year Following Bereavement" *Journal of Psychosomatic Research* 12 (July, 1968), pp. 297-306; Colin Murray Parkes, "The First Year of Bereavement" *Psychiatry* 33 (November 1970), pp. 444-467.

Emotional Reactions. A natural reaction is to express the sorrow through tears and through a constant retelling of experience surrounding the painful loss as well as the rehearsing of the detailed memories of the loved one. Reactions to grief often include guilt feelings. "If I had only taken him to the hospital sooner, this might not have happened" is frequently heard. At times like these people can be very unreasonable in their guilt. Another common reaction is that of angry feelings. Anger may surface in the form of specific complaints against the physician, other family members, the church, and even God.

Spiritual Reactions. It can be observed how closely the physical, emotional and spiritual reactions intertwine. How one feels physically certainly relates to ones mood swings. A person who is run down physically—whose diet is inadequate—will be more inclined to be short with people and to become angry, to feel guilty and to become depressed in ways that are reflected in his spiritual life. A person's spiritual life is severely tested when he is physically and emotionally drained.

Wholistic Guildelines to Ministry with the Grief Stricken

A wholistic approach to helping the bereaved takes into consideration the whole person: physically, emotionally, socially and spiritually. How can ministry most effectively meet these needs? Specific guidelines are suggested to assist in this ministry.

1. *The proclamation of the Word.* There is simply no substitute for preaching theological themes that pronounce hope to the individual. Preventive mental health can be provided by preaching. Preaching is a form of counseling; it

can minister to people's emotional needs as well as to their intellectual needs. Sermons dealing with the practical areas such as "Coping with Grief" speak to the entire congregation. Every person has dealt with this subject or will in the future. People in the congregation desire to hear what the Bible says on the subject from their own preacher.

2. *Christian education on the subject of "death."* Christian educators must not leave this growing field of interest to a secular approach. The Biblical perspectives must be heard and what better place than in Bible School and special interest groups on prayer meeting nights. Children must be taught in the church and most of all in the home on those special occasions when children are inquiring about death.

3. *Be present.* In the initial times of grief, the bereaved may be experiencing shock. They may not be very communicative, but they nevertheless need the presence of a trusted Christian friend. Support is crucial. They need a person to lean on, to touch them physically, to meet some simple needs that may overwhelm them. A word of caution about doing too much. The more the bereaved person can comfortably handle, the more personal phone calls and occasions that force them to confront their loss and handle basic responsibilities, the better. Don't take over but support them.

The presence of a close friend or a loved one early in the grieving process is important. Make sure someone is there. A Christian can fill in for those times when relatives cannot be present. Being present is far more important than the frequent concern, "What do I say?" There are no simple formulas. Let the bereaved set the pace.

4. *Encourage talk about the lost loved one.* As the bereaved gets over the shock, more and more discussion will

focus on the lost loved one. Sometimes this process of sharing memories of the past—painful and pleasurable—begins immediately. Listen and encourage the grief process. The more they talk the sooner they will get better. As a friend or counselor, it is very helpful to initiate the grief process. The listener gives the person permission to share a part of his or her life. This can be one of the most rewarding experiences of the caretaker's life.

5. *Give attention to physical needs.* One of the most helpful ideas is to bring in food or provide a meal after the funeral. Encouraging the person to eat out or to share in meals at church can be helpful. If transportation is a problem, provide a means for the person to go shopping. "Meals on Wheels" and other community programs are helpful in some cases. Draw attention to community resources when they are needed. Without leaving the impression that physical deterioration is the norm—lest it become a self-fulfilled prophecy—become aware of the person's physical condition especially where health problems and increasing age are a factor.

6. *Remember social needs.* As time goes on more and more of the grief process will probably be dealt with. Attention to the social needs of the person who may be alone or lack transportation is important. Most churches have many social occasions—movies, occasions to dine, and various other outlets—which may need to be encouraged.

7. *Be accepting.* Sometimes in a time of grief anger may be ventilated toward the caretaker or other people. The caretakers must absorb this and not take it too seriously.

8. *Consider the ministry of various support groups in the church.* Classes, women's groups, Bible Study groups and groups designed especially to help people with grief

need to be created in the local church.[7] The discussion of legal and financial problems by professionals would assist in coping with some knotty problems. Groups involving people who have successfully dealt with their grief will give the most-recently bereaved courage to face their grief. They will also provide insights to cope with the adjustment of life without the loved one.

9. *Provide reading material.* Give the sorrowing books or pamphlets for devotional needs and to assist with the grieving process. Booklets on grief such as one by Edgar Jackson, *Understanding Grief,* (New York: Abingdon Press, 1957) or Granger Westberg's, *Good Grief,* (Philadelphia: Fortress Press, 1962) can be helpful in facilitating the grief process. When the bereaved recognizes the experience that seems so devastating is common to other people and he is not "losing his mind," this alone can be helpful. Books that integrate Scriptural insights with the experience of loss are especially helpful. If you suggest that the person read his Bible, provide specific references. It can be frustrating to say "read the Bible" without direction into specific Scriptures that would be helpful. Write the Scriptures down so the person can remember them and turn to the references in times of need.

10. *Include a ministry to the bereaved in the church's shepherding procedures.* A ministry to the bereaved must not be left to chance. Too many neglected individuals attest to the very slip-shod approach that many congregations take to this ministry. Perhaps the church fits right in with a death-denying society and does not care to become involved.

---

7. John B. Oman, *Group Counseling in the Church* (Minneapolis: Augsburg Publishing House, 1972). Carl W. Pruitt, "The Widow's Group," *The Lookout,* 93(September 20, 1981):7.

A procedure that follows up on the ministry of the minister, his calls and his sermon at the service, should be implemented. People who see people from the church at the funeral home and are aware of the follow-up of the church to meet their needs will appreciate this witness to the church's message of hope. Some system needs to include a ministry to people who are not members of the local church, but whose minister helps by preaching the sermon. A systematic involvement of church members, at the funeral home and in a concerned ministry, will open the door for the Gospel in this time of maximum human need.

Scriptural Resources

Both the Old Testament and the New Testament bring vital insight to the subject of dealing with death. One of the most frequent laments of the bereaved is, "Why did this happen?" As one reads the Old Testament it becomes clear that God did not intend for man to die. It was disobedience to God's will that ushered in death (Genesis 2:17). It was the Evil One who was responsible for the temptation and fall of man. Implicit in the frequent question as to why this has happened is a fear that the bereaved person has fallen out of favor with God and He is punishing them personally by taking the loved one. Jesus clarified this point by His statement that the timing of death is not due to personal sin (Luke 13:1-4). Sin is involved in the sense that Adam's sin caused each person to suffer the consequences through death (Romans 5:12-14).

Modern man seems no less confused on the question than ancient man. Job's friends wanted him to acknowledge the sin that they were convinced had brought his calamity

29

upon him. This creeps into the Christian's life in times of trouble. A person's emotions seem to take over for one's better judgment and God is blamed for sickness and death. In the midst of grief anger surfaces and the bereaved complains to God. In view of theology a more fitting target of anger would be the devil who tempted man and caused his fall. God sent His Son with His redemptive message which ultimately resulted in Christ's death (John 3:16; I Corinthians 15:3; Hebrews 1:1-3). By His death and triumphant resurrection—death—the last enemy is overcome (II Timothy 1:10; I Corinthians 15:26).

Christ has thus removed the sting of death by His own atoning death. Therefore the Christian along with the apostle Paul may look forward to a positive gain (Philippians 1:21) in sharing in the glorified presence of the Son of God (II Corinthians 5:8).

The fact that the sting of death, the fear of ultimate annihilation or ultimate damnation, is removed does not make death a welcome guest. Death is the shadow we must walk in on the way to the eternal glory. Death represents physical pain and emotional separation from earthly ties. Paul considered it an "enemy" and certainly it is none the less for us.

The Christian knows that finally the troubles, sorrows and death shall be done away.

> And God shall wipe away all tears from their eyes; and there shall be no more death, neither sorrow, nor crying, neither shall there be any more pain; for the former things are passed away (Revelation 21:4, KJV).

No earthly person could fully comprehend the horror of sin which resulted in man's death. This was what Christ came to destroy, death and the Evil One. In accomplishing

30

His redemptive work He took upon Himself the sins of the world and in so doing died a uniquely horrible death of separation and sorrow (Mark 15:34). As the Lamb of God slain from the foundations of the world He is uniquely qualified to bring comfort as we approach death. He certainly understands the horror of death but also knows first hand the glories prepared for the faithful.

As Christ comforted His disciples who faced the loss of their Lord, He comforts us with peace beyond that which anyone else can give.

> Let not your heart be troubled: ye believe in God, believe also in me. In my Father's house are many mansions: if it were not so, I would have told you. I go to prepare a place for you. And if I go and prepare a place for you, I will come again, and receive you unto myself; that where I am, there ye may be also. . . . Peace I leave with you, my peace I give unto you; not as the world giveth, give I unto you. Let not your heart be troubled, neither let it be afraid (John 14:1-3, 27, KJV).

DISCUSSION QUESTIONS: *Dealing with Death*

1. Explain the strange paradox concerning death in society and in the approach of many Christians.
2. What Scripture provides the focal point of this chapter. How can it best be interpreted in the light of other Scriptures?
3. Discuss the grief process. How does the experience of grief involve one physically, emotionally and spiritually?
4. Discuss the significance of a wholistic approach to helping the grief stricken. Explain how the guidelines are wholistic.

5. Brainstorm on how your local church or class might implement some of these and other suggestions in ministering among the bereaved.

6. In helping a sorrowing person why is attention to the person's physical needs important? How about the social needs?

7. What unique role may a caretaker who has been through a similar situation have? How could this be administered to provide maximum benefit? Can you think of any potential difficulties with this model?

8. Do you think the shepherding program where you worship covers a ministry to the bereaved? If so how does it work? Ask some of the people involved to explain how it works. Could other classes help? What could your Bible School class, a study group or college class, or group of interested individuals initiate?

9. Role play a grief situation in class. Try to stay with the person's feelings—be supportive. Help the grieving person get out his feelings concerning the loss. Help him rehearse some of the events from the lost person's life. Here is a suggested role play situation: A woman of 53 lost her father very suddenly of a heart attack. She and her father were quite close. Her mother died two years ago. (To do this role play you will need a person to re-enact the role of the bereaved and one person to be the counselor. Assign four others to write down observations and suggestions. Others may want to come in later with their suggestions. Be sure that observations are well balanced with supportive and positive reflections.)

10. Have a person who has been through a grief experience share what was hardest. What resources were found

in Scripture meditation, in the sermons, and from family and friends. (Be sure the individual's grief is not so fresh as to be difficult for them and for the observers).

11. What Scriptural resources were found to be most helpful. Explain your answer.

Chapter Three

DEALING WITH DEPRESSION

An Immense Problem

Of all the problems treated in this book depression is potentially the most serious. According to figures based on the National Institute of Mental Health (1978) and the President's Commission on Mental Health (1978), 53,500,000 individuals suffer from mild to moderate depression. Each year two hundred thousand individuals attempt suicide and twenty-six thousand or more die from suicide. (Incidents of suicide may be much higher since a large number are never reported as suicide).[1] Probably 80% of all those who commit suicide were depressed at the time.

Depression ranges from the "blues" to the depths of despair in an acute depressive disorder. Everyone experiences depression at some level. No one is immune. Christians experience it and the Scripture indicates that even as great a man as David had serious bouts with depression. In fact, Psalm 42 and 43 were probably written under the inspiration of the Holy Spirit to help us deal with depression.

Scriptural Focus

Why are you downcast, O my soul? Why so disturbed within me? Put your hope in God, for I will yet praise him, my Saviour and my God (Psalm 42:5, NIV).

---

1. James C. Coleman, James N. Butcher and Robert C. Carson, *Abnormal Psychology and Modern Life* (6th ed.) (Glenview: Scott Foresman and Company, 1980), p. 4. The figures clearly indicate that the suicide threat is not limited to the United States but is a serious problem in several countries around the world, p. 583. Coleman also provides a good overview of depression in this popular text.

Ray Stedman insists that repetition of this refrain indicates that this Psalm "is intended to teach us how to handle our blue moods . . ." He goes on to maintain that "the answer to each blue mood is, 'Hope thou in God,' wait for God. He is working out his purposes and if you hang on you will yet praise him."[2]

Context

The probable time of composition is the year of David's flight from Jerusalem because of Absalom's revolt. David was driven into exile. Although there is no specific mention of this in the psalm, many scholars believe it to reflect this low point in David's life. Clearly the psalm represents a time of deep depression. David does not accept this mood as irreversible; he did something to change it.

G. Rawlinson writing in the *Pulpit Commentary* depicts the setting of this Psalm: "The psalm is chiefly an outpouring of sorrow and complaint; but it is still an 'instruction,' inasmuch as it teaches the lesson that in the deepest gulf of sorrow (v. 7) the soul may still turn to God, and rest itself in hope on him (vs. 5, 8)."[3]

Most people who are depressed can relate traumatic situations that led to their depression. David was certainly no exception. The kind of grief David was experiencing at this particular juncture in his life is one of the most common stressors resulting in depression. David actually lost his son

---

2. Ray C. Stedman, *Folk Psalms of Faith* (Glendale: Regal G/L Publications, 1973), p. 131.

3. H. D. Spence and Joseph S. Exell, eds., *The Pulpit Commentary*, The Psalms by G. Rawlinson, E. R. Conder and W. Clarkson (Grand Rapids: Wm. B. Eerdmans Publishing Company, 1950), Vo. 8:330.

in a very real way before his actual death; his rebellion could well have triggered a loss reaction. Other losses such as status, loss of financial position and, of course, the death of a significant person may give rise to the symptoms of grief.

Scope of the Chapter

This chapter will begin by exploring typical characteristics of the depressed person, some of the treatment approaches, and additional Scriptural resources available. A second look at Psalm 42 and 43 will complete the chapter.

I. *David Provides a Detailed Description of Depression.*

1. *Dejection and loss.* The general appearance of the depressed individual is one of dejection and sadness. In this psalm David is dejected. The present situation in David's life certainly contributed to those feelings of dejection. David was driven into exile. There he was a fugitive in his own kingdom. Coupled with this loss of his kingdom was a son who had rebelled against him. Not only had he rebelled against him and betrayed him, he was actually out to kill him.

David's cry at the time of his son Absolam's death unleashes all that pent-up frustration and grief he had experienced over a long period of time.

"O my son, Absolam, my son, my son Absolam! Would God I had died for thee, O Absolam, my son, my son!" (II Sam. 18:33, KJV).

Losses often result in a depressive reaction. Job provides one of the earliest Scriptural examples of depression over the loss of his houses, his substance, his children and his health (Job 6:2, 9).

36

2. *Insomnia.* Insomnia frequently accompanies depression. Waking and failing to go back to sleep is a common pattern.

David suffered sleeplessness. "My tears have been my food day and night" (Ps. 42:3, NIV). Many a depressed person could identify with David's sleeplessness. Not only does the depressed person have difficulty falling off to sleep —he often finds himself awakening long before his usual time.

One of the basic reasons people seek medication is "to get a good night's rest." Medication may be helpful in this regard. Unfortunately, it also presents a double threat. A person may become addicted to this easy access to sleep and potential to alter his mood level. Also sleeping pills and other medication for depression provide accessibility to one of the most frequent means of suicide.

3. *Physical exhaustion.* The depressed person is often run down physically. When a person becomes overextended physically and emotioally, the door is wide open for depression. Many housewives, business executives, students and others leave themselves in a precarious position as they push hard to prepare their work, close a business deal or study for exams.

In my experience as a professor and counselor on a college campus, I have observed that the times prior to and immediately following examinations are the times when more students are depressed than any other time. Sometimes they simply overextend themselves both physically and emotionally. Undoubtedly the kind of high expectations the good student has of achieving superior grades contributes to his depression while the poor student's sense of desperation contributes to his already low self-esteem surrounding his grade performance.

Several Scriptural references record occasions when depression may well have been related to physical exhaustion. Elijah became depressed to the point that he wanted to die. He was greatly discouraged over the rebellion of Israel. The problem seems to have been complicated when he completely depleted his physical and emotional energy. The angel comforted him by meeting his need for food (I Kings 19:4-8). This may also have been a contributing factor to Jonah's wish that he might die. Jonah was extremely angry with God that He had spared the city. Perhaps the very fact that he had worked so desperately contributed to this narrow legalistic and negative thinking pattern as well as his physical exhaustion. Although this passage is not as clearly related to physical exhaustion as with Elijah's fatigue, the hot sun and the long wait would have added to his already apparent wish to die.

David may well have been exhausted physically and mentally from his race to flee Absolam. The constant pressure together with his flight may have added to his depression.

When David claimed that his tears had been his meat day and night, this is an indication that he had not even eaten. Depression affects a person's appetite. The inability to eat obviously determines one's physical condition. Without proper nourishment a person's physical well being will rapidly deteriorate.

4. *Sensitivity to rejection and a tendency to withdraw.* A depressed person is extremely sensitive and easily hurt. Most individuals recognize that they handle criticism according to the kind of day they have had—how they feel about themselves at that time. David was no different. He was going through a lot of trouble and he was sensitive. He was sensitive toward those who had mistreated him. Most of all

he was sensitive toward God and questioned whether God had forsaken him: "Why art thou so far from me?"

A depressed person feels abandoned—forsaken. This is what David was experiencing. Elijah and Jonah withdrew to be alone. One of the earliest descriptions of depression found in the book of Job describes his sensitivity to the crude handling of his feelings by his "friends" and supposed "comforters." Job exclaimed that his friends were "miserable comforters . . ." (Job 16:2).

5. *Overgeneralization and magnification of negative thought patterns.* When depressed a person draws an extremely broad conclusion based on inadequate evidence. David makes many sweeping generalizations: he is parched (42:1-3), overwhelmed (42:6-7), forsaken by God (42:9-10—nearly the entire Psalm contains that theme) in absolute gloom (43:2), broken (42:10), laid low (43:5). It is characteristic of the depressed individual to view everything in catastrophic terms, the worst conceivable extreme.

When depressed the positive tends to be minimized and the negative to be maximized. Depression not only strikes a person's emotions; it also interrupts the thinking process as well. Somehow the negative thinking patterns must be broken to permit the person to be free to enjoy life again.

Life is not as gloomy as the depressed person views it. The cloud of gloom hangs over the depressed individual, hiding the sunshine. One may liken it to wearing dark-colored glasses. A person gets up in the morning, puts on sunglasses and views the job, family, sickness, future vocation plans and all of life through those dark lenses. In fact, the whole gamut of the past, the present and the future is affected by this dark picture.

6. *Hopelessness and meaninglessness.* Viewing life through his dark glasses life looks bleak. For David meaning was tied

to his personal relationship with God and his faith in God's purpose. A strong focal point of Psalms 42 and 43 is this reassurance of hope. This hope provides an anchor amid the waves that threaten to overcome him.

Prayer gave David access to the Divine presence. Though his complaints were many and his pain was nearly devastating the availability of prayers as a vehicle to express his uttermost feelings provided a great source of therapy. David was getting at the source of his trouble. God was the power that controlled life's events. He was taking his complaint straight to the top, no intermediaries.

David was open and honest. He expressed his real feelings. He did not try to hide his anger or his disappointment. Thus he vented the angry feelings, experienced catharsis and kept the channels of communication open, rather than allowing his anger to block his access to God.

Closely associated with David's prayer life was his confidence in God's Word. He anticipated God would "send out . . . light . . . truth" that would "lead" him. Likewise David anticipated the worship experience to be renewed. The temple was not available to him presently but he looked with renewed hope to that future occasion.

Psychologists are becoming increasingly aware of the role that meaning and hope play in an individual's ability to deal with crisis. (This aspect in treating depression will be treated later under "Therapies and Treatment of Depression").

7. *Correlation between guilt and anger.* Many psychologists see a close correlation between guilt and anger. People handle angry feelings differently. One person may bottle up his anger—hold it in. As a result of attempting to keep a lid on this pent-up emotion he turns the anger on himself and becomes depressed. As a general rule therapists

encourage "getting out the feelings—getting it off your chest." The Scripture encourages believers not to let the sun go down on your wrath (Ephesians 4:26).

A problem can develop with the individual whose problem is the opposite from the repressive. This is the person who assures everyone that they need not worry because he is always perfectly honest and people always know how he feels. The tendency when this announcement is made is to take three steps backwards and hope to escape the sudden unleashing of this person's anger.

The person with the short fuse does not have the problem with anger building up. His problem is that he may unleash so much anger that he feels guilty for hurting people. The Scripture admonishes "to be angry and sin not" (Ephesians 4:26). When an individual is destructive to another person, this is sin. As anger is expressed in harmful ways there is a tendency to increase the anger. To justify himself a person is easily inclined to tear his enemies down —dehumanize them in order to justify their cruel treatment. This can set in motion a vicious cycle.

The key to dealing with angry feelings is to share our feelings without attacking the other person. It is most appropriate to stay with "I" statements and feeling statements such as "I feel angry" and to stay away from accusing "you" statements, such as, "You did this to hurt me." It is impossible to know someone else's intention—that involves an interpretation. The only thing we can know for sure are our own feelings. Avoid sweeping generalizations, such as, "You always do this to me." Words like "all" and "always" usually provoke a negative response since the other person tends to become upset at the generalization. Most people try to get out their angry feelings by taking it out on the other person

41

in an extreme way—to hurt the other person. This has the effect of increased guilt when it is overstated.

Psychologists have long recognized the role that guilt plays in depression. Guilt is a major contributor to depression. David may have experienced guilt feelings. His own son betrayed him. A typical response of a parent might be, "If I had done things differently, my son would have responded differently. If only I had listened to him more . . . if I had spent more time with him." Of course there is no way of knowing for sure, but similar thoughts could well have been on David's mind.

In times of loss people are inclined to experience guilt. Sometimes the guilt is inappropriate. There is a strong tendency to question the judgment which at the time seemed the best thing to do.

A clear example of appropriate guilt is found at another occasion in David's life. David expressed his and the accompanying depression when he stated:

> When I kept silent about my sin, my body wasted away through my groanings all day long (Psalm 32:3, NAS).

In this passage David paid a price in depression with its physical and mental pain. David held his feelings of guilt in. They affected him dramatically.

David had done some things in life in which he should have experienced guilt: adultery and murder. Fortunately, David finally brought his sin out in the open, repented and found healing. The 51st chapter of the book of Psalms vibrates with the principle that when a person seeks God's forgiveness, He provides forgiveness and renewal.

> Have mercy on me, O God, according to your unfailing love; according to your great compassion blot out my transgressions. Wash away all my iniquity and cleanse me from

my sin. . . . Create in me a pure heart, O God, and renew a steadfast spirit within me (Psalm 51:1, 2, 10, NIV).

The Relationship of Depression to Learned Behavior.

When it comes to the relationship of Solomon's depressive reaction to faulty learning the detailed evidence is lacking for any definite statement. However, the book of Ecclesiastes is insightful in revealing extremely pessimistic thinking patterns. David may or may not have transmitted to his son, Solomon, depressive behavior patterns. To what extent Solomon may have learned a sense of helplessness is highly speculative.

A child can be rewarded by attention and sympathy when he is ill. Children who observe their parents reacting to their down times by going to bed, taking pills, withdrawing, or venting their anger on the children are quite likely to follow their parents in this regard. Behaviorists insist that people receive some side effect or benefit from the patterns they develop. If, for example, a child who feels unloved gains sympathy and attention through illness, he may continue this mechanism to achieve attention later in life.

II. Treatment of Depression

Picking up with the previously-mentioned problem—threat of suicide—a referral to a psychiatrist may be made when chemotherapy is called upon to take the edge off the depression or in cases where mood swings such as manic depression need to be controlled by drugs.

Too much of a drug can mask the mood and not allow enough pain to be present to provide motivation for therapy.

43

The commonly-dispensed medication by physicians is merely a stop-gap procedure. Most physicians do not have the time to listen to people's problems. It usually takes a great deal of time and special training to assist the person with coping resources to deal with depression. A psychiatrist is especially well equipped to prescribe and monitor this medication in conjunction with psychotherapy.

A number of approaches are effective depending on the severity of depression. Most therapists use a variety of approaches depending upon the needs of the client. A combination of these are employed by many therapists called eclectic therapists.[4] Some suggestion as to some of the strengths of a limited number of therapies follows.

1. *Psychoanalysis.* The stereotype that most people have of psychotherapy is a patient lying on a couch while a bearded shrink takes copious notes of the crazy behavior of the patient. Psychoanalysis is the process which best fits this popular conception. In this model a person presents his problem to the therapist who analyzes the problem and comes up with a cure. This is much like going to a physician who makes a diagnosis, provides treatment and hopefully a cure follows. (Although the "medical" model is still popular,

---

4. James O. Palmer, *A Primer of Eclectic Psychotherapy* (Monterey: Brooks/Cole Publishing Company, 1980). (This text is intended to integrate the variety of therapeutic theories for the beginning practitioner in graduate school studying psychotherapy.) Howard Clinebell, *Basic Types of Pastoral Counseling* (Nashville: Abingdon Press, 1966). Clinebell's "revised model" is eclectic, designed for ministerial students. A most recent thrust of his theory may be found in *Growth Counseling* by Howard Clinebell (Nashville: Abingdon, 1979). From a conversation with Dr. Clinebell I understand he is in the process of revising his *Basic Types of Pastoral Counseling* which at the present time is still in print.

Robert A. Harper, *Psychoanalysis and Psychotherapy 36 Systems* (New York: Jason Aronson, 1974). Harper's succinct presentation of the major therapeutic schools provides a survey of the immense variation in the field of psychotherapy as practiced today.

many therapists seriously question its basic assumptions.) The psychoanalyst is in an authoritarian role as he or she interprets the patient's feelings and directs the session. The patient is in a more passive role.

Sigmund Freud[5] viewed many problems as related to repressed sexual and hostile impulses. In his view it was important to retrace the patient's life, uncovering these unconscious conflicts by employing his particular techniques. The depressed person would be seen as involved in an out-growth of these internal conflicts. Freud claimed that depression was often tied to an elevated superego.[6] That is, one's realistic expectations in keeping strict rules of religion and society contributed to his problem. (This is not to say that all psychoanalysts are unreligious[7] but it is important to be aware that some may follow this line of thought.) At the same time it is well to recognize that Freud was not in favor of the kind of unrestrained sexuality and overt aggression evidenced in contemporary society.

Freud's was the first professional approach to therapy, but in the course of time many new techniques began to form. Karen Horney, Alfred Adler, Carl Jung, and Harry

5. Sigmund Freud and Oskar Pfister, *Sigmund Freud Psychoanalysis and Faith*. Ed. Heinrich Meng and Ernst L. Freud. Trans. Eric Mosbacher (New York: Basic Books, 1963). This delightful dialogue between Sigmund Freud and Oskar Pfister, a minister and psychoanalyst provides reference to a continual sharp conflict between these two friends on the issues of religion and psychoanalysis.

Sigmund Freud, *The Dynamics of Transference*, Std. ed. Vol. 12 (London: Hogarth Press, 1955).

6. Joseph Rychlak, *Personality and Psychotherapy* (Boston: Houghton Mifflin Company, 1981), pp. 92-93.

7. Millard J. Sall, *Faith, Psychology, and Christian Maturity.* (Grand Rapids: Zondervan Publishing House, 1975). This text illustrates the value of psychoanalysis within a Christian context. Other systems are also treated in this introductory text. The book provides a good beginning point for the layman interested in the integration of therapeutic psychology and the Christian faith.

Stark Sullivan were all critical of Freud's work. However, these and others, such as, Erich Fromm merely provided various deviations from Freud's original theory and practice.

2. *Behavioral Therapy.* In contrast to psychoanalyst insight into the internal world of the client, the behaviorist is an action-oriented approach which focuses on solving problems in one's external world. Since it deals with the everyday problems of behavior, it can be more easily measured by the therapist and the client. The basic assumption of the behaviorist is that maladaptive patterns have been learned but by systematic work these can be replaced by learning more appropriate patterns. These patterns can be modified by a system of rewards or positive reinforcement. The behaviorist maintains that while knowledge of the background of a problem may be helpful, it is not necessary for producing significant change. This system is much briefer and can be monitored more accurately.

Patterns of behavior such as maladaptive ways of dealing with anger, which contribute to depression, can be changed through behavior modification to relieve depression. A more assertive style of life may be suggested and a systematic program set up to implement these changes.

In the course of therapy the behaviorist is more inclined to take charge. He may appreciate the individual's resources but moderates his intervention according to the needs of his client. To put it bluntly the behaviorist insists that "the direction of the process belongs in the hands of the skilled therapist and not the sick patient."[8]

---

8. W. Stewart Agras, Alan E. Kozdin and G. Terence Wilson, *Behavior Therapy* (San Francisco, W. H. Freeman and Company, 1979). Michael T. Nietzel, Richard A. Winett, Marian L. MacDonald and William S. Davidson, *Behavioral Approaches to Community Psychology* (New York: Pergamon Press, 1977). Martin Sundel and Sandra Stone Sundel, *Behavior Modification in the Human Services* (New York: John Wiley and Sons, 1975). Harper, *Phychoanalysis and Psychotherapy 36 Systems,* (1974), p. 114.

3. *Client-centered Therapy.* The concept behind this non-directive technique of Carl Rogers[9] maintains that each person has within himself the potential for healing and personal growth. In the course of therapy the depression may bottom out as the client receives support and experiences catharsis. An advantage to this approach is the maximum opportunity for the client to get in touch with his own resources and to feel better about himself as a result of this supportive thrust. This approach is probably most effective in dealing with a certain crisis and when patterns are not too deeply entrenched.

4. *Gestalt Therapy.* Another system, Gestalt therapy[10] helps the client get in touch with feelings, emotions, bodily sensations and opens a person up to life's experiences. The therapist assists the client to become aware of all aspects of his personality: emotional, physical, spiritual, and social. This is helpful in encouraging an awareness of all of life's perceptions as well as the somatic distress and mood changes of the depression. Insight into areas of one's personality that have previously been blocked to one's awareness can be a benefit of the Gestalt emphasis.

Since the depressed person is often obsessed with past failures and future fears the Gestalt focus upon the present can be helpful. Freeing up the client from bondage to his past and future can make him more open to celebrate life's joys and experience his sorrows as well. When a person can be fully present he will, according to the Gestalt therapist,

---

9. Carl Rogers, *Client-centered Therapy* (Boston: Houghton Mifflin Company, 1951).

10. Frederick Perls, *Gestalt Therapy* (New York: Julian Press, Bantam, 1977). Excerpts from the work of this pioneer in Gestalt therapy may be secured in his book *Gestalt Therapy Verbatim* (New York: Real People Press, Bantam Books, 1976).

be more fully human—a more responsive and more responsible individual.

5. *Rational Emotive Therapy.* The rational emotive therapy of Albert Ellis[11] stresses that depression alters one's mood because of the negativistic and catastrophic thinking of the person that sets him up for depression. RET attacks sweeping generalizations, such as, "I can't," "I am the worst person in the world," "I should be able to please everyone," and "I should be competent at everything I do." All the sweeping absolutes that are irrational and need to be squared with reality are challenged. An attempt is made to restructure a person's belief system with the unreasonable "shoulds," "oughts," and "musts" that stand in the way of a positive self-image and a fulfilling life.

6. *Reality Therapy.* Another popular cognitive approach, reality therapy (RT) pioneered by William Glasser,[12] is an attempt to apply reasoning and responsibility in the context of a warm trusting and personal relationship. When a therapist probes the client's background and the role of parents, colleagues and peers in his problem, some clients assume the responsibility lies with their parents or other causes in their environment. RT places responsibility squarely on the client for his treatment.[13]

---

11. Unfortunately Albert Ellis is another striking example of an unreligious person. Not only is he unreligious in his unorthodox sexual views but his offensive language often leads a Christian to discount completely his approach to psychotherapy. Paul A. Hauck, *Reason in Pastoral Counseling* (Philadelphia: The Westminster Press, n.d.) contends that RET offers a rationale that can be applied in complete harmony with a Christian point of view in spite of the negative embellishments that Ellis' personality embodies.

12. William Glasser, *Reality Therapy* (New York: Harper and Row, 1965).

13. This is not to say that other therapists from other systems have not recognized the problem of denying responsibility. A world-renowned psychiatrist and psychoanalyst, Karl Menninger, sets forth a powerful presentation to challenge modern man to reclaim responsibility for his actions in *Whatever Became of Sin?* (New York: Hawthorn Books, Bantam Books, 1978).

7. *Transactional Analysis.* The TA approach to therapy developed out of the theories of Eric Berne[14] and his followers. It considers the past important to see where conflicts arise but it is wholistic like Gestalt therapy. The purpose is to integrate emotions, thoughts and behavior. TA has a strong educational component. In recent years many family problems that contribute to depression have been clarified and adjustments made to improve these intimate human relationships.

8. *Existential Therapy.* Like TA and Gestalt this is another wholistic approach. As with client-centered therapy the individual is the one who knows what course of direction is best. Viktor Frankl, an Austrian psychiatrist, applied the lessons learned in a German concentration camp in the late 1930s and early 1940s to psychotherapy.[15] The focal point of his work has consisted of stressing the value of meaning in all of life's experiences as the key to mental health.

The sense of hopelessness and meaninglessness that many people experience today has led psychologists to coin a new term — "existential anxiety." No doubt the sense of meaninglessness rampant in this is a factor contributing to depression. Since the Christian message provides a context to enhance the meaningfulness of life, it appears natural

---

14. Erich Berne, *Transactional Analysis in Psychotherapy* (New York: Grove Press, 1961). A popular version of his work, *Games People Play* (New York: Grove Press, 1964) had phenomenal success remaining on the best-seller list for over two years. Another extremely popular book by Thomas Harris, *I'm OK, You're OK* (New York: Harper and Row, 1967) sets forth the theory and application of TA.

15. Viktor E. Frankl, *From Death-Camp to Existentialism* (Boston, Beacon Press, 1959).

that some collusion be possible employing the approaches of logotherapy.[16]

Resources for Dealing with Depression in Psalm 42 and 43

David provided a caricature of the impact of depression but his approach is also insightful as a paradigm of coping with depression.

David permitted every available emotion to surface. Psychologists are aware of the tremendous value of "getting it off your chest"—of expressing catharsis. David appears to have achieved this therapeutic relief.

David does not merely vent his emotions; he thoroughly engages his mind as he summons a new attitude toward his trouble. David is not resigned to depression; he does not merely wallow in self-pity which is a tendency when depressed. Instead he expectantly awaits for renewed strength. David insists "I must wait for God." He opens himself up to the possibility for God to act. He senses that a new day is dawning or deliverance is around the next corner. John Goldingay states, "The psalmist knows this truth. He knows that he will be able to keep going if he can live in hope. Where there is hope there is life.[17] He anticipates God's grace and deliverance. His heart is filled with praise. He begins to thank God before He answers his prayer. "Praise

---

16. Donald F. Tweedie, *Logotherapy* (Grand Rapids: Baker Book House, 1961). This is a helpful book in evaluating this approach from a Christian perspective. Another source for the minister may be found in Clinebell's book.

Howard Clinebell, "Counseling on Religious-Existential Problems" in *Basic Types of Pastoral Counseling* (Nashville: Abingdon Press, 1966), pp. 244-265.

17. John Goldingay, *Songs From a Strange Land* (Downers Grove: Inter-Varsity Press, 1978), p. 42.

will then celebrate what sight sees. And in the meantime faith bridges the gap between prayer and its answer, and looks forward to praise."[18]

This psalm provides a great resource against the most severe threat of depression—hopelessness. When "hopelessness" sets, in suicide may emerge or another desperate option. David helps the depressed person call on those intangible qualities of faith and hope in God which can make the difference between life and death.

In my own experience as a therapist I have known many people who survived repeated bouts of depression through hope in God. By relying on the spiritual resources available as well as the methods of therapeutic psychology in the hands of a concerned Christian they are now living more abundant lives. They, like David, have a story to tell. "Hope thou in God."

DISCUSSION QUESTIONS: *Depression*

1. How extensive is the problem of depression today?
2. What Scripture is focused on in this chapter?
    A. What does it say about depression?
    B. What does it say concerning the resolution of depression?
3. Describe specific characteristics of depression as experienced by David.
4. Explain the correlation between guilt and anger. Include the following:
    A. What problem may the person who has a short fuse experience?
    B. Distinguish between inappropriate and appropriate guilt.

---

18. *Ibid.*

51

5. Is it possible to learn depressive patterns? Explain your answer.

6. Name the founder of each of the following approaches to psychotherapy as well as the basic thrust of their approach.
   - A. Psychoanalysis
   - B. Behavioral therapy
   - C. Gestalt
   - D. Rational-Emotive therapy
   - E. Reality therapy
   - F. Transactional analysis
   - G. Existential therapy

7. Choose two of the above and explain how you might treat a depressed person within that particular framework.

8. What does eclectic mean?

9. Explain how the following professionals might be of help in treating depression.
   - A. psychiatrist
   - B. marriage and family therapist
   - C. minister/pastoral counselor

10. What are the resources for dealing with depression in Psalm 42 and 43?

11. How does this passage help to bring together basic approaches to psychotherapy in the treatment of depression.

12. Share personal reactions to this chapter concerning
   - A. your own "blues"
   - B. your part as a helper to the depressed

13. What have you learned about
   - A. depression
   - B. the role of the Scripture as related to depression

14. What do you need to learn beyond this chapter and how would you suggest to proceed with that learning experience?

Chapter Four

COPING WITH ANXIETY

Biblical Reference

Jesus said, ". . . I tell you, do not be anxious about your life . . ." (Matthew 6:25, RSV). The Apostle Paul likewise insisted, "Have no anxiety about anything" (Philippians 4:6-7, RSV).

Relevance to the Contemporary Problem

Contemporary psychologists call this the "Age of Anxiety." What a commentary on our times—that it should be characterized by the term 'anxiety.' This description suggests some very important factors concerning the 20th century.

Much of our modern life sets the stage for anxiety. Certainly the road to peace and tranquility has never been easy. However a number of factors give occasion for anxiety. (1) The pace of life is problematic. Many people set unrealistic expectations for themselves. Schedules to keep and deadlines to meet find a vast number of people on a treadmill of ceaseless, often meaningless, activity. Constant pressure without adequate intervening times for rest is devastating to anyone's mental health. Our Lord provides a model in this regard. He kept a tremendous pace of activity, yet withdrew on occasions from the pressures of His ministry for solitude such as when he heard of the death of John the Baptist (Matthew 14:13). (2) The economic situation. Inflation has cut drastically into modern life. In spite of sky-rocketing interest rates and constant increase of basic commodities such as food and fuel, most people insist on attempting to continue the lifestyle to which they have become accustomed.

53

This materialistic bent is in obvious contradiction to the Lord's admonition to seek first His kingdom and to trust Him for daily provisions (Matthew 6:33). (3) In addition to the troubled economy in personal life, the explosive world situations are alarming: threat of atomic warfare, overpopulation, mobility, burgeoning crime rate, changing values of society, uncertainties about child-rearing practices and questioning of religious beliefs. Also, modern man lacks trust in God's providential care.

For most people life presents many intimidating situations beyond man's control. Man is simply unable to control all the variables of health and prosperity. Jesus intended for this passage from Matthew 6:25 to teach that life involves a trusting relationship between man and God. When a person can acknowledge that all things are in the care and keeping of the One who loves us more than we can ever appreciate, then he can cease to worry about his lack of control.

Unfortunately, instead of getting a clear perspective on a life of trust as God intended, people rush to find simplistic solutions to their problems. The Lord never promised simple answers. The Scriptural approach clearly insists that the Christian meet his problems head on and, with God's help, work through them. The process of working through them, even of suffering, is clearly to be a growth-producing experience for the Christian (James 1:12).

Obviously, many attempt to cope with anxiety through various inappropriate methods. Attempts to cope with anxiety have led to unprecedented drug and alcohol problems. Drug problems may result from receiving anti-anxiety medication. This medication is appropriate to manage acute cases, but when prescribed as constant medication it can lead to addiction as the dosage increases to provide the same relief. Often people are searching for a simple answer or quick cure which can lead to an abuse of a drug.

People who turn to alcohol to relieve their symptoms are also using an inappropriate method of coping. They, as with persons taking medication or street drugs, have another problem which can become seven times worse than the first. Alcohol does not help in any way to get at the problems which create the need to escape. Physicians have long recognized the relationship of anxiety to illness. In some situations anxiety may be causal and certainly in most instances it aggravates the treatment.

Only the Lord Himself knows how many homes have disintegrated as a result of the inability to cope with a high anxiety level in one of its many destructive forms. Over and over again this scourge of our times destroys interpersonal relationships, leaves children homeless and in some instances contributes substantially to the spiraling suicide rate.

Scope of the Study

A Scriptural perspective is urgent as already indicated. To assist in the understanding of anxiety a definition is in order as well as treatment procedures. In summation Scriptural application will conclude the chapter.

Anxiety defined.[1] Anxiety is unrealistic fears. In light of

---

1. For an extensive treatment of anxiety and fear or unrealistic fear, see David Sue, Derald Wing Sue and Stanley Sue, *Abnormal Behavior* (Boston: Houghton-Mifflin Company, 1981). Part Two includes "Anxiety and Fear" in Chapter 6 and "Anxiety, Somatoform and Dissociative Disorders" in chapter 7, pp. 148-206.

Also see James Coleman, James N. Butcher and Robert C. Carson, *Abnormal Psychology,* "Anxiety Disorders" (Glenview: Scott, Foresman and Company, 1980), pp. 207-223.

all the problems in society and those crises that occasionally confront everyone, a person would be less than human if not affected. When mental health professionals use the term "anxiety" they are usually referring to levels of fear that are out of proportion to the external danger. The anxious person experiences such strong feelings that he is disoriented due to physical and mental distress.

Physical manifestations of anxiety disorders run the gamut from jitteriness, inability to relax, sweaty palms, diarrhea, difficulty in falling asleep and irritability, to panic attacks accompanied by a choking or smothering sensation, dizziness, trembling and sense of losing control.

Creative use of anxiety. Anxiety is not always a bad word. Psychologists now recognize that anxiety fosters creativity and growth. The public speaker, the musician and the athlete all learn to channel the energy of anxiety to serve their purpose. The performer speaks of getting up for the performance. Many an athlete has taken another team for granted or has relaxed only to meet devastation at the hands of a lesser team.

Too much anxiety can cause the football player to overreact, drop the ball or jump off sides. Anxiety can be counterproductive on the ball field or in our lives. Anxiety is counterproductive when it interferes with our coping. To be a disorder it must be at the stage where it is counterproductive and stands in the way of effective living.

Causes of Anxiety

Learned behavior. One basic cause of anxiety is learning. For example, I have had people caught in the clutches of anxiety come for therapy, who seemingly did not have a worry in the world. They were independently wealthy, had beautiful, talented and successful children, and a reasonably happy marriage. What was the problem? Everything this person had, he was afraid would be taken away. Come to find out the seeds of this distrust were planted years before by a parent who was always on "pins and needles" about every little detail as well as the overall picture which was bound to explode at any moment.

All parents transmit basic skills of survival to their children: look both ways when you cross the street and don't ride with strangers, for example. Unfortunately, parents also transmit other messages, or tapes as transactional analysis calls them, which affect attitudes and set the stage for much of learning that follows. Destructive patterns may need to be recognized and more appropriate learning be encouraged.

The family structure needs to be explored, evaluated, and changes be made—lest destructive patterns be transmitted through the family. Therefore, it is preferable in many situations to get back into the family unit since this is the origin of many problems. The family provides the setting in which the client most generally needs to learn to relate more effectively. Usually where one person in the family has a problem that comes to attention, others are in need of education in more effective interpersonal relationship skills.

Family therapists insist that looking for an "identified patient" is inappropriate. A child, for example, usually is best treated in the context of the entire family. The "identified patient" is "the family" or the inadequate "family system." Family therapists help alter the family system so that it will run more smoothly.

Situational anxiety. Each individual must meet certain anxiety-producing events such as sickness or death or loss of a job. Some anxiety in the face of specific situations is predictable. These feelings run their course and are limited by specific situations. A certain amount is normal under trying circumstances. It can be a stimulus to doing a better job, exercising healthy caution, or a stimulus to meet a great challenge. But it can also be a danger signal to be heeded. If the danger signal is heeded, new roadways of adventure, learning, and personal growth may be traveled. Good can come out of anxiety as with any of life's experiences (Romans 8:28).

Internalized conflict. Anxiety is related to conflicts within the individual. The person experiences himself or herself drawn in two or more directions, neither of which provide a satisfactory solution.

Sigmund Freud's theory concerning the origin of anxiety contends that conflict exists between a person's basic instincts or tissue needs such as the drive for sexual intercourse and society's standards which insist this is only appropriate within marriage. In religious terms we would think of the conflict between what the Bible calls the flesh and the dictates of one's conscience.

It is possible for a person to have an overly-sensitive and misguided conscience. If a Christian feels that not only is sexual intercourse outside of marriage wrong but that the sexual expression is also wrong within marriage, then the conscience is overly-sensitive and misdirected. If this be the case that person at the intellectual level or the emotional level has an overly-sensitive conscience; it is not the fault of the Bible or the Christian religion but rather the fault of incorrect teaching or inappropriate shaping of the conscience in one's youth. A distinction must be made between the practice of religion which may be misconstrued and the truth found in the Bible. Unfortunately many psychologists who see people emotionally disturbed also see religion that is likewise sick. Too often they judge the Christian religion as being sick when in fact it is the disturbed person who is sick and not the religion. I am indebted to Wayne Oates' chapter "Hindering and Helping Powers of Religion" in *Religious Factors in Mental Illness* (Association Press: New York, 1958) for this view.

The Christian is bound to experience some conflict in trying to live the Christian life (Romans 7:7; Galatians 5:17). However, the Christian is aware of these struggles. The problem is the putting off of the resolution of conflict. The anxiety-ridden person puts off the process of grappling with conflict and therefore is in a constant state of conflict. Some psychologists believe conflicts are buried in one's subconscience and thus leave a person in continual conflict without a full awareness of the cause of the anxiety.

A certain amount of conflict is normal but when conflict stands in the way of normal functioning then it needs to be resolved. Some people experience conflict over nearly every decision—large or small, and cannot remember when this was not true for them. Decisions never seem to be the right ones. Other people feel anxious and have no idea where that anxiety comes from. This "free flowing," non-specific character of anxiety is characteristic of the anxiety-ridden person.

Most people in times of severely stressful situations experience anxiety. This anxiety is situational. However, many people experience anxiety that is altogether unrelated to circumstances but nevertheless invades and continues nearly all the time.

Inadequacy and inferiority. The roots of anxiety are often found in childhood. A child who is unjustly criticized will very likely react adversely to criticism as an adult. As an adult he may read even constructive criticism as rejection.

The child who receives positive affirmation of abilities and yet is not protected from realistic evaluation has a legacy of great value. Parents who feel good about themselves are able to transmit this affirmation to their children. Although the childhood years are vital to the establishment and growth of the self-image, this is not to say adults do not have needs for affirmation. When a person endures a traumatic experience such as the death of a loved one or the loss of a job, the healthiest self-image is tested. The person who ordinarily feels good about himself will have a great resiliency to respond to the situation.

A person with a poor self-image may have difficulty processing the good impressions others have. I recall a young man who was a brilliant attorney. But as far as he was concerned, he was an absolute failure. His view certainly did not square with what I saw. To me the young man was a gifted musician, handsome, had a successful practice, and was highly regarded in his profession. In short, he apparently had everything going for him. However, there was one thing against him; his negative concept of himself threatened his ruin.

The Scripture sheds light on the subject of our self-concept. Jesus emphasized the importance of good feelings about ourselves as a basis upon which to evaluate our attitude toward others. He seemed to take it for granted that we will love ourselves when he said, "You shall love your neighbor as yourself" (Luke 10:27). Unfortunately, many people have a terrible self-image and it adversely affects everything else in life.

Treatment. Much of anxiety springs from inferiority feelings. The anxious person looks for someone whom he can lean upon and receive affirmation. Since the causes lie in insecurities, therapy usually requires several sessions. As the person shares his fears in the protective and supportive environment, those fears begin to diminish as they are brought out in the open and examined. The binding effect lessens as one's fears are explored in detail. The process of sharing with another caring human being who listens without judgment has a vital healing impact. As he shares he becomes less fearful and more confident. His views, his plans, his ideas for growth are honored and enhanced by the counselor's presence.

The counselee is encouraged to share the most sensitive aspects of life which appear to be most anxiety arousing. These occasions may center around relationships with authority figures or heterosexual relations or school work or thoughts about future goals in life. The roots of the anxiety are discovered and insight follows. When painful areas are rehearsed over and over again, they soon tend to diminish.

Focus may be directed to the specific areas of need in a practical way. If the person is anxious regarding heterosexual relationships, the counselor might have the person keep track of the feelings surrounding these relationships. Increased exploration into the reasons behind these difficulties will be pursued. As attention is directed toward these situations, it may be important to make some changes in the midst of those encounters. Perhaps a young man who is interested in a certain girl needs some supportive therapy as he would muster up enough courage to talk with this potential girl friend rather than going into the library where she is every day and leaving after he says, "Hello." What would he talk about? How would he approach the subject? Sometimes the therapist might do some role play. If the young man gets up his courage to try it in therapy which is a programmed setting, but also a difficult situation, he may be able to deal with the actual situation. Coping with the anxiety in advance will enable the person to cope in the midst of the real encounter with the girl friend.

By fantasizing the actual encounter, the feelings in his mind surface. By thinking about the feared situation, one learns to become more familiar with the sensations. The temptation for the person that is anxious is to immediately flee the object that threatens. The therapist can help the person bring to his awareness all the possibilities that may result. For example, the therapist could say, "Tell me the worst thing that could possibly happen." By actually experiencing the sensations of being rejected and recognizing that he can survive, the person is lead to conclude that the fear of rejection is worse than the actual rejection. One can become better prepared for the actual conversation, how to proceed as well as to assess the impact should the date not materialize.

Here it is essential to recognize another treatment procedure to help the person who is anxious in the presence of the opposite sex. Group therapy where one has occasion to share feelings with a prospective dating partner and to get feedback and encouragement from peers, both men and women, brings the individual closer still to dating situations. Opportunities to flush out those fears and to feel the support of people who to some degree can identify with his struggles may provide an added supplement to the more in-depth process of individual psychotherapy.

Scriptural Resources

A person becomes fearful when he senses that everything is out of control. The presence of a caring person who understands what is happening, who has helped other people survive, removes the panic.

The Christian can take confidence in the recognition that God is in control and He lovingly cares for us as His children. If he cares for the birds of the air, how much more so he cares for us (Matthew 6:25-27).

As the Psalmist called to mind His God who was his ever-present help in trouble, so can the Christian celebrate his presence and thereby experience a rest in the Lord. This resting in the Lord is a kind of mental equilibrium—a vital balance that psychologists speak of.

> God is our refuge and strength, an ever present help in trouble. Therefore we will not fear, though the earth give way and the mountains fall into the heart of the sea. . . . Be still and know that I am God . . . (Psalms 46:1, 2 and 10, NIV).

This Scripture moves one to quiet reflection upon a God who stands beside us in every anxiety-provoking situation and who challenges us not to be afraid but to place all our confidence in Him. The anxious person can find great comfort in the God of all comfort.

> Come unto me, all ye that labour and are heavy laden, and I will give you rest. Take my yoke upon you, and learn of me; for I am meek and lowly in heart: and ye shall find rest unto your souls (Matthew 11:28, 29, KJV).

"Rest" is not limited to the spiritual realm but is extremely needful in the physical areas as well. For the Christian, his body is the temple of God (I Corinthians 6:19). That temple

63

should be cared for properly. If a Christian refuses to care for himself, he will develop physical and emotional problems. Proper diet, physical exercise, adequate relaxation, and appropriate sleep are absolutely necessary to good mental health.

Marion H. Nelson comments: "Paul knew of the pressures a pastor is under when he wrote Timothy to 'take heed unto thyself' literally, keep on giving attention to yourself (I Timothy 4:16). Paul's principle was that Timothy should not neglect attending to his own physical, psychological and spiritual needs. He was not to become fatigued so that he would be unable to meet the needs of others.[2]"

Nelson goes on to relate that one must be careful in going overboard and caring for others by denying oneself.[3] He cautioned against making unrealistic demands upon one's physical and emotional energy that can lead to fatigue.

Some people receive their basic gratification from doing for others. When people gives so much on the job or in the community that they suffer severe anxiety or even a nervous breakdown—they are doing no one a favor—not their family —not others who depend upon them—and certainly not themselves. It is not uncommon for people to push themselves beyond their limits and then to collapse in what is generally called a "nervous breakdown." Then the person is forced to rest and get away from pressures. It is far better to pace oneself, "to take heed to oneself" than to reach

---

2. Marion H. Nelson, *Why Christians Crack Up* (Chicago: Moody Press, 1960), p. 100. In Chapter 9 Nelson treats "Spiritual Causes of Nervous Tension . . ." Also see Chapters 6 and 7, "Physical Causes of Nervous Tension" and "Psychological Disorders."

3. *Ibid.*

the point where the body and mind will no longer carry the unrealistic burden.

God can use our anxiety as motivation to seek help. Apart from that pain we would not seek deliverance. God can use that anxiety to further His purpose. When anxious, it is difficult to ignore the problem; it comes into focus, commands our attention and forces movement in the direction of resolution. Energy is bottled up and cries out for resolution. This is a tremendous opportunity to redirect this energy in productive healing channels rather than in malfunction. When a person wants deliverance badly enough to make important changes, growth will follow as he achieves insight and moves in the appropriate life-saving directions and away from the life-draining avenues.

Raymond L. Cramer translates Matthew 5:3, "Blessed are the poor in spirit: for theirs is the kingdom of heaven" as "Congratulations when we find ourselves in a difficult situation because satisfying results will follow if certain conditions are met."[4] He reiterates:

> By all means, don't be afraid to recognize and face up to your emotional problem, for as you do, there *is* an answer. Congratulations to the poor in spirit—those who obviously are in need of help, who cower and are thoroughly frightened, and who recognize their need.
>
> God *rushes* to the attention of a person with needs. The person with needs—who recognizes his condition is to be congratulated . . . he is to be envied . . . he is a candidate for the kingdom of heaven![5]

---

4. Raymond L. Cramer, *The Psychology of Jesus* (Grand Rapids: Zondervan, 1959), p. 17.

5. *Ibid.*, p. 21.

DISCUSSION QUESTIONS: *Anxiety*

1. What did Jesus and Paul say about anxiety? Discuss the difference between anxiety and concern. Jesus claimed we should not be anxious about our life, but does this mean we should not have concern for providing for necessities of life?

2. Discuss the difference between worry, fear and anxiety.

3. Why should our age be labeled the "Age of Anxiety"?

4. Is anxiety always destructive? Under what circumstances may it be helpful? Can you recall situations when it served you well? When it didn't?

5. Describe the relationship of our family background to anxiety.

6. What is meant by situational anxiety? Do some people feel anxious nearly all the time?

7. What was Freud's view of anxiety as conflict? Does the Christian have conflict? What unfortunate conclusion did Freud draw concerning religion and psychopathology? How would you correct his misconception?

8. How does a poor self-image relate to anxiety? What Scripture is mentioned in this regard? Can you think of others and how they would be helpful with the problem of inferiority feelings?

9. What treatment approaches are mentioned? How would you personally try to help the anxious person.

10. What Scriptural resources are suggested? How are they applied to the anxious person?

Chapter Five

CHILDREN OF BROKEN HOMES

Biblical Reference

Children from broken homes have always been a concern of the church, the family of God. One of the earliest insights into the ministry of the New Testament Church included a provision for their daily necessities (Acts 6:1-4). However, it is James who most clearly exemplifies the temper of both the Old Testament and New Testament Scriptures regarding children of broken homes:

> Pure religion and undefiled before God and the Father is this, To visit the fatherless and widows in their affliction, and to keep himself unspotted from the world (James 1:27, KJV).

Context

James insists that no elaborate forms of worship can take the place of practical service toward those in need. The warning of James had already been sounded earlier when the Psalmist reminded the people that God "is a father of the fatherless and a judge of the widows" (Psalms 68:5). Zechariah likewise complained of the hard hearted tendency of the people and demanded that they execute true justice by showing mercy and compassion to every person and not to oppress the widow, the fatherless and the poor (Zechariah 7:6-10).

Relevance of the Scripture to the Contemporary Problem

If there was ever a time when the church must take seriously the admonition to care for the fatherless and widows it is now. More and more are turning to divorce (over one million in 1976). By 1973 statistics indicate that one child in seven under age eighteen—or about 10 million children —was living with one parent due to divorce or desertion. Add to these statistics some five million widows and widowers who are attempting to rear their children alone and the extent of the problem is startling.

Comment

The Scriptural admonition in James 1:27 as well as the Old Testament supporting passages provide a poignant warning to the church today. The contemporary church would do well to ask herself whether there was ever a time when people were more caught up in the external trappings of religion. When beautiful buildings and bulging budgets became the obsession in churches, then the real business of the church is lost. William Barclay contends:

> It is perfectly possible for a church to be so taken up with the beauty of its buildings and the splendour of its liturgy that it has neither the time nor the money for practical Christian service; and that is what James is condemning.[1]

Another consideration may block a ministry among children of broken homes: the stigma of divorce and death. Consider the trauma existing among Christians who find it difficult to understand how any Christian could divorce. To be understanding and caring toward the divorced is not tantamount to endorsing it. Perhaps some Christians also avoid a ministry to those broken by divorce as a way of avoiding reflection on the possibility that this could happen

---

1. William Barclay. *The Letters of James and Peter,* The Daily Study Bible Series (Philadelphia: The Westminister Press, 1960), p. 72.

to them. A hard line may help to provide considerable insulation from doing some needed reflection on one's own marriage. If this is true regarding divorce, it may be even more true of the widowed. Although the widowed does not carry quite the negative stigma of the divorced, who would question that this is still a death denying society. A ministry to those affected by death can hardly help but touch the discomforting thought of the fragility of life.

Obviously whatever personal and theological reflections come to mind regarding the broken home, children are least to blame and undoubtedly the severest victims of the loss of their parent or parents.

Scope of this Study

This chapter first focuses on the centrality of the parental coping skills and how they affect children. Then an exploration of how homes particularly broken by divorce impact upon children. Often remarriage appears to be a simple solution to problems and yet many problems are inherent in the blended family. The next concern revolves around how to identify the signs of stress in children. Scriptural resources available to enhance the healing process and finally suggestions as to the role of the church in this ministry complete this chapter.

Importance of Parental Coping

A divorced mother exclaimed, "Suddenly for the first time I heard what my son had been saying all along. It is so obvious now but I couldn't hear his needs because my pain overwhelmed me." Until the adults have dealt with their pain

69

and made the necessary adjustments, it will be impossible to meet the child's needs. When the very mention of, "Why did Daddy leave?" or "Why did God let Mommy die?" provokes anger or tears, a conspiracy of silence may develop among the very ones whose emotional needs cry out for expression. Parents must remember that "we'll talk about it later" to a child is "never." That child may not approach the subject again.

If one parent now struggles with the full responsibility of the children twenty-four hours a day, resentment may build up against the children. The constant responsibility coupled with the emotional drain of depression, angry feelings, doubts, and fear may leave the parent wondering how it is possible to help the children with their adjustment.

When a parent realizes his or her pain blocks communication with the children, this is a sure sign that help is needed. Other signs of concern are a general inability to function in one's normal way, and extreme bouts of depression. In coping with the grief reactions and the adjustment problems, a friend—another widow or widower or a divorced person who has successfully navigated a similar journey—may be a wise counselor. Many ministers are able to provide counsel to grieving persons. If a person's problems demand more time or training than the minister possesses, most ministers are able to recommend a competent professional therapist.

Counseling may involve the children directly in the sessions, or it may simply free the distressed parent to channel new energies to meet the needs of the other family members. The sooner positive feelings replace the negative depressive patterns, the sooner he or she will be able to pass along this healing to loved ones affected by the divorce or death. The apostle Paul describes the process in II Corinthians 1:3, 4, KJV,

70

". . . the God of all comfort; who comforteth us in all our tribulation, that we may be able to comfort them which are in any trouble, by the comfort wherewith we ourselves are comforted of God."

Homes Broken by Divorce

A home broken by divorce can be even more damaging to children and to family relationships than a home broken by death. In the case of death, family and friends pull together to help cope with the loss and go on providing the best care possible for the children. With divorce the loss is not permanent, and the closure of the wounds may take longer to heal because they are opened frequently. The problem expressed by many divorced people accents this when they complain, "Divorce is worse than death because you must continue seeing the person." When children are involved, the couple must face former mates as they negotiate details concerning the children's welfare. It may seem cruel but generally it is best that details be fairly explicit and structured regarding visitation rights. Then children can count on certain times when they will be able to spend time with their other parent.

Is Remarriage a Solution?

The problems of a broken home are not as easily solved by remarriage as is often believed. The reconstruction of a home broken by death or divorce brings its own set of problems into the new relationships. In addition to the adjustment period demanded in any marriage, the remarriage where children are present places the additional pressure of an adjustment of several people living together. Parents

71

have no opportunity to establish a wholesome relationship between themselves before assuming parent roles. Whether the new home will absorb the abrupt transition depends both upon the attitudes of the new parents and the children involved.

One of the problems that often emerges involves the discipline of the children. If the new parent assumes a different style of parenting than the children are prepared for, the stepparent may be resented by the children as well as the real parent who sees the role as an infringement on the existing pattern of parenting. Usually the home climate is better when the stepparent is a father. Stepfathers usually assume less direct responsibility than real fathers, often limiting their contact to "play time."

Many men are disappointed in their role of stepparent. They resent supporting another man's children and hearing the children express a preference for their real father. The stepchildren also provide a constant reminder of his wife's first husband and her love for him.

If the parents have adequate opportunity for a courtship period and abundant opportunities alone during the initial adjustment period, they may well have greater occasion to develop secure relationships with each other. If their relationship is secure, meeting their needs satisfactorily, they will be less threatened by the parenting problems. The more time they have together and especially the more open communication on such topics as discipline and feelings of jealousy, the freer they will be to invest energy into the parenting role. To swing from the problems of getting ready for a wedding into the problems of parenting immediately places demands on stable mental, physical and spiritual resources.

72

Signs of Stress in Children

Children express their feelings in a variety of ways depending upon their age. Restlessness, bad dreams, and fears of being left alone in Bible school or other places are common among preschoolers. Older children are more likely to demonstrate emotional stress through moodiness, bed-wetting, and inappropriate outbreaks of anger. Among adolescents rebelliousness, aggressiveness, depression, withdrawal from ordinary activities, and use of drugs or alcohol are ways they communicate their anxiety and anger. All those who have contact with children under a divorce or bereavement situation would do well to discuss these changes with the parents so that they will be more available to assist the child or to make a fitting referral to the appropriate professional.

The book of Romans provides hope amid the crises of life when it insists that good can come out of every situation. Romans 8:28 certainly does not teach that such tragedies as death or divorce are good, but it does claim that out of them can come good. What a family will make out of an unfortunate circumstance is really up to it. The fellowship of the church can assist by helping bear that burden. The church has a responsibility to strengthen the resources of every family that it might prosper and grow in this age of dissolution of family life. Certainly the family of God also has a responsibility to families and especially to the innocent victims of the premature breakup of the family unit through the death of one of the parents or due to separation, desertion or divorce.

Although it is seldom done, divorce counseling that helps to negotiate details concerning the children would be very beneficial. Especially would it be important for the child to hear from both parents the facts, reassurances that he is loved by both parents, promises of future visits with the absent parent, and clear arrangements for the visits.

Most families broken by divorce suffer the loss of the father. The effect of this loss is more extensive than was formerly realized. Some contend that the effect may be greater than the absence of the mother, a concept psychologists and the courts have been very reluctant to consider. Both in the Jewish religion and in New Testament times, fathers maintained a decisive role in child-rearing. The Scriptures teach, and modern psychology acknowledges, the vital role both the mother and father contribute to the emotional well-being of children.

During adolescence father-daughter contact appears to be a strong force in shaping feminine sex role development. Several patterns of difficulties are suggested as possible results of father absence: general ineffectiveness, severe anxiety, shyness, discomfort around males, and aggressive promiscuity.

If a boy is five or younger when his father leaves or dies, his masculine identity may falter and he may exhibit low self-control or inability to function.

A mother can compensate to a great degree for a father's absence by encouraging assertive, independent, and responsible behavior. Steps may be taken to bring into the son's life men who will serve as positive models. Friends, relatives, teachers, scout leaders, and others can provide such models.

Scriptural Resources for Parents and Children

One of the complaints of divorced people is the calloused approach of many church people. Darlene Petri shares her personal experience as the brunt of this attitude in a chapter in her book on divorce entitled, "Sticks and Stones."[2] She plays on the familiar childhood poem, "Sticks and stones may break my bones, but words will never hurt me." She emphatically rejects that ditty exclaiming that although words do not break bones they do indeed break the spirit. People can be cruel. Perhaps no people are more cruel than children to other children. Children are quick to observe that playmates living with one parent are different from them. For this reason they may subject them to ridicule.

Heartless people of all ages need to read again the Scriptures that forewarn us against judging (John 8:1-11; Matthew 7:1-5). Those who are the recipients of judging need to get in touch with the healing power of forgiveness toward their self-appointed judges (Matthew 18:22).

Severe feelings of hostility toward the ex-mate need to be dealt with. Jesus' directive from the Sermon on the Mount certainly speaks to this situation (Matthew 5:23-24, KJV).

> Therefore if thou bring thy gift to the altar, and there rememberest that thy brother hath ought against thee, Leave there thy gift before the altar, and go thy way; first be reconciled to thy brother, and then come and offer thy gift.

Becoming aware of God's grace and forgiveness relates dramatically to a person's self-image.[3] Surrounding oneself

---

2. Darlene Petri, *The Hurt and Healing of Divorce* (Elgin: David C. Cook, 1976), p. 87. This book also contains a chapter on children of divorce, pp. 71-85, in which the author shares personal lessons learned.

3. The importance of the self-image may be examined in Walter Trobisch, *Love Yourself* (Downers Grove: InterVarsity Press, 1976). Don E. Hamachek, *Encounters with the Self* (New York: Holt Rinehart and Winston, 1975). James Dobson, *Hide or Seek* (Old Tappan: Fleming H. Revell, 1974). Paul D. Meier's *Christian Child-Rearing and Personality Development* (Grand Rapids: Baker Book House, 1977) treats the self-concept in Part One of his four-part book. An extensive bibliography is an additional plus of this source.

and chidren with caring people provides a basic context for renewed self-acceptance. A firm realization that God cares personally apart from the former mate works wonders.

It is vital in all relationships that one's behavior be appropriate. Paul reminds us of the importance of loving and avoiding injurious acting out.

> For all the law is fulfilled in one word, even in this; Thou shalt love thy neighbor as thyself. But if ye bite and devour one another, take heed that ye be not consumed one of another (Galatians 5:14-15, KJV).

Those whose homes are broken by death probably experience some bitterness toward the mate but may be even more angry with God for taking husband, wife, daddy or mommy from them. Angry feelings toward a mate who died are hard to handle. After all it was not their fault that they died. As unreasonable as this sounds, the bereaved often hold it against their mate or parent. "How could he dare die on me and leave me with all the responsibility of these kids?" All the unfinished feelings rush to the forefront. "Why didn't Daddy spend more time with me?" "I wonder if Mommy really loved my sister more than me." When death strikes, especially when it comes suddenly, it often leaves in its wake a multitude of unresolved reflections. In retrospect one can usually come up with a long guilt list. "If only I had taken her to the doctor sooner." "If only I had spent more time with him." These are a couple of frequent complaints.

The Scripture will assist with the myriad of feelings of the bereaved. At times Christians tend to bury angry feelings, especially those directed toward God. Most people would do well to follow the lead of David in the Psalms. He shared every conceivable emotion with God, including his anger toward Him. When the bereaved person is open and honest with God in sharing his complaints and doubts he usually experiences relief. (It certainly helps to convey this to a friend who permits this ventilation as well.) The reading of Psalms is especially helpful because the troubled person who doubts God's presence can identify with David.

> Why standest thou afar off, O Lord? Why hidest thou thyself in times of trouble? (Psalm 10:1, KJV).

> How long wilt thou forget me, O Lord? for ever? How long wilt thou hide thy face from me? How long shall I take counsel in my soul, having sorrow in my heart daily? (Psalms 13:1-2, KJV).

Of course David went on to attest to His mercy and His salvation and concluded that chapter with the words:

> I will sing unto the Lord because he hath dealt bountifully with me (Psalm 13:6, KJV).

God knows us better than we know ourselves. The question is whether we are going to relate our prayers to Him out of our actual feelings or attempt to hide them as if they were not there. Wayne Oates sets forth this need for honesty:

> The regular ventilation, catharsis, bringing to light, and resultant insight into one's negative or hostile feelings in one's prayers puts them into their rightful context with the Eternal. It lowers their importance along with the correction of our self-concept, and it makes for better health.

> With the modern loss of this kind of frankness in prayer illustrated in the Bible, people have tended to look upon their prayers as a means of communication between God and their *ideal* selves, and not their *real* selves. Prayer as a means of access to the real self then loses its meaning.[4]

---

4. Wayne E. Oates. *The Bible in Pastoral Care* (Grand Rapids: Baker Book House, 1971), p. 116.

It is appropriate to pray for the former mate. God is able to grant healing of those feelings of bitterness. The continual festering of angry feelings are hard on one's mental, physical and spiritual health. To continue to harbor destructive feelings can be harmful to children whose self-image is geared to their relationship to both of their parents. It is in the best interest of the child to have an amiable relationship with the ex-mate if at all possible. An on-going relationship is inevitable in most cases involving visitation rights and various details that occur from time to time.

Forgiveness also applies to oneself. The haunting refrain, "Did I do all that I could to preserve the marriage?" has kept many divorced people awake nights. God's grace covers all iniquities. Petri maintains:

> Praying for the former mate and asking God's forgiveness for both of you can help so much. Ask God for power to forgive your former spouse of any injustices against you, and He will not ignore your request.[5]

After unloading all the negative feelings, and the positive feelings surface; pray for God's grace to cover all inadequacies. No mate is perfect, no child. Most guilt in the bereaved situation is abnormal, not based on reality, but God's grace covers the real shortcomings and all sins as well. A fitting Scripture meditation at this juncture would be a passage in Hebrews which reads:

> Try to stay out of all quarrels and seek to live a clean and holy life, for one who is not holy will not see the Lord. Look after each other so that not one of you will fail to find God's best blessings. Watch out that no bitterness takes root among you, for as it springs up it causes deep trouble, hurting many in their spiritual lives (Hebrews 12:14, 15, TLB).

---

5. Petri, *The Hurt and Healing of Divorce*, p. 91.

It is crucial to remember that children experience the same wide range of emotional reactions as adults to loss. They are vulnerable to guilt feelings. They may blame themselves for the divorce or even for the death of the parent. Care must be exercised to extricate them from such inappropriate feelings if they arise. Children need the comfort of God's Word. Too often adults focus on Scriptures as a means of correction at the neglect of a well-rounded selection that also treats reassurance and hope and grace and love. Familiar Scriptures already known to the child are extremely helpful. Young children look at concepts in concrete terms and abstractions allude them. Permit the stories of the Old Testament and the characters of the New Testament to speak to them. A child can appreciate God's love and His presence. He or she can appreciate that God is the good shepherd who loves us and cares for us (Psalm 23).

How the parents use their spiritual resources provides a model. How one copes with life's severest struggles when there are no simple answers, when faith is really called for, speaks forcefully to the child. At the same time the trust of a child points to that passage which states:

> Suffer the little children to come unto me . . .; for of such is the kingdom of God. Verily I say unto you, Whosoever shall not receive the kingdom of God as a little child, he shall not enter therein (Mark 10:14, 15, KJV).

An important Scriptural perception that relates to every trial emerges from Romans 5:3. This passage helps any person realize that troubles provide the occasion for growth both for parents and children.

> Therefore, since we have been justified through faith, we have peace with God through our Lord Jesus Christ, through

whom we have gained access by faith into this grace in which we now stand. And we rejoice in the hope of the glory of God. Not only so, but we also rejoice in our sufferings, because we know that suffering produces perseverance; perseverance, character; and character, hope. And hope does not disappoint us, because God has poured out his love into our hearts by the Holy Spirit, whom he has given us (Romans 5:1-5, NIV).

The Role of the Church

The church must become involved more directly in this ministry to children of broken families. We obviously should cover preventive measures to assist families in meeting the challenge of adjusting to marriage and the challenge of parenthood at each stage of the child's development. We also may intervene in the marital difficulties of reconstituted families. Groups that are designed to meet specific needs of each congregation may be formed. For example, groups designed especially for the widowed and the divorced may be appropriate. Groups for parents of preschoolers through adolescents, marriage enrichment groups, and seminars are helpful. This may be accomplished best by a minister-counselor who is trained in both ministry and the insights of counseling and is qualified to supervise various groups, teach, preach, and do marital therapy. The time has come when the local church can no longer bury its head in the sand.

Above all, the church must continue to teach the abiding moral values which are so much under attack in this secular society and keep reaching out with the healing ministry in word and deed.

DISCUSSION QUESTIONS: *Children of Broken Homes*

1. How do the shortcomings in the Old and New Testament times regarding those from broken homes compare to the situation today? Explain your answer.
2. Explain how important parental coping is.
3. Do you feel a home broken by divorce is more difficult to deal with than one broken by death? Explain your answer.
4. What problems are often present in remarriage. Give suggestions as to the resolution of these.
5. What is the attitude of your class or your church toward divorced people and toward the bereaved? Suggest ways in which this may be improved?
6. How can divorced people deal with their feelings toward their former mates. Give specific Scriptural suggestions.
7. What are some of the danger signs that a parent may have difficulty with a child in dealing with the broken home?
8. When may a counselor be needed? Who can help?
9. How important is the father's role and what suggestions may compensate for his absence.
10. Discuss the possibility of support groups in your church.

Chapter Six

THE STRUGGLE FOR MEANINGFUL MATURITY

The Nature of Man

All of us are amateur psychologists and theologians to some degree so think for a moment of one of the most profound questions of human existence, "What do you see when you see a man?"

That question touches upon your view of the nature of man. Is he basically angelic or demonic—good or evil. Is he basically animalistic or uniquely human and separate from animals! Obviously, answers to this question reflect upon a person's views concerning the dignity of man. How a person answers the question provides insight into how highly he regards people. Is he optimistic or pessimistic?

A low view of man suggests he is merely the result of his conditioning or his lower and basic drives of aggression and sexual drives.

A Balanced View

A Scriptural approach brings into perspective both the negative and the positive aspects of man—his degradation and his nobility. The Bible never glosses over sin even in its finest heroes, such as, David, Moses, and the Apostle Peter. As Paul insisted: "All have sinned and fallen short of the glory of God" (Romans 3:23). The best of man and the worst are all portrayed vividly in the Scripture.

Scriptural Perspective

Genesis 1 teaches that we are made in God's image.

Then God said, "Let us make man in our image, in our likeness, and let them rule over the fish of the sea and the

82

birds of the air, over the livestock, over all the earth, and over all the creatures that move along the ground." So God created man in his own image, in the image of God he created him; male and female he created them (Genesis 1:26, 27, NIV).

Yet we only need to read into the third chapter of Genesis to be faced with the first in a long and unbroken array of offences since the fall of man. Their disobedience in eating the forbidden fruit was followed by their son Cain's murder of his brother Abel (Genesis 4).

Obviously, God recognized that we have the potential for fellowship, or He would never have sent His son. Embedded in Genesis 3:15 is a prophecy that the creator would send His son to deal a mortal blow to the Evil One and rescue man from the clutches of Satan. "And I will put enmity between you and the woman, and between your offspring and hers; he will crush your head, and you will strike his heel" (Genesis 3:15, NIV).

The Psalmist reveals insight into the dignity and the grandeur of man as well as the glory of the Creator when he exclaimed:

When I consider your heavens, the work of your fingers, the moon and the stars, which you have set in place, what is man that you are mindful of him, the son of man that you care for him? You made him a little lower than the heavenly beings and crowned him with glory and honor. You have made him ruler over the works of your hands; you put everything under his feet: all the flocks and herds, and the beasts of the field, the birds of the air, and the fish of the sea, all that swim the paths of the seas. O Lord, our Lord, how majestic is your name in all the earth! (Psalm 8:3-9, NIV).

The New Testament abounds in references to man's growth potential as amplified in the following references:

Instead, speaking the truth in love, we will in all things grow up into him who is the Head, that is, Christ (Ephesians 4:15, NIV).

Like newborn babies, crave pure spiritual milk, so that by it you may grow up in your salvation (I Peter 2:2, NIV).

But grow in the grace and knowledge of our Lord and Savior Jesus Christ. To him be glory both now and forever! Amen (II Peter 3:18, NIV).

Relevance of the Problem in Contemporary Society

Evidences of man's inhumanity abound in present-day society. The death camps of World War II amply illustrate the depths of degradation. Those same prison camps, however, abound with evidence of highest tribute to the dignity of man. The daily newspapr is replete with the most startling cases of theft, child abuse and murder. Between the headlines one can also see noble tributes to the spiritual leaders of the times in which we live.

Psychologists Differ in their Views of Human Nature

Some psychologists stress the baser side of man. Sigmund Freud focused on the animalistic side of man, especially his aggressive and sexual drives. He saw this baser element residing in his unconscious. Like a gigantic iceberg the Id impulses that reside beneath the surface could occasionally emerge and effect our lives. In contrast to Freud, Abraham Maslow postulated that indeed we do have physiological drives such as a need for food to sustain our bodies but we also have transcendent qualities. We may override these lower drives for some cause we believe in.

Why is it that some reach to the heights of human dignity while others sink to the depths of utter degeneration?

Scope of this Chapter

This chapter proposes that there are certain principles of maturity that can be determined which relate to human growth and development. When these principles are followed they maximize the highest human potential.

The Relationship of the Child to the Adult

Another approach to the question, "What do you see when you see a man?" involves his developmental history. The person answering the question from this perspective would respond that he sees a child. Both psychologists and theologians would agree that the childhood experiences inevitably determine to a large extent the adult years.

Babies are pretty much alike when they are born. They go through the same sequences in physical maturation. They become different because of the unique genetic inheritance and the specific environment in which they grow.

The unique blending of heredity and environment may be exemplified in an observation of a neighbor of mine years ago. This man was unique. I always thought no one in the world could look like him. He had a gate, a swagger when he walked. He conveyed the impression "when you see me coming you better step aside." (At least as a child growing up he conveyed that impression. His size and the barroom brawl stories he spun for me tended to confirm the imprint on my mind.) There could never be another quite like him. Then he had a son. You guessed it. His son was the spittin' image of the old man. He walked like him and talked like him and any kid half his size tended to step aside when he appeared. My mother and I were often amused to watch them across the road playing in their backyard. I can see

85

the scene from thirty-five years ago as if it were yesterday. The man and his miniature swaggering along behind him. My concern as I look back is whether his son ever developed the drinking problem his father struggled with. My neighbor often conveyed to me, just a child, how destructive alcohol was and how badly he wanted to stay off the bottle for the sake of his son.

Sequence of Growth Specified

As a seed develops and matures into a flower which we see so beautifully arrayed, we become aware that there is a specific pattern of growth. An infant changes and matures into an adult by following an established pattern of principles relating to growth and development. This maturational sequence is specific enough so that it can be identified, observed, and recorded. The sequence is the same for all individuals. The developmental process is not limited to one aspect of growth, however, since each child grows in five ways: mentally, physically, emotionally, socially and spiritually. This sequence should not surprise us when we recall that Jesus grew in wisdom, stature, and in favor with God and man. Within this Scripture is our outline. For the Christian all these areas are important. Herein is our basis for Meaningful Maturity.

The word "maturity" according to the dictionary, means "to bring to maturity or completion; the termination of the period; the final stage in a cycle or erosion." The word "maturity" can give us the wrong impression. We never become "arrivers" but "becomers." We are always in the process. Hopefully this process is meaningful. The whole Christian life in Christ brings meaning.

Children, for example, will grow up, given some care, but they may not necessarily mature. Maturity demands discipline, motivation, and goals. The Apostle Paul spoke of pressing toward the mark. Meaningful Maturity is not accidental. It involves struggle, tension, and conflict. We have to work at it. There is always the temptation to resist maturing meaningfully.

Role of Discipline

Students in college who have their first crack at freedom often lack discipline. They put off doing that term paper or studying for that final exam. We all get into these ruts at times. To the other extreme, we can become so goal oriented that we are compulsive drivers that need to decide some goals and perspectives.

While I was writing my dissertation I was working at the mental health clinic and had a church. I was pushing so hard that it was difficult for me to relax. A turning point for me was when I gave up some of my clients and some of the group work I was involved in to spend more time with my family. I had so many goals.

Scriptural Focus

We all need to grow in certain basic ways, but we are all specific and unique. No two people are the same. It is up to each one of us to work on maturity that is meaningful to us. May we look at each of these areas from the life of Christ and His growth and see how they apply to us.

And Jesus grew in wisdom and stature, and in favor with God and men (Luke 2:52, NIV).

I. *Wisdom (mentally)*

Not only should we grow in wisdom, but we must ask questions: Is it meaningful? Why do we want to increase our knowledge or our education? To achieve prestige, money, fame, fortune (this is the goal for many today). How about increasing our image in society or for ourselves?

One time in group therapy with a psychologist, we discovered that we had both failed the first grade. He jokingly insisted that it was a prerequisite for getting a doctorate. He was implying that perhaps we were proving something to ourselves. I experienced something of an anti-climax when I got my doctorate and I wondered if I had to keep proving myself. Big achievements like this have a way of turning out like this if they are an end in themselves.

The ultimate goal for our learning must be to serve God. You will remember that Solomon was an educated man. Listen to what he had to say about it in Ecclesiastes 1:13-18.

> I devoted myself to study and to explore by wisdom all that is done under heaven. What a heavy burden God has laid on men! I have seen all the things that are done under the sun; all of them are meaningless, a chasing after the wind. What is twisted cannot be straightened; what is lacking cannot be counted. I thought to myself, "Look, I have grown and increased in wisdom more than anyone who has ruled over Jerusalem before me; I have experienced much of wisdom and knowledge." Then I applied myself to the understanding of wisdom, and also of madness and folly, but I learned that this, too, is a chasing after the wind. For with much wisdom comes much sorrow; the more knowledge, the more grief (Ecclesiastes 1:13-18, NIV).

The summation of the whole thing for Solomon was to fear God and keep His commandments.

Be warned, my son, of anything in addition to them. Of making many books there is no end, and much study wearies the body. Now all has been heard; here is the conclusion of the matter: Fear God and keep his commandments, for this is the whole duty of man (Ecclesiastes 12:12, 13, NIV).

II. *Stature*

In contrast to wisdom or our mental development our stature or our physical maturity may seem rather unimportant. But as a matter of fact, our appearance is important. In the study of adolescence we know it is extremely important to boys and girls. Not just to girls as we traditionally thought.

It is important to girls and boys that they be sexually appropriate. That the boys look like boys and the girls look like girls. The Scripture accents the body far more than we often consider. Our bodies are the "temple of God." The New Testament teaches a bodily resurrection not merely a survival of the soul. The Greeks taught that the body was evil and was to be destroyed while the Christian realizes God is the Creator of our bodies. All things are given to enjoy (I Timothy 6:17). There are many wholesome ways in which we can enjoy life in the flesh. Eating may be enjoyed as well as sustaining our bodies. Sexual relations are to be enjoyed within the bond of marriage. Exercise, whether it's tennis, or golf, or walking or whatever, is enjoyable and important to our health. All work and no play makes Jack a dull boy or Jane a dull girl. A constant diet without relief can make Jack or Jane a pretty bored and even sick guy or gal.

Sometimes we can neglect this area of care for our physical bodies. Appropriate stewardship demands attention to physical needs.

III. *In Favor with God and Man*

In proportion to His advance in wisdom, Jesus grew in favor with God, not that he ever *lacked* the favor of God. He showed an understanding and spirit like His own. To my mind no statement can possibly sum up better what God would expect of us as we grow through childhood and adolescence and into adulthood.

Jesus once summed the law and the prophets up in a statement concerning love to God and our fellowman. In the Christian religion these two concepts fit together.

> Jesus replied: "'Love the Lord your God with all your heart and with all your soul and with all your mind.' This is the first and greatest commandment. And the second is like it: 'Love your neighbor as yourself.' All the Law and the Prophets hang on these two commandments" (Matthew 22:37-39, NIV).

Psychosocial Development from a Scriptural Perspective

It is interesting that great psychologists although not drawing from Scriptural teaching have through their studies of man's behavior drawn similar conclusions. Erick Erikson, a psychologist whose work has been popular, stressed what he calls a psychosocial theory of development. Erikson insists that the key to our maturity is to come to grips with the struggle with society at each stage of our development. We either learn or fail to learn lessons through life. At each stage of life a conflict is present. For example, with the infant it is trust vs. mistrust.

The severe problems that may develop when distrust is rampant may be illustrated in some cases of childhood schizophrenia, while lifelong struggles with trusting may also be apparent. The child who cannot trust his parents conjures up negative pictures of the heavenly father as harsh and cruel. Early impressions may adversely affect the concept of a loving heavenly father.

The child who is not permitted to exercise a sense of autonomy in a kind and loving way according to Erikson becomes hung up in this stage and experiences shame and doubt. The central focus during this period revolves around the challenge of the parent to become nurturing and inviting rather than demeaning during the potty training stage.

The transmission of a sense of worthlessness affects the openness with which a child views himself as either good or evil. If the parent can nurture the child's sense of autonomy during the trying period of potty training, the child will more likely emerge with positive feelings about himself. Rigid parent demands that are unrealistic, in light of the child's control over his sphincter muscles, can result in internalized rage and shame over his inability to meet next to impossible parental demands.

The next stage Erikson addresses is industry vs. inferiority. As the child enters school a tremendous challenge awaits him. His ability to cope with the academic and socializing world of school may result in feelings of inferiority that may plague one's sense of adequacy to the task of work. Of course, the child may experience this new world with good feelings about his ability.

Many Christians unfortunately view Christianity to be basically work. They must earn their salvation instead of fully appreciating the role of God's grace in salvation. These people are stuck in this stage that affects a wholesome outlook on the role of work in life and a healthy spiritual view of work and grace.

The crisis to be resolved during adolescence is the crisis of identity or role confusion. If the adolescent is able to bring some resolution to the disturbing probes into who he is as a man or a woman, the meaning of his life and what to do with it, he can achieve some preparation for his vocation and readiness for marriage.

During this stage a person is hopefully ready to make a decision regarding his relationship to Christ. The religion of mother and father is processed and some decisions made in light of the adolescent's emerging intellectual abilities to cope with the doctrines of Christ and the church. Hopefully, the child moves into the adult world in reconciling this and many other important decisions that affect his life.

Sherrill sums up this stage in the following synopsis.

> The drama of childhood has its sequel in the drama of adolescence. In the former, the central problem was individuation. In adolescence the central problem is that of becoming psychologically weaned from the parents. The nature and degree of the weaning which is achieved during adolescence have much to do with the kind of growth which can take place within the adolescent years and with the later adequacy of the individual for the more mature responsibilities of adulthood.[1]

When a youth works through identity crisis then the stage is set for intimacy. If the battles of earlier days leave a person thoroughly confused over who he is and the direction of his life, then marriage, the most intimate of all human relationships, would not be advisable. Today a great deal is made of finding oneself. Too often a couple marries to

---

1. Lewis Joseph Sherrill, *The Struggle of the Soul* (New York: Macmillan Company, 1951), p. 75.

seek answers concerning themselves and to meet needs that should have been resolved prior to the commitment of marriage. One viable explanation for the problems of many marriages resides in the inability to cope with the commitment to work with another person. If a person lacks adequate self-esteem to cope with life's stresses, it is unlikely he will achieve satisfaction in sharing his life closely with another person. Marriage will test the stability of one's developmental health.

Intimacy also relates according to Gleason with an individual's capacity to establish a closeness with God as often expressed in the songs of faith as a "friend," a "brother," the "lover of our souls," and "companion." Not only does the Christian desire the nearness of God in that profound relationship but the fellowship in the church family draws upon a person's capacity for closeness as well.

> In this view the essence of the church (the body of Christ) becomes a group of human beings risking intimacy, sharing with one another the joys, the hurts, the whole range of what it's about to be human, and thereby, attaining in its fullest moments the divine.[2]

Generativity vs. stagnation encompasses the next developmental stage according to Erikson. Erikson describes generativity.

> Generativity, then, is primarily the concern in establishing and guiding the next generation, although there are individuals who, through misfortune or because of special and genuine gifts in other directions, do not apply this drive to their own offspring. And indeed, the concept generativity is

---

2. John Gleason. *Growing Up To God* (Nashville: Abingdon Press, 1975), p. 92.

meant to include such more popular synonyms as *productivity* and *creativity*, which, however, cannot replace it.[3]

The most obvious religious reference is the charge God gave shortly after the creation of man and woman. God blessed them, saying to them, "Be fruitful, multiply, fill the earth and conquer it. Be masters of the fish of the sea, the birds of heaven and all living animals on the earth" (Genesis 1:28, NIV).

The need for industry typical of the child going to school for the first time is reactivated. It is not only work but the sense of creativity in one's work that comes under scrutiny.

A man near the age of retirement confided in me:

> My job is no longer exciting. It used to be a joy to go to work, now it's a chore. I'm no longer treated as if I have something to contribute. They assume I'm not interested. They will not call me in on the continuing education programs and inform me of the new systems. They assume I'm content to sit and wait till I retire. They do it quite unintentionally because they assume that's the way they would be. When they get to the place where I am they will probably also want to be creative. If I cannot continue to grow I don't want to work. Since I am no longer able to do that on my job, I will retire as soon as possible.

A person's job is important. Meaningful vocational activity is crucial. To stagnate is the fear. However, nothing becomes more important than one's family, the relationship to the next generation. It is the next generation, one's offspring, that provide continuity to life.

The central issue in the final stage is whether an individual

---

3. Erick H. Erikson, "Eight Ages of Man" in *Childhood and Society* (New York: W. W. Norton and Company, 1963), p. 267.

can get in touch with a sense of integrity in the life that has been lived. If an individual can look back and acclaim that it's been a good race, well worth the effort; then life has had fulfillment. On the other hand, despair results when life has not maintained a sense of integrity concerning life experiences.

Perhaps the Apostle Paul expressed it best of all when he shared his personal testimony concerning his own life.

> For I am already being poured out as a drink offering, and the time has come for my departure. I have fought the good fight, I have finished the race, I have kept the faith. Now there is in store for me the crown of righteousness, which the Lord, the righteous Judge, will award to me on that day —and not only to me, but also to all who have longed for his appearing (II Timothy 4:6-8, NIV).

In summary it must be acknowledged that man has immense potential for meaningful maturity. The Lord himself provides the perfect model of development. Developmental Psychologists help to bring into bold relief the issues to be met throughout the life cycle. The Scripture facilitates the task of reconciling the crisis in each stage of development.

DISCUSSION QUESTIONS: *The Struggle for Meaningful Maturity*

1. How do psychologists differ regarding the nature of man? How does the Bible relate to the question of man's nature? What is meant by a balanced view?
2. What is the relationship of the child to the adult?
3. Name and describe the five aspects of the development process.

4. Explain how the word "maturity" can give us the wrong impression.
5. Why ask, "Is wisdom meaningful?" Do some people accumulate knowledge for inappropriate reasons?
6. Is physical development important? Explain the role of physical development and self-image as we grow. What causation do you personally take in caring for yourself physically? How might you improve the care of your physical body?
7. What impact does a child's early relationship with parents have upon his concept of a loving heavenly father?
8. Describe the importance of potty training and how it relates to development?
9. How important is a child's early school experiences? How do they effect self image and grow and work?
10. What developmental crisis takes place during adolescence? What issues does the adolescent deal with?
11. How are the issues of adolescence related to intimacy in marriage? How does intimacy and a person's capacity for closeness come into focus when one becomes a Christian and is added to the community of the church?
12. What does generativity mean? How can stagnation develop?
13. Explain the use of the term integrity? What does Paul acclaim? What aspects of your life will add integrity to your life?

Chapter Seven[*]

THE TWO-CAREER MARRIAGE

Biblical Illustration

The role played by the wife in Proverbs 31 speaks forcefully to the current problem of many couples caught in the throes of a two-career marriage. Unfortunately times have not changed; the weight of the responsibility for the success of a two-career marriage still rests unequally on the wife's part. In spite of equal rights, society still places considerable expectations upon the woman's role as basically a wife and mother. Although this passage sets forth in detail the wife's role, it does convey how the husband is to respond to her career.

Context

At first glance it is rather ironical that in this age of women's rights, the model for a two-career marriage emerges out of an era in which society provided women with very few legal rights. However life then was seldom as bad as it might have been theoretically.[1] In actual practice women were afforded considerable prestige commensurate with the responsibilities within the home and in the market place.

The husband mentioned in Proverbs 31 was a well-known council member who helped rule the city. It may well be that he derived considerable civil benefits from his wife's managerial skill and industry in running the household. Her abilities as an affluent businesswoman certainly never hurt his prestige as a city manager.[2]

---

[*] A portion of this chapter was originally published as an article in the *Christian Standard* entitled, "Adjusting to Vocational Requirements in Marriage" by Carl W. Pruitt and Millie Pruitt in September 20, 1981.

1. E. W. Heaton, *Everyday Life in Old Testament Times* (London: B. T. Batsford LTD, 1956), pp. 68-69.

2. S. R. Driver, A. Plummer and C. A. Briggs, *International Critical Commentary*, "A Critical and Exegetical Commentary on the Book of Proverbs," by Crawford H. Toy (Edinburgh: T. and T. Clark, 1899), pp. 546-547.

One of the chief problems of the career woman today is that of ambiguity concerning her role.[3] To be successful in a career militates against the role of wife and mother. Success at one appears to contradict success in the other. Women may burn up considerable energy caught in this conflict. If a woman is looking for permission to be a responsible mother and wife as well as a successful businesswoman she can find a model in this passage. This woman certainly has it "all together" as Staton suggests in her book, *What the Bible Says About Women*.[4]

Relevance of the Scripture to the Contemporary Problem

Nearly half of the laboring force today are women. Recognition of both financial pressures and personal needs have led more and more women to seek employment. The demands of time and energy place tremendous emotional drain on a marriage. At the present time one of the most serious problems facing a married couple is the pressure of blending their careers with the marital relationship.

A useful strategy for answering this challenge of a dual-role marriage is to compare their dual-role with others. Unfortunately, there are few models to emulate. Many marriages that appear to deal with this problem are the very ones which sometimes come apart at the seams to the utter shock of those who would emulate them. Not infrequently the reason for the breakup involves friction within their careers.

---

3. Susan A. Darley, "Big-Time Careers for the Little Woman: A Dual-Role Dilemma" in *The Changing Family*, ed. Jerald Savells and Laurence J. Cross (New York: Holt, Rinehart and Winston, 1978), p. 276.

4. Julia Staton, *What the Bible Says About Women* (Joplin: College Press Publishing Company, 1980), p. 255.

When we turn to the individual husband and wife within the dual marriage model, one is hard pressed for an adequate model. Models are especially difficult for the wife. The role requirements for being a good father and husband are not contradictory. Men can integrate their careers and their marriage and family life much easier than women. Susan Darley sums up a woman's struggle to find a fitting role model:

> Most of the woman's colleagues are likely to be men, which makes them dissimilar on an important dimension, and of the few colleagues that are women, not all will be married or have children, and so they too may be importantly different and thus not ideal social-comparison referents.[5]

Comment

In the example chosen from Proverbs 31 there is that much-needed model for a woman. This beautiful portrayal of a wife and mother and career woman provides implicit direction for the husband as well. He should not be jealous or envious of his wife's success. Her husband was supportive and proud of her and perhaps most important of all was not ashamed to praise her. Within this Scripture there is much to pattern for the husband as well as the wife (Proverbs 31:28).

It is possible that this career woman conducted a business on an international scale with a very valuable industry of that time.[6] She was also a realtor and investor. Scripture says that she considered a field and bought it. She seemed to receive pleasure from her work. In addition to the labor in the market place she worked willingly with her hands

---

5. Darley, "Big-time Careers for the Little Woman," p. 276.

6. H. D. M. Spence and Joseph S. Excell, eds., *The Pulpit Commentary, Ecclesiastes, Song of Solomon*, by W. J. Deans and S. T. Taylor-Taswell (Grand Rapids: Wm. B. Eerdmans Publishing Company, 1950), Vol. 9:598.

around the house. Although she represented a wealthy household with maidens, she as the head of that large household was not above performing menial tasks. She ground the corn and prepared for the next day's meal. She probably provided clothing also by her own hands. (This does not suggest that present-day wives have to do manual tasks that are customarily done by modern conveniences.)

She worked long and hard at her business and in her home. She was not arrogant or conceited. She received personal satisfaction and performed her labor of love to her family and to the poor and needy in the community.

Although this approach has applauded the woman's skills as a businesswoman, it is as a homemaker and wife that she has enjoyed great veneration throughout history. Her children and her husband who had the best opportunity to appraise her life do so in the most glowing terms. Her work is praised "in the gates"—praised of men and God.

If one woman were chosen as the Ideal—one would be hard pressed in all literature to surpass this woman whose renown has become synonymous with the Ideal Woman. This Ideal Woman successfully combines her career and her role as wife and mother. Her husband trusted in her and gave her freedom to invest her cosmopolitan and domestic gifts to the fullest. Many women after comparing themselves, to this model, may feel very inadequate because they do not possess the gifts of this unusual woman. Julia Staton rightfully insists that we are not to take every point literally but we are to note the main trends and principles that this woman followed. She goes on to maintain an important point for woman to consider. The husband and wife found in Proverbs 31 most perfectly embodies the Ideal Two-Career Marriage.

. . . we to assume that every woman must be this busy or out buying and selling real estate. We do not know the age of this woman or the age of her children. Certainly a woman with toddlers or with several children would not be expected to be so active outside the home. No woman's talents and capabilities are the same. We are each unique individuals with unique home situations. God does not expect us to be "superwomen," but He does expect us to be His women, doing our best for Him with what interests and abilities we possess.[7]

For most people this task of blending two careers with marriage has been less than ideal. The two-career marriage presently in vogue is nothing new, however some of the pressures are unique to our times.

The Scope of this Study

To supplement the Scriptural model, contemporary dynamics of adult life provide additional insights. In present day marriages there are a number of adjustments that need to be made during the course of a couple's life together. After exploring a life span approach to a couple's struggle with a dual career marriage, Scriptural resources will be explored further.

In this presentation an attempt has been made to focus upon vocational plans prior to marriage, in early marriage, in the middle years and in the later years.

I. Vocational Plans Prior to Marriage

Failure to clarify the husband-wife role prior to marriage is a major cause of discord and eventual divorce. In our

---

7. Staton, *What The Bible Says About Women*, p. 256.

experience as marriage therapists, this oversight, deliberate or careless, has disastrous results. In Wes Robert's and H. Normal Wright's marriage preparation manual, *Before You Say "I Do,"*[8] they encourage couples to work through, with the help of their workbook, the answer to the question, "Woman's Place—Where Are You?"

This is one of the central issues in marriage. The working through, the questions they ask, help to bring out where each partner is. In some cases conflict is readily apparent. Other times differences may be buried to emerge at some vulnerable point in the marriage years later. Take, for example, a recurring theme of the husband who views his role as the provider and decision-maker. He marries a shy woman whose father modeled this approach and whose mother reinforces it reluctantly as the way it is supposed to be. The woman sits on her feelings of being a second-class citizen available for his pleasure and his career and to raise his kids. One day she says, "Enough is enough, I've had it!" One of the trends that recurs in our practice over and over again is the desperate man whose wife has finally filed for divorce as the result of this problem.

It would be helpful if premarital counseling would be required by law. Instead of the emphasis upon divorce laws that make it easier to get out of marriage it would be more helpful to make it more difficult to get into a marriage. Certainly ministers ought to require it before they become involved in planning a wedding service. Serious premarital counseling could help the couple get acquainted with their family background, the roles taught by their parents and how these have

---

8. Wes Robert and H. Norman Wright, *Before You Say "I Do"* (Irving: Harvest House, 1979).

affected them. Encouragement needs to be given to facilitate communication and to check out how well the couples have shared on vital issues of vocational expectations. Assessing the readiness through interviews and testing of emotional stability may be accomplished in three or four sessions. More extensive exploration of the issues that evolve would enable the couple to anticipate some problems and work through recognized conflicts.

At Kentucky Christian College we have instituted pre-marital counseling. Some couples have become involved in some counseling over a period of a year, thereby giving adequate opportunity to assess their readiness for marriage, share goals and develop important communication skills. For most couples extensive counseling for a year would be impractical for several reasons. Premarital counseling should be provided by the church. The normal one to three sessions is inadequate to analyze issues such as vocational concerns. Obviously short-term premarital counseling alone is too little too late for most couples. The couple that is set on getting married often views counseling as merely a require-ment for marriage. Inadequate motivation is prevalent. The reasoning may well be, "after all we're in love." The mis-conception that love conquers all prevails.

As far as counseling is concerned post-marital counseling for individual couples or for groups of couples soon after marriage may be even more effective. After a few months the couple begins to come down from cloud nine and is forced to deal with some serious realities. Issues revolving around vocational concerns would be a major part of such counseling. The marital support and insight of other couples coping with similar problems is effective in defining and implementing needed adjustments in a relationship. An excellent resource for setting up such a group may be found in Howard Hovde's book *The Neo-Married*[9]: Hovde's approach is structured in such a fashion as to provide a context for discussion. This style would be helpful for the leader who would be uncomfortable with less structured group therapy.

Beneficial questions for discussion for most couples should focus on the following issues:

1. What are the priorities in life of each partner?
2. What about educational plans? Who will work and who will go to school?
3. In the case of dual careers, what plans are there for both meeting their career needs?
4. How do they both feel about the wife working?
5. How do they both feel about the wife working after children are born?
6. How committed are both to a career goal?
7. How important is the career goal when it conflicts with family time?
8. What are the feelings of each partner on the possibility of relocation? Some vocations such as the military, the ministry and construction work usually demand frequent moves.
9. What salary range will the job be in? How frequently will one or both of them be paid? If one is in business for himself or a salesman, the salary will vary and it may take time to build the business.
10. How much security does the job provide? How much risk is involved? For example, being in business for oneself has advantages of freedom and often greater financial potential but can demand considerable greater financial risk than most 9 to 5 jobs.

---

9. Howard Hovde, *The Neo-Married* (Valley Forge: Judson Press, 1968).

One serious decision emerges among college students when the wife also desires a career, although she may work while her husband goes to college. This is apparent on our campus. Wives who work to put hubby through sometimes become resentful if their careers were interrupted. Dad has many of his needs met academically as well as socially. Mom works and takes care of the kids around the clock for the fulltime student. This can become a very uneven relationship. Some attention to her needs must be provided. Occasionally a slight modification such as giving the wife a chance to take a class or two can do a great deal for her morale. Certainly a more even distribution of the chores involved is helpful. It is critical that the fulltime student give attention to his marriage and his responsibility as a parent.

On a more personal level we will illustrate some of the issues we worked through during our courtship.

1. Millie was to work until Carl finished graduate school.
2. Although Millie always wanted to be a minister's wife, she also viewed her work as teacher and later as a guidance counselor in the public school as a ministry as well.
3. We decided Millie would work when we had a family but only after they were in school.
4. We planned to be clear when negotiating the terms of a contract with a church that we viewed her work as a ministry and would have dual careers.

Due to the mutual comfort we each shared with this contract we had with each other, the problems many couples have in this regard were avoided. Of course, we both had our careers outlined and have basically shifted only slightly from them. In fact, quite independent from each other, we seemed to navigate toward counseling. Presently we have distinct careers, Millie as a guidance counselor and Carl as professor. We share a private practice of marriage and family counseling.

II. *Vocational Adjustment in Early Marriage*

The adjustment problems depend upon the interaction of the social and economic situations. The male blue collar worker tends to marry earlier. Consequently, he settles into his job sooner, has his family and retires earlier. His whole life is accelerated. In contrast, the professional man generally goes to college, marries later, waits longer before his family begins and retires later in life. He usually has a greater emotional investment in his career.

The female worker, like the man who has no special training and works basically for economic reasons, also wants to get out of the house to meeting social needs often thwarted by an early marriage.

In the case of the professional woman she has unmet career needs. She also may have labored hard to get through college or partially through before marriage and beginning her family. She anxiously wants to see her career goals realized now that her maternal needs of a family are realized.

The early years of marriage for most couples involves getting established. Young couples are usually conservative. They are concerned with the practical necessities of meeting the demands of a growing family. Career changes are likely to be more prevalent later in life.

During these years the seeds of what Wayne Oates calls workaholism may be implanted. Concern with financial security and career goals tends to be addictive for some people—both professional and blue-collar workers. This is most often the problem of the husband and father. As women become more active in the job and the demands for their skills increase this will undoubtedly become a problem with them. These inroads into the time together for each other and for family poses an immense problem in some families. Suggestions for recognizing and breaking this problem are treated extensively in Wayne Oates delightful *Confessions of a Workaholic*[10].

Our earliest married years were spent when Carl was in graduate school and Millie taught school. In our marriage we struggled with the distribution of tasks around the house. Carl attempted to help with some of the tasks but lacked skills as a cook. He did, however, run the vacuum and clean the house, do some shopping, and the laundry. The first year teaching Junior High English was a tremendous adjustment. Millie was exhausted emotionally and physically. Getting dinner together was all she could manage.

We learned early in our marriage to anticipate each other's work schedules and to cover when the other one was tired. Even to this day, we anticipate each other's heavy teaching schedules and/or counseling days and cover for the other. Now it involves taking care of the kids while the other stretches out for awhile and regroups.

III. *The Vocational Adjustment in the Middle Years*

The suggestion has been presented that ideally couples should verbalize, work through their vocational roles. However, the fact of the matter is that often couples fail to do this and perhaps most important of all they change.

For example, a wife may be content to be a housewife for five, ten, fifteen, or twenty years. Then one day she changes.

---

10. Wayne Oates, *Confessions Of A Workaholic* (Nashville: Abingdon Press, 1978).

According to Gail Sheehy "thirty-five is when the average American woman re-enters the working world." In my experience this is a time when many women are saying, what's in this for me, this is my last chance to have a sense of satisfaction with my identity. Often as Sheehy describes, a woman is interested in career advancement and satisfaction beyond making ends meet at the very time when a husband is beginning to settle down. Change is threatening to him. Few couples move in the same direction at the same time in their careers.

A couple in their early forties comes for marriage counseling. One of the issues that emerges is the area of vocational adjustment. The wife went back to work after the youngest child entered school. She became quite successful as a salesperson in women's clothing. She received rapid advancement and opportunities to travel to various conventions in cities like San Francisco, New Orleans and Las Vegas. She invited her husband to go along but he refused. He also failed to give her much praise for her success. In the course of counseling a particular session revealed the reasons. He had been the sole bread-winner, prided himself in providing a high level income, and received an ego boost from the dependence on him. He was uncomfortable with her traveling because he was concerned she would become involved with another man. He never verbalized his fears and his sense of loss until the counseling session. Instead he went along with her but indirectly attempted to sabotage her good feelings about herself. He carried around a lot of hidden anger. She, in turn, could not understand why he was not proud of her while everyone else seemed to be. The one person from whom she most needed support withheld it.

activities, leisure activities, and relationship activities provide a key to a more stimulating life.

Vocational adjustment in the later life must be linked with a discussion of widowhood. Since women usually outlive men and generally marry older men, they are more apt to survive their husbands. The widow often is forced to get along on less retirement income. If she is widowed earlier she must fall back on her vocation, if indeed she has one. Many widows are vocationally unprepared for widowhood.

Since there are more widows and fewer eligible mates, the chances for remarriage are considerably less among widows than for widowers. The surviving spouse faces a host of emotional and practical adjustment problems, not the least of which is financial. Once again the importance of life-long vocational career planning comes into focus.

In New Testament times widows were even more unprepared for widowhood than today. If their families did not care for them as directed by Old Testament law (Deut. 24), their plight fell upon the church (Acts 6). Lydia, the seller of purple, provides a bold contrast to the economic situation of both the ancient and the modern widow. Lydia is a representative of women throughout history who have business acumen (Acts 16:14). Lydia's business was lucrative. She was probably wealthy. Although we cannot be sure, tradition has it that she was a widow with children.

In our personal experience with widows in several different church settings, we have observed that some have accumulated financial resources through their husband, their own business adventures, or through professional job security. However, most are financially insecure in comparison with the norm of society. It might be said that widows are unfortunately more representative of the widow of Nain than the seller of purple from Thyatira. This is a sad indictment upon our times as well as on ancient times. Perhaps it is wise for women to look upon this as a clear warning to look ahead, for the day may come when no one will take care of their needs. At the present juncture society is beginning to open new fields to women. Whatever a woman's status, married or single, she would be well advised to place at least a foot in the door of some vocation to protect herself and/or her family for the possibility that she will be thrown back upon her resources as a single woman.

Due to the insight provided by developmental psychologists such as Erik Erikson[11] and more recently Sheehy in her best seller, *Passages*[12], Americans are becoming aware of the dynamics of adult life. The theological framework for a study of a life-scope approach is found in works by John Gleason in *Growing Up to God*[13] and Lewis Sherril's *Struggles of the Soul*[14]. An awareness of these changes is a first step in coping with career adjustments in marriage. In the midst of shifting roles of men and women in today's society, few issues are more vital than this one.

Scriptural Resources for Dealing with Vocational Adjustments

The present state of the economy has forced most people to adjust to spiraling inflation. Suddenly we cannot afford some luxuries we have taken for granted. The time has come

---

11. Erik Erikson, "Eight Ages of Man" in *Childhood and Society* (New York: W. W. Norton, 1950), *Identity and the Life Cycle* (New York: International University Press, 1959).

12. Gail Sheehy, *Passages* (New York: Dutton, 1976).

13. John Gleason, *Growing Up To God* (Nashville: Abingdon Press, 1975).

14. Lewis Joseph Sherrill *Struggles Of The Soul* (New York: MacMillan Publishing, 1955).

to refocus priorities and take seriously the model of a simpler life provided by our Lord Himself. His life-style was devoid of the trappings of "things" that most of us are all wrapped up in. Unfortunately, Americans appear to judge their lives in relationship to the accumulation of gadgets and conveniences. Our feelings about ourselves may be intricately tied to how we keep up with the "Joneses." The Lord's admonition from the Sermon on the Mount provides a vital directive to those of us who are caught in a bind between our materialistic desires and our shrinking dollar. The Lord challenges us to "seek first the kingdom of God, and His righteousness; and all these things shall be added unto you" (Matthew 6:33).

Some of the best advice we ever had as a young couple came from a minister friend who was also a father figure to us. He cautioned us not to get in debt. This advice served us well early in our marriage. In retrospect, I wish we had practiced more of this same discipline throughout life. Perhaps others share this same desire to re-evaluate their perspectives. Dr. David Mace in February, 1981, series for *Marriage and Family Life*[15] sets forth a beautiful example of a full life and yet a life that is relatively free of many accessories that bog us down. We heartily recommend the reading of this series of acticles.

People on fixed incomes and the unemployed find financial problems of the current recession have struck devastating blows. Perhaps no better word can be offered than that of patience during this session of crisis (Galatians 5:22). Most of us are short on patience, especially in times of adversity. James and Paul both remind us that growth can emerge out of all these difficult circumstances if we are patient

---

15. David Mace, "Simple Living in Today's World," *Marriage and Family Life* (February, 1981), pp. 8-10.

and give the Lord a chance to work in our daily lives (James 1:2-4; Romans 8:28).

Dual careers can become what Wade and Mary Rowatt call dueling careers in their book, *The Two Career Marriage*[16] (Westminster Press, Philadelphia, 1980). When our careers as married couples tend to aggravate existing problems, contribute to jealousy on the job or over the salary, or the prestige the other commands, it is high time to take a serious look at the marriage and family life. Handling two careers taxes communication. The lack of energy left for each other can contribute to a serious drain on the relationship. A careful reading of a selected passage in Proverbs will lead us to a basic principle. It is better to have less and have unity in the marriage than to have plenty and have strife (Proverbs 15:16, 17 and Proverbs 17:1). Dual careers are not worth a divorce. A few extra dollars are not worth the high cost that divorce can rain on a couple and their children. Not even the high calling of the ministry is justified at the cost of a serious threat to marriage and family life. Whenever a career or careers clash with the continuity of the marriage and family bond, attention must be given to the survival of that basic commitment.

Two-career marriage calls for the highest quality of reciprocal marriage and family relationship, as well as all other interpersonal contacts.

Conclusion

The vocational adjustments required between a couple are as varied and as complex as each person involved. These

---

16. Wade and Mary Rowatt, *The Two Career Marriage* (Philadelphia: Westminster Press, 1980).

adjustments depend upon our personality, our moods, our image of ourselves and where we are in our life cycle.

The struggle with two careers can be a real blessing or a real curse. In the final analysis, it is up to each couple what they will do with the challenge.

In our marriage our careers have blended together. We have felt positive stimulation to share our separate and mutual career goals. We have worked together to achieve these goals. We have felt a healthy pride in each other's achievements and wept with each other's failures. We have come to appreciate each other more as persons, as companions, and as professional colleagues. Our careers have added a dimension of intimacy that would not have been there otherwise.

Today, many couples feel that they have to both work. Whether they both work or not, they would be wise to trim their life-style down in keeping with the runaway inflation. They need also to keep Biblical priorities in mind. Apart from the financial remuneration, we have gained mutual satisfaction from our careers. We have sensed a ministry in the blending of our lives. It has not always been easy and we have had our share of ups and downs, but we would do it all over again. Of course, we would make some changes, some of which we tried to share with our readers.

DISCUSSION QUESTIONS: *The Two-Career Marriage*

1. How were times different when Ecclesiastes was written? How alike?
2. What does Proverbs 31 provide for a woman today who is adjusting to a two-career marriage?
3. Explain the ambiguity around a career for most married women?

4. What basic question needs to be clarified by a couple before they are married? Why does it need to be worked through completely?

5. Why does the author feel post marital groups may be even more necessary than premarital counseling? Why or why not? What program of guidance, premarital or postmarital, do you feel would be best?

6. How relevant for you are the questions the author focuses on for premarital direction? Are there other questions that should be raised? Discuss these additional areas where guidance would be helpful.

7. What practical suggestions do you feel are helpful for a couple when both work? Discuss specifically
   A. Sharing chores around the house
   B. Sharing in caring for the children
   C. Sharing financial expenses

8. Discuss the importance of Biblical priorities regarding financial guidelines.

9. How approximate are the illustrations of what happens in the middle years? What other problems arise during this time in life?

10. Discuss the unique career adjustments in the later years.
    A. Retirement
    B. Widowhood

11. What Scriptural resources were especially helpful in this chapter?

Chapter Eight*

WHEN YOUR KIDS GROW UP

Biblical Illustration

The Parable of the Prodigal Son provides a most gripping illustration of a child leaving home. Under the best of circumstances, parents struggle to cope with the experience. The Parable of the Prodigal Son is especially insightful because it deals with a child leaving home under the most trying conditions. Unfortunately, the circumstances have a frequent counterpart today.

Context

For a child to leave home was unusual in the first century. The empty nest was seldom a problem. Children in those times remained at home. Families were large and all lived together in an extended family. This was, of course, a feature of the patriarchal age. The eldest son's role was typical and the youngest son's departure strikingly exceptional. This very fact of a son leaving was dramatic, to say nothing of the freedom which incited his need to kick the props out and the riotous living that further added to its traumatic quality.

Relevance for Today

A parent exclaimed to me recently, "We haven't experienced the empty nest syndrome. It is wonderful. We have a great relationship." Upon closer inquiry, I learned that they were living close enough to visit occasionally. I also learned that they were close as far as values and life-style. The children were continuing to fulfill their expectations.

---

* A portion of this chapter was originally published as an article in the *Christian Standard* for February 1, 1981.

It is when the children move far away physically but especially spiritually that a parent suffers the most intense hurt.

When this chapter first appeared in its original form for publication, I received a letter from a mother who convinced me to revise my work to treat an aspect of this problem I had overlooked. She wrote, "If they were living decent moral lives and happily married I could accept this, my husband and I get along well. . . . It worries us both as we love them so much. . . ." As this mother continued to pour out her heart to me, my heart ached for her. I really didn't have the answer personally but it occurred to me how profoundly this parable speaks to this identical situation. Is not this something of what God experiences when one of His children leave home, waste themselves in riotous living in that "far country" of sin. Of course when we attempt to fathom Divine love we must remind ourselves that God loves our children more than we do. Certainly we can know assuredly that our Heavenly Father understands our sorrow.

There is no simple panacea to the dilemma of parents who stand by and observe their children's lives in the far country. Parents often realize that to interfere in any radical way only drives a deeper wedge between them and their grown children. When children are young we can and must exert a strong spiritual influence on their sense of values. When they grow up and leave, they are out from under our dominion. There is little that can be done to legislate their morality. We are severely limited even as our Heavenly Father is limited because of the free will of His children. At this juncture, it is what we have already done in their lives that becomes vital.

The insights of contemporary psychology and the truth of God's Word reaffirm the validity of early training on the later development of children. Often some great crisis comes and our child hits bottom. Homesickness sets in. Then the child like the prodigal is in a fever to come home. He is ready to turn around and look at himself. The Scripture claims that "he came to himself." Helmut Thielicke sets forth this process of repentance and the influence of home.

> . . . it was because the father and the father's house loomed up before his soul that he became disgusted with himself, and therefore it became a solitary disgust, a disgust that brought him home. It was the father's influence from afar, a by-product of sudden realization of where he really belonged. So it was not because the far country made him sick that he turned back home. It was rather that consciousness of home disgusted him with the far country, actually made him realize what estrangement and lostness is. So it was a godly grief that came over him and not that worldly grief which produces death (II Cor. 7:10)[1]

Helmut Thielicke provides an interesting perspective when he calls this parable and title of his book on parables *The Waiting Father*. The Scripture describes God, the father in this parable, as "waiting." As God was patient with us in our pursuits in the "far country" of sin so also does He anxiously wait the return of our physical children. He never abandons us in our painful wait. He stands beside us. Often there is not much that we can do but stand and wait and hope and pray. As in this picturesque parable, perhaps one day our children will come to themsleves and come home, not to us most of all, but to the Father who also stands and waits.

---

1. Helmut Thielicke, *The Waiting Father* (New York: Harper and Row, 1959), pp. 17-29.

Looking Forward to the Empty Nest

Under less traumatic circumstances, parents look forward to the empty nest but still find it a difficult experience. "Enjoy your kids while you can. They will be grown up and gone before you know it." How remote that advice sounds when the children are young. When they are crawling around getting into everything and you are changing diapers and handling sibling squabbles, their leaving may even sound wonderful!

But the day comes, and you're the one who anxiously awaits a letter or a phone call. We wonder how the kids are doing, and we experience the emptiness others warned us about. Somehow we thought we would be different; we would be happy for them; we would revel in our new freedom. But we can't shake the sadness and loneliness. What happened? Why is it so difficult?

In this chapter we will attempt to trace those feelings and explore why this stage in life is so traumatic. We also want to suggest ways to handle this experience that will be mutually beneficial to parents and children alike.

Why is it so hard? First, when our children leave home, it represents a loss. We have invested enormous emotional energy into their lives. Much of our world is wrapped up in our kids. Certainly, it is normal to miss them.

This loss is uniquely difficult to handle. If a loved one died, we would mourn them, eventually overcome the pain, and be free to pursue other interests. In a very real sense we do not permit ourselves to grieve when our children leave home. We are supposed to rejoice in their independence, their happiness in their family, and their successes. Friends, especially those who haven't been through this, try to pass it off: "You should be happy your son found such a wonderful girl and has such a great opportunity on the West Coast." And you are happy for them, but you are also sad that your lives will no longer be intertwined, as they once were.

So feelings are all bottled up inside. Depression settles in because you will not allow those feelings of sadness to surface. It is unseemly to show anything but happiness in our children's good fortune. In failing to get in touch with those angry feelings because of traumatic changes in our lives, we pay a price, usually in more extreme depression.

The impact upon the mother. The loss of the physical presence may well affect the man and the woman in similar ways. They both experience the loss we have described, if they are a close family. The extent of this loss will depend upon a number of factors, such as how much they have anticipated the loss, how deeply involved they have been in recent years with their children, and how they have looked beyond their children to a life together.

The loss is not merely physical. For the woman, it usually represents a loss of her basic role. The cessation of the menstrual cycle abruptly reminds the woman that she is no longer able to bear children. At the very same time, she begins to feel a void created by the loss of her grown children, who are no longer the center of her life.

Some studies intimate that the more deeply religious mother invests a greater degree of her self-image in the mothering role. Due to this increased investment, she may suffer the more intense depression when the role dissipates.[2]. The wife and mother who views her mission in life solely in

---

2. Pauline Bart, "Depression In Middle Aged Woman" in *Female Psychology: The Emerging Self* ed. Sue Cox (Chicago: Science Research Association, 1976), pp. 349-367.

terms of homemaking sets herself up for depression. If her only satisfaction comes vicariously through her husband and children, this change can be a devastating loss of esteem.

The loss experienced by the father. Traditionally, we have regarded the empty nest syndrome as basically a mother's problem. However, there appears to be a strange reversal between men and women that takes place in the middle years. Men seem to become more passive and more nourishing, while women become more dominant. Women now appear to feel pressure to succeed in a career, while men are backing off from their relentless climb to the top of the corporation ladder[3]. Perhaps men become bored or tired or merely refocus priorities on family life.

If it be true that a man's family becomes increasingly important during the middle years[4], it is happening during the strategic period when his children are in the process of their disengagement. The empty nest may be a far more devastating experience for the man than has been realized. He reaches out at the moment his children coincidentally pull away, leaving him longing for an intimacy he may never have known. In the past, accustomed to being career oriented or in meeting others' expectations, he now, for the first time, looks to his children to meet his heightened generative needs, but finds too little, too late.

The woman grieves at what she once had and lost as a basic role of life, while the man discovers the significance of a nurturing role just as the growing children negate that function.

What to avoid. Obviously, some parents interfere to a fault. The Scriptures provide some negative models for

---

3. Gail Sheehy, *Passages* (New York: Dutton, 1976), p. 405.
4. Erik Erikson, *Childhood and Society* (New York: W. W. Norton, 1950).

parents. Rebekah's role in deceiving her sick husband and insuring that Jacob would be the recipient of her husband's inheritance has to rank high on a list of classic interference by a mother (Genesis 25). This move resulted in the deep grief she experienced later in having sent Jacob away to flee his brother's wrath. Her sorrow surfaced in her embittered cry, "Why should I be deprived also of you both in one day?" Rebekah succeeded in helping Jacob escape from Esau's revenge. In the process their family life was destroyed. Rebekah and Isaac would bear separation and regret. Rebekah would never see her favorite son again and Jacob would suffer the loss of his father, mother, and brother. Isaac moved nearer to his death without his favorite son. Rebekah would mourn because of the distress she had created by her bold act of interference. Still another familiar example of an interfering mother is found in the familiar example of James and John whose mother tried to secure a top spot for her sons in Jesus' kingdom (Matthew 20:20-22). Even Mary, the mother of Jesus, attempted to put pressure on Jesus to make his move prematurely in beginning his ministry (John 2:1-5). Later, she undoubtedly was responsible for sending Jesus' brothers to fetch him home when he was in the midst of that very ministry (Matthew 12-46-49).

What can be done. To begin with, we need to take a second look at the concept of the empty nest. Although birds commonly force their young to fly on their own, humans usually have considerable more difficulty in trying their wings. In our enthusiasm to avoid "interfering" we can go overboard.

1. Establish a new parenting role. Countless mother-in-law jokes add to some of our own rightful reluctance to take on responsibility of a new family. At the same time this reluctance may push us away from providing appropriate

counsel to the fledgling who suddenly is on his or her own. The flourishing business of marriage and family counseling and the spiraling divorce rate may be related to a mobile culture that separates children from their parents by physical and emotional distance. Other organizations provide assistance, but often it is too late when they are called in. Insightful parents could be helpful in a number of areas to a young couple.

Who says we have to push our children out of the nest like the mother sparrow? Children do not suddenly become mature when they walk down the aisle to the marital altar or go off to college. The opportunity may then be presented to assist with the real issues of the adult world. Parenting may be learned to some extent from observing and absorbing the emotional climate of the home. But, a thousand and one specific questions remain unanswered. As the child grows older, he usually appreciates his parents' wisdom more and more. With all the jokes to the contrary, many in-laws have abrogated a responsibility that was taken for granted far more in times past when generations lived close by, and their venerable patriarchs were respected and looked to for direction.

Obviously, some parents interfere to a fault. We have always been aware of this problem. Perhaps we have not said enough about the opportunity for children and parents to fully appreciate each other in an adult-to-adult relationship in which children can benefit from the accumulated wisdom of their parents.

Of course, parents can't preach to their children or parent them in the way they did when they were children. But we can be available when we are needed. "How do you make ends meet in this age of inflation? What dishes can you fix that are interesting, quick, and reasonable?" are the kinds of concerns a young couple faces today. In these days of spiraling inflation, parents who have survived harder times can usually provide some assistance in sharing how to stretch that shrinking dollar.

The Old Testament patriarchial system confirms the insight of transmitting from generation to generation the wisdom of age. The Wisdom Literature of the Old Testament, as well as the Pastoral Epistles in the New Testament, abound in a continuity of parental admonition. Scripture manifestly demonstrates that our elders should have a greater input in our pilgrimage than the contemporary independent family units allow.

So, all is not lost; a new parenting role emerges which may be as important to our children and very enriching to ourselves. Without the direct responsibility in the lives of our children we can participate in more limited and yet meaningful ways.

Grandchildren are enjoyed in a beautiful sense because we have the pleasures without the direct responsibility. As many grandparents, we may participate at special times in their lives, such as when that grandchild is born. Many exciting adventures unfold in the lives of our children. Granted, there are times of trials, as well. But we love our children and we want to be present with them during the hard times as well as the good times. New chapters are written daily in our children's pilgrimage. The book is far from over when our children leave home. They will continue to bless our lives and we theirs as we graciously temper our continued parenting role.

In addition to taking a careful look at the role of a parent to an adult child who has left the nest, we must consider realistically reinvesting our lives in other directions beyond our children.

2. Be flexible. An important ingredient in making this adjustment is flexibility. If all we can focus on is "helping our children," we are going to be extremely frustrated most of the time because we are severely limited in ways we can help. The fact that our children do not live at home and are now adults imposes obvious limitations. As already stated there would be great benefits from appropriate encouragement, insight, and healthy support to our children. Once the children leave home, however, an unlimited investment would be inappropriate.

A mother, for example, should be flexible and change her expectations of her children as they grow older. If her personality is rigid she may expect adult children, even if married, to act as they did when they were children who were dependent upon her. When they are no longer dependent upon her, she may feel resentful. Since hostility toward children is unacceptable, she may turn the hostility inward and become depressed. The hard-working mother may expect more from her children and her husband. She may expect them to fulfill her needs and bring her satisfaction. If her children fail her by not having a good marriage or achieving her high career aspirations, or even by forgetting to call her, she is likely to be severely distressed. She may even conclude she is not wanted or cared for and that no one is interested.

3. Reinvest energies into meaningful channels. Our mental health is dependent to a great extent upon a positive self-image. When a woman's self-concept comes mainly from a mother or wife role then she is in a difficult situation when children leave. The self-concept of these women must

126

change. She needs to realign her self-concept to fit her shifting position in her maturing family. If her life already has been full and meaningful apart from these relationships this refocusing will be much easier.

Many psychologists insist that depression is related to angry feelings turned inward. Others contend that this phenomenon may be equally related to existential depression or a sense of meaninglessness. If a mother can reinvest her energies into other meaningful channels as her children grow older, she is going to be increasingly fulfilled in other outlets. The stress should be on meaningful experiences. This may include going back to school, entering business, or embarking on a profession. However, it need not be anything this dramatic. Volunteering to help in a community, taking a part-time job, or increasing one's work for the church may provide alternative emotional support.

4. Be cautious. A word of caution may be needed as one considers altering one's life-style to include wider possibilities. Change usually produces some personal anxiety. The anxiety of embarking on a new adventure hopefully will be offset by the excitement of a worthwhile challenge of personal growth. Changes also tend to provide occasion for tension with others who unfortunately tend to see us in a very stereotyped role. When a mother's interest shifts from the dominant caretaking concerns of mothering to fulfilling her potential in an achievement-oriented society, she may experience some resistance from others, especially her husband. He may feel threatened by the shift of interest and may question how he fits into this new picture. The husband has also suffered the loss of his children and may very well have a deepening need for companionship to fulfill the vacuum created by the empty nest.

When the last child leaves, the couple will have more time for each other. If they provided a healthy background for these opportunities for togetherness, this can be a very rewarding time. Even in the merry-go-round of activities while the children are home, a couple may learn to capture special moments of sharing simple experiences: a walk through the woods, bird-watching, work in the yard, and various occasions spent apart from the children. As one grows older, life becomes simpler, less cluttered. Simple pleasures of the moment can be appreciated more as they are cultivated.

5. Look ahead to the grandest homecoming. What is said of the opportunities to cultivate a deeper relationship with our mate may also be said of the opportunities to renew and enrich our relationship with the one most significant in our life, the person of Jesus Christ. This person has come through strongly for us in times of other losses and we know that all life's events and relationships have optimal limits. All our relationships have beginnings and endings.

As we live our lives to the fullest in all these earthly relationships we must never forget that the spiritual realm transcends all earthly existence. There is one whose relationship exceeds all the others. Both we and our children know that He has prepared a home for us where there shall be no more separation. This, after all, is the ultimate homecoming.

DISCUSSION QUESTIONS: *When Your Kids Grow Up*

1. Explain the most trying circumstances for parents to deal with regarding the empty nest. What Biblical perspective does the Scripture provide?
2. Why is the empty nest difficult under the best of circumstances?

    A. How does it affect the mother?

    B. How does it affect the father?

    C. Explain the loss experienced and why this is an especially hard loss to cope with?

3. What should parents avoid?

    A. Discuss the negative models found in Scripture.

    B. Discuss other Scriptural examples of interfering parents.

4. Can you think of other examples of the empty nest syndrome in the Bible?

5. Name and discuss the suggestions for dealing with the empty nest that you feel are most helpful? Can you think of other ideas for coping?

6. Can you come up with more specific ideas for reinvesting energy when the kids leave home? (Clubs to join, hobbies, volunteer positions, etc.)

7. What does the author mean by the need to "capture special moments of sharing simple experiences." Brain storm ways you can capture more special moments to enjoy your marriage.

8. How does this chapter help you to understand your parents? What struggle did they have in dealing with this when you left home? What was it like for you to leave home? How are you presently coping with leaving the nest? How has your relationship changed with your parents?

9. Discuss your relationship to your parents by drawing a pendulum of 0 to 10. 10 is complete dependence and 0 is completely a peer relationship.

10. Discuss the Scripture found in Genesis 2:24 which reads, "Leave your father and mother and cleave unto your mate. . . ."

Chapter Nine

UNDERSTANDING AND MINISTERING AMONG THE AGING

With the advance of medical science's life-prolonging medicines and improved living standards, we have suddenly become aware of a new minority group which we have labeled "senior citizens," golden agers," "older Americans," or a similar designation. This group outnumbers the college and university persons by about three times. The aged outnumber most racial and ethnic groups. As a minority group they are increasing in gigantic proportions compared to the rest of the population due to the increasing life expectancy. This expanded life expectancy has greatly affected the average age of the membership in the church. Churches now have a much older membership. Recent studies indicate that "the church has twice as many—or more—older people as at the turn of the century."[1]

In spite of this growing segment of her constitution the church has given relatively little attention to ministering among older members.

Scope of this Chapter

The design of this chapter is to contrast contemporary attitudes toward aging with a Biblical approach, enhance understanding of the aging process, and to share concepts of ministry that relate to older persons.

---

1. William M. Clements, ed. "Introduction: The New Context for Ministry With The Aging" in *Ministry With The Aging* (San Francisco: Harper and Row, 1981), pp. 1-20.

I. *A Contemporary View of Aging and the Biblical Perspective*

The contemporary view of aging and the Biblical perspectives provide a vivid study in contrasts. Throughout Scripture the aging are portrayed in an honored place. A long life was to be greatly desired. "Honor thy father and thy mother" is followed by a promise of a reward, "that thy days may be long upon the land which the Lord, thy God, giveth thee" (Exodus 20:12, KJV). Today, people frequently say, "I hope I don't live to be old." The fear of physical deterioration, the fear of loneliness, the fear of abandonment, and perhaps most of all, the fear of the loss of an honored place usher in dreaded thoughts of growing old. The writer of Proverbs exemplifies the wisdom of this book and the position of the aged when he attests to their honor, "My son, forget not my law; but let thine heart keep my commandments: for length of days, and long life, and peace, shall they add to thee" (Proverbs 3:1, 2, KJV). The blessings or the benefits of age were to be anticipated—not to be dreaded. Judeo-Christian religion honored the old. This is not to say that youth was not honored. One of the blessings of age was an honored place. The values encased in the Bible were engrained in generation after generation. "Thou shalt rise up before the hoary head, and honor the face of the old man" (Leviticus 19:32). That honored place is conspicuously missing in the present culture. The Biblical perspective honored the young. The Apostle Paul could emphatically say, "Let no man despise thy youth. . . ." In the same pastoral letter Paul goes on to warn "Rebuke not an elder, but entreat him as a father; and the younger men as brethren; the elder women as mothers; the younger as sisters, with all purity. Honor widows . . ." (I Timothy 5:1-3, KJV).

The Biblical perspective indicates a well-balanced view. The Old Testament Scripture sets value on old age as well

131

as youth, "The glory of young men is their strength: and the beauty of old men is the grey head" (Proverbs 20:29, KJV). (Today grey hairs are to be avoided. Dye to color grey hair is big business. Few people would boast of the beauty of grey hair.) All of life should be honored. Cedric Tilberg tries to pull together an appreciative awareness of the entire life cycle:

> There is no inherent reason why we should not be as proud to be called "old" as to be called "young." Every period of life is important to God, regardless of whether it is nearer the beginning or the end of our time on earth. But, in a society that exalts youth and undervalues the later years, people strive to act and appear "young." Perhaps we will arrive at a positive image of aging only when we can say with open self-assurance, "I am old."[2]

A Full Life to be Envied

To live a full life is to be envied according to the Old Testament. Child mortality was high; diseases, accidents, hunger and war were prevalent. When a person survived these to live to old age it was considered a blessing. Nobody can control the length of life: "Which of you by being anxious can add one cubit to his span of life?" (Matthew 6:27, RSV).

Rolf Knierm interprets the above passage: "Therefore, if death can come at every age, the real danger for human life does not lie in aging and old age. It actually lies in premature death which cuts short the full age of humans. Aging

---

2. Cedric W. Tilberg, ed., *The Fullness of Life* (New York: Division for Missions in North America, 1980), p. 12.

and old age are not periods of transition between life and death, and not at all the first phase of death. They belong to life. In view of the ever-present danger of death, however, they are not to be taken for granted either. But if age is granted, it is appreciated as a blessing, as a gift of life reaching its fullness despite the frailties of mortal life's last phase."[3]

The Old Testament continually emphasizes the length of life. Old age is seen as an intrinsic part of human life. In the Biblical geneologies the number of years appears more important than the fact that they died. From Methuselah's time when they lived to 800 and 900 years (Genesis 5), to the 600 years of Shem's era (Genesis 11:16-25, 32), to Abraham's period of 175 years to the much shorter and contemporary 70 to 80 years (Psalm 90:10), duration of years is important in the Old Testament. Old age is looked upon as more desirable. "The days of our life span amount to seventy years, and in their full strength to eighty years" (Psalm 90:10). Old age is definitely a sign of a blessed and fulfilled life.

Physical Problems of Aging

Although aging is viewed as the fullness of life, this does not mean that the adverse conditions of aging were not realized in Scripture. Perhaps the most familiar passage that strikingly sets forth the distress of aging are these words from Ecclesiastes 12:1-7, NIV:

> Remember your Creator in the days of your youth, before the days of trouble come and the years approach when you

---

3. Ralf P. Knierim "Age and Aging in the Old Testament" in *Ministry With Aging,* ed. William Clements, p. 22.

will say, "I find no pleasure in them."—before the sun and the light and the moon and the stars grow dark, and the clouds return after the rain; when the keepers of the house tremble, and the strong men stoop, when the grinders cease because they are few, and those looking through the windows grow dim; when the doors to the street are closed and the sound of grinding fades, when men rise up at the sound of birds, but all their songs grow faint; when men are afraid of heights and of dangers in the streets; when the almond tree blossoms and the grasshopper drags himself along and desire no longer is stirred. Then man goes to his eternal home and mourners go about the streets. Remember him—before the silver cord is severed, or the golden bowl is broken; before the pitcher is shattered at the spring, or the wheel broken at the well, and the dust returns to the ground it came from, and the spirit returns to God who gave it.

Another passage setting forth the negative aspects of aging is found in II Samuel 19:34-37, NIV:

But Barzillai answered the king, "How many more years will I live, that I should go up to Jerusalem with the king? I am now eighty years old. Can I tell the difference between what is good and what is not? Can your servant taste what he eats and drinks? Can I still hear the voices of men and women singers? Why should your servant be an added burden to my lord the king? Your servant will cross over the Jordan with the king for a short distance, but why should the king reward me in this way? Let your servant return, that I may die in my own town near the tomb of my father and mother. . . .

From these two selections alone the reader can readily observe the following negative characteristics of the aging process: weakening physical condition, failing eyesight, loss of sense of taste, body is bent. These references of a

134

weakening condition are realistic assessments of the aging process. They do not undermine the very positive view the Scriptures present of living a long and satisfying life.

II. *The Church's Ministry Among the Aging*

There are two broad areas where the church can serve. First, provide services to those who are alone and in some way incapacitated. Secondly, provide opportunities for Seniors themselves to serve. We may say we are treating how we can minister to Seniors and how we can minister with Seniors. Those who are able have tremendous potential to minister among us. My doctoral dissertation entitled "Ministering With Widows Through Small Groups" intentionally used the preposition "With" rather than "To." William Clements entitled his recent work *Ministry With The Aging* for similar reasons. Seniors have a need to be independent, useful and productive. They also possess through their experience and interest, and their available time, unlimited capacity to minister to each other and to others. The last part of this presentation will deal with their ministry. The first part will concentrate on the ministry to those who are unable to serve others and limited in their abilities to care for themselves. They are most profoundly in need of ministering.

Ministering to the Aging

First of all we can provide care for those who are alone and incapacitated. Even among those incapacitated, it is not appropriate to make decisions for them they can make for themselves. A person does not come to the place where the younger automatically take over life decisions for the elder. However, they, as with some of the young, need assistance occasionally to maintain themselves because of certain limitations.

The church has historically led in movements to provide Nursing Homes and Convalescent Centers. I am personally acquainted with two of the directors of church related homes and have the highest regard for their ministry. I have a sense of well being that my loved ones and I personally have these kinds of facilities available. Most of all I feel they provide a community of fellowship with Christians. At one time during a local ministry we had five people in the County Home and two in private homes. I had good feelings about the care provided in most of them. What is saddest for me is that I long for these people to have more meaningful contacts with those with whom they share common friends, a common cause in Christ and fellowship in the Gospel.

Support for institutions is important. However, this is not the complete answer. If the local church neglects her ministry to her members that are aged and in need, no amount of institutional care can compensate for this loss. The local church has responsibility beyond financial support of institutions for the care of the aged. She must be involved on a personal level to those who reside in rest homes. Any public institution can suggest ways church groups can minister. Brotherhood Homes carry suggestions in their papers on ways churches can help. During Christmas many homes have more help then they can handle and during the rest of the year almost none. The local congregation bears a responsibility to minister to these people. Regular visits by the Minister should be a priority. Others in the congregation can send birthday cards. Although ministering should not be limited to specific occasions, neither should we overlook their importance. Birthdays, Easter and Christmas are times that are especially lonely. What is said concerning those in institutions also applies to shut-ins.

There are unlimited ways we can minister to Seniors. Another suggestion is to have a special Extension Department. Guy Leavitt has authored a book in the Standard Publishing Company's *Training for Service* series entitled *Home and Extension Department.* In this book he details how to set up an Extension Department in the Bible School.

An idea that we utilized from the book was a tape ministry to shut-ins. We have provided some musical concerts on tape, sermons and Bible School lessons, and have taken them to the shut-ins and the hospitals. This would be a tremendous ministry if sufficient interest is secured to administer it. This puts the person who is isolated in touch with his class and his teacher. The person is able to follow the lesson in his own home. The shepherding program of the local church should reach the shut-ins or hospitalized. Regular phone calls and calling lists need to be worked. Systematic checking on the shut-ins is essential. In this ministry do not neglect what the youth can do for shut-ins. Older people need these contacts with the young.

The congregation must be alert to the possibility that the older person may become incapacitated suddenly. Many of the elderly have no relatives to handle their affairs in such a crisis. In my most recent ministry prior to assuming a teaching ministry, such an occasion happened. Fortunately, we had a remarkable group of ladies in a recently formed widows group that were able to provide around the clock care with the additional assistance of a number of other church members. In the three weeks from the time of incapacitation until we were able to get her in a nursing home, it demanded a tremendous effort on the part of a number of people. We were able to cut the red tape, find a vacancy in a nursing home and move her in; a less patient and sturdy support group would have given up the task.

When elderly do not have relatives available or close friends who are both caring and physically strong themselves, a great part of the responsibility falls upon the church family. Cedric Tilberg recommends in this situation

> that every older man or woman designate a family member or friend to take necessary actions. This may involve "power of attorney" or some other arrangement. It is particularly important for elderly persons who have no family members nearby.[4]

The church must be prepared to assist the elderly to capitalize on the services provided in the immediate community. This involves making the elderly alert to the services and providing transportation to and from the cite where services are being offered.

> Services are often organized on a one-time basis in connection with community functions such as a health fair. Tests for diabetes, blood pressure and other services are given. A woman's organization in one congregation used the skill of one of its members, a retired nurse who checked blood pressure at meetings.[5]

The church can help raise the consciousness of the community to the conditions of the nursing homes to be sure they meet basic guide lines for such institutions. Often the system of monitoring such facilities is inadequate. However, appropriate measures may be made where these guidelines

---

4. Cedric Tilberg, *The Fullness of Life*, p. 78.
5. *Ibid.*, p. 77.

are not insured. As citizens of an earthly government, as Christians, and as concerned children whose parents and eventually ourselves may be called upon to use these available resources, we must exercise our responsibility.[6]

Obviously not only those incapacitated in the extreme situation previously mentioned need supportive services of the church. Supportive services such as house cleaning, assistance in shopping, transportation, cutting grass and minor repairs are some of the most common needs. Bible School classes and youth groups may meet some of these needs. At times such groups within the church may take on such projects but it must be coordinated by the church board or shepherding committee to be sure these rather simple means of helping are not left to mere chance. It has been my experience that church people are sometimes slow to see obvious services and, when it is recognized, at times careless in implementing them effectively. If these kinds of services are provided it will enable older people to remain at home and in a rather independent and happy role in life rather than be forced to enter a nursing home. When ill they will be able to come home sooner or remain at home longer.

In recent years state and government have become involved in providing assistance. If earthly governments recognize justice toward the elderly, can the Church provide less? If the state is concerned with fairness and basic human rights can the Church be involved any less? Just laws are needed to safeguard human rights. Sometimes Christians may become involved in helping to establish justice.

---

6. Tilberg focuses squarely on the Christian's responsibility in the last chapter of his book *The Fullness of Life*.

However, the Christian is to go beyond justice. Laws and institutions and systems can be fair or just or equal. People can reach beyond justice to love.

Christians are subject to the law of love written in their hearts (Romans 2:15). Man is created in God's image as the crowning glory of His creation. We are responsible to see that dignity and honor is not irradicated. As Christians we must play the role of advocate in behalf of the elderly, as well as all others in need, to see that justice is done.[7] Beyond that we must supersede justice with grace and mercy and love.

Jesus once said, "Unless your righteousness surpasses that of the scribes and Pharisees, you shall not enter the kingdom of heaven" (Matthew 5:20, NAS). In commenting on this verse J. W. McGarvey and Philip Pendleton insist that:

> The laws of Moses regulated civil conduct, and being state laws, they could only have regard to overt acts. But the laws of the kingdom of Christ are given to the individual, and regulate his inner spiritual condition, and the very initial motives of conduct: in it the spirit-feelings are all acts (I John 3:15).[8]

Present state and government policies deal with justice and rights of Senior Citizens. Surely as Christians our concern for justice and our loving care for the aging as well as other minority groups must surpass that of civic responsibility. Christians are challenged to be the conscience of societies' policies and to surpass them in loving treatment toward all disadvantaged people.

7. *Ibid.*

8. J. W. McGarvey and Philip Y. Pendleton, *The Fourfold Gospel* (Cincinnati: The Standard Publishing Foundation, n.d.), p. 237.

140

Caring for the aged who are incapacitated leads naturally to the subject of caring for the dying. Many people, including some ministers, are extremely uncomfortable with this aspect of ministry. Since their own mortality has not been worked through, they avoid ministry that places them in direct contact with the aging; especially if they are dying.

Elisabeth Kubler Ross's book, *On Death And Dying* has had a tremendous impact upon professional and lay people as well. Although there is a growing sensitivity to this subject, it certainly has not eradicated the denial of death. It takes considerable motivation for people to process their own feelings about their death to the place where they are able to really be fully present with another person at the time of his death.

Speaking from my own experience, although my training prepared me for coping with this ministry far more than most people, there were times when I knew my feelings blocked my abilities to minister to the dying. As I look back I feel good about many occasions but there were times that I missed opportunities which if I had not been overloaded with my own problems and the grief of other's, I would have been more present.

In this chapter many ideas are presented for ministry to the aging but our own feelings may well be a bigger obstacle to this ministry than the lack of good ideas to implement in caring for the aging.

The Role of Motivation and Mortality. If there is one factor that blocks a minstry to Seniors it is the problem of motivation. I am far more concerned about our motivation than our ideas. If you stop and think about it you may have many ideas. You are probably aware of someone now who would profit from your ministry. A few minutes of your time would benefit them immeasureably. We can pass it off by saying we do not have the time. We know this is an excuse. If we are to minister to Seniors we must meet the real problem head-on. We do what we want to do. Can we be honest about that? I remember a conversation with a person to whom I had suggested how much one of our older members would benefit from a visit. She mentioned she had not seen anyone from the church, especially a church officer, for a long time.

> I said, "She needs to know you care." He responded, "I could not do that—I cannot stand being around people who are that sick. Isn't she dying?" "Yes, she is," I replied. He said, "I am glad you are visiting her. I really appreciate it because I just cannot do it."

I am glad that this illustration does not speak for everyone, however it speaks to many of us. To my mind this is what the ministry is all about: reaching people in the midst of profound need. If there is a time in which the Christian message must be communicated, it is to the aging and dying. As great a prophet as John the Baptist sent a messenger to Jesus to inquire for him while he was in prison prior to his death. "Art thou he that should come, or do we look for another?" Jesus reassured John. "Go and show John again those things which you do hear and see." After the messenger left, Jesus stated to the audience, "There hath not risen one greater than John the Baptist . . ." (Luke 7: 19-28). If so great a man of God as John the Baptist needed reassurance how much more so do the rest of us.

It is my experience that Christians need reassurance in their final hour. Dare we deny them? If just when people have the greatest need, when they are dying, we abandon them; what does it say about our faith in the resurrection hope? I wonder what must go through a person's mind who is old and feeble in a home, and not visited because he reminds us of old age and our own death.

One way we may deny our own mortality is to avoid the aged. Until we come to grips with this in our own lives we cannot begin to approach the subject of ministering to the dying. This applies especially to those who are in convalescent centers or hospitals and have physical problems, but it may also explain our reluctance to visit the shut-ins as well.

Closely associated with the denial of death is the denial or avoidance of the whole range of human suffering. The sights and sounds of the mental hospital, county homes, convalescent centers, are not places most of us would choose to visit. Unless we have a sense of mission we will not go. If we have a close relative we might, but to choose to minister to these people on a regular basis as a part of our concept of ministry is quite another matter.

Recently after completing a Clinical Pastoral Education Program in a mental hospital, the Chaplain asked me to take a new class of Chaplains on a tour of the hospital. Specifically I was instructed to take them in the afternoon to one particular cottage where we would have a short devotional service. This was the worst, or at least one of the worst, in the hospital. I resisted the direction as I was aware of the effect. The Chaplain said, "It will give them something to talk about in group." Their reactions to the patients as they stepped into the room was one of horror. The smell alone, apart from the sight of deformed bodies and minds, was nearly devastating. We had a little service, mingled among our new congregation, meeting each one personally, sang some hymns, had a prayer, and went back to the main building. The new Chaplains went on their rounds to their respective wards, then met for group that afternoon.

143

It was a study to see how each one handled his feelings. One Chaplain went on about how much he had learned from the nurse on his ward. The nurse was very willing to initiate him to the hospital and what was going on in her ward. This was an active ward. (That is a ward which had quite a few admissions and releases.) The patients were generally less chronic and it was a good place to work. One could find satisfaction in observing the progress of the patients. The nurse was young and attractive, which helped too. He had successfully denied the unpleasant experience of an hour before and was well into what promised to be an interesting and rewarding experience at the hospital. On the other hand, another fellow had left the service to go to his ward. His was a ward filled with chronic patients. The staff appeared to be too busy to talk with him. He attempted to minister with no noticeable response from the patients. His ward was, for all practical purposes, identical to the building we had all visited together. Instead of finding a meaningful refuge from the feelings he experienced previously, his ward merely intensified his despair. He angrily asked that poignant question, "What am I doing here?" How often I have asked the question myself. It is not easy ministering to people in pain. Not only is there discomfort aroused in me but also the question of what can I do. This young man experienced a torturous sense of futility at the very depths of his being. Amid such intense suffering what could he do. Many of these very sick people were unable to respond appropriately. Sometimes they were unable to express what they did feel.

Often we anticipate a response that the sick may not be able to give us. The Chaplain Supervisor previously experienced this in going to that same ward. He went there every week for several months with little or no response. Undoubtedly this was hard and the fact that he seemed to be unable to accomplish much, made it all the more difficult. He gave up and stopped going for a period of time. When he went back there was shock and disbelief as one of the patients exclaimed, "When you did not come back we thought you were dead." A rumor circulated that he had died. The staff had even been convinced he was dead. There was a sense of celebration that he had come back from the dead. Behind this was the touching experience that they were convinced his ministry was so significant that only death could keep him away; whereas he had felt by their reactions that they were not aware of his presence. How indeed aware they were! Our presence among the aged and ill is often more significant than we can imagine. We must have a commitment to serve Seniors when they are in need. This may involve coming to grips with our mortality and with our Christian hope. It may mean facing human suffering beyond our present ability to imagine. In the final analysis our ministry will then become the very essence of serving or ministering.

Ministering with the Aging

In order to understand our attitude toward the aging and to depict the emphases in the second part of the chapter, I would share an old Balinese legend:

Once upon a time the people of a remote mountain village in Bali used to sacrifice their old men. A day came when there was not a single old man left, and the traditions were lost. They wanted to build a great house for the meetings of the assembly, but when they came to look at the tree-trunks

145

that had been cut for that purpose no one could tell the top from the bottom: if the timber was placed the wrong way up, it would set off a series of disasters. But then a young man entered the circle and said: "If you promise never to sacrifice the old men any more, I will be able to find a solution." They promised. He brought his grandfather, whom he had hidden; and the old man taught the community to tell top from bottom.

Does this legend speak to our society in the 80's? Do we ostracize the old from the community? Most important for our considerations, does this story relate to the way the church treats the elderly. If it does, I suggest it is high time to bring them out of hiding. They may well enable us to discern the top from the bottom.

Perhaps we should hear once more God's direction through Moses. "Ask . . . of your elders, let them enlighten you" (Deuteronomy 32:7). Perhaps we need to recall the role of the elders of Israel. According to the book of Numbers, God said to Moses, "Gather unto me seventy men of the elders of Israel, whom thou knowest to be the elders of the people, and officers unto them . . . and they shall bear the burden of the people with thee, that thou bear it not thyself alone" (Num. 11:16, KJV). Perhaps we should note a sentiment that seems to have prevailed in history that the rulers both civil and religious should be men of age and experience. The Greeks and the Romans had their assemblies of elders as well as Israel's Councils, composed of men distinguished for their age, wisdom and experience. We are aware that many of our government officials are elderly men. In the New Testament the term "elder" describes mature men who by virtue of their experience, prudence and moderation are voted by the congregation to be overseers of the interests of a local congregation (Acts 14:23).

146

If we were to conclude our presentation after exploring our ministry to them we would be robbing them of the opportunity to serve. When it comes to ministering there is so much we can learn from the elderly. The breath and depth of their human experience is vast in comparison to the young. The elderly have gone through much stress and strain. They are uniquely equipped out of their experience to minister.

Sam Stone, editor of the *Christian Standard* in an editorial (*Christian Standard*, August 23, 1981) states that

> . . . senior citizens also have responsibilities. They are not only to be served, but to serve. God has always used mature, trained, and able older saints for strategic tasks in His Kingdom. Think of Noah (he was 600 years of age when the flood came—and he lived to a ripe old age of 950!). Think of Abraham (he was 75 years old when God called him). Think of Moses (an octogenarian, he overcame handicaps, survived the plagues, and led a grumbling people for 40 years in the wilderness).

Mr. Stone's point is well taken; the elderly are also challenged to minister from their experiences and skills. One retired couple became involved in an extensive ministry to hospitalized in a large suburb congregation. An eighty year old widow blessed the lives of a countless number of shut-ins through her telephone messages of good-cheer and started a Bible study in her home.[9] A ninety-three year old woman who could not read invited others to read to her from the Bible and influenced twenty-five people to come to the Lord.[10]

---

9. Donna Schmidt, "A Ministry of Calling," *The Lookout*, 92, (Sept. 28, 1980):4.

10. Dale Williamson, "Not Too Old To Serve," *Christian Standard*, 116, (Aug. 23, 1981):12.

Some elderly people may find a market for their skills on the staff of a local church. This would uniquely apply to older ministers who desire to cut back their activities and yet want to be used in a meaningful way. Judy Norris describes the fulfilling retirement her husband found in a less demanding ministry after his retirement. Other church workers without a professional background may find a nitch on the staff of a local congregation. Probably most will find a context for meaningful volunteer work in the community and in the church. A model for programs that help to bring purpose into the life of the retired volunteers while at the same time maintaining a supportive ministry to the elderly is found in the Shepherd's Center as described by Elbert C. Cole's work *Lay Ministry With Older Adults* in William Clements book *Ministry With The Aging*. Home services are provided by the center and administered by people who are themselves over sixty-five. Most of the services are free of charge to those over sixty-five who are unable to perform the services for themselves.

The ways of involving the elderly in ministering with the congregation are limited mainly by our own imagination. Only as the minister and church officers become involved with Seniors can this ministry take place. They need to act as enablers to place people in relationship to each other. As the pastoral needs of parishioners come to attention they can share specific ways these Seniors can provide support for each other. They may involve as small a detail as communicating the news of hospitalization to the class of a Senior, with a suggestion that they send cards. Another simple example would be a suggestion that a Senior who is handling his leisure creatively provide support to another member who is experiencing anxiety adjusting to his new retirement.

This pastoral care could result in a new lease on life rather than a death certificate that retirement can represent. The importance of support during times of transition is critical as we grow older. The rising mortality rate when the elderly are moved from one home to another is substantiated. The mortality rate the year following bereavement is also well documented. The church, as a caring community, must realize the vital life saving quality of pastoral care to the aged. Often we pass off the loss of functioning to age, whereas the loss may be more closely related to emotional factors than strictly physiological change. The sociological and psychological factors are at least as vital as physical deterioration. The person who appears increasingly senile may be experiencing depression. Inability to communicate may be related to loss of hearing, a common problem in aging. Opportunity and encouragement to socialize should be presented by the family of God.

If Seniors are given opportunity to support each other they often will respond. A pastoral care thrust needs to be incorporated into the Bible School ministry through classes. Seniors must not be limited in their opportunities for service to a ministry among their age group. How can the young people profit from their elders? How about young married couples? The middle aged? Opportunities that cut across age lines are a necessity if we are to truly be one in Christ. We all have the same fears and anxieties. We can find support in each other.

Ministry to Seniors is the same as ministry to Juniors. Whether we are ten, thirty, fifty, seventy or eighty, ministry takes place when we allow people to touch our lives. It is the task of the church to break down all the barriers that separate us and, certainly in our culture, age is one factor that divides us. Our outward man may change, our ability to produce in this success-saturated society may change but our inner man may deepen as new joy can be born until the day we die.

I would like to share the story of a painter, Asher Lev, who experienced the ministry of his own father. In Chaim Potok's book, *My Name Is Asher Lev*, this younger painter relates this account about himself:

> I drew . . . the way my father looked at a bird lying on its side against the curb near our house. "Is it dead, Papa?" I was six and could not bring myself to look at it. "Yes." I heard him say in a sad and distant way. "Why did it die?" "Everything that lives must die." "Everything?" "Yes." "You too Papa? And Mama?" "Yes." "And me?" "Yes," he said. Then he added in Yiddish, "but may it be only after you live a long and good life, my Asher." I could not grasp it. I forced myself to look at the bird. Everything alive would one day be as still as that bird? "Why?" "So life would be precious, Asher. Something that is yours forever is never precious."

We each share a common humanity. May we allow the elderly to enter into ministry to us. This may be more essential than serving them. Our enthusiasm to serve may get in the way of listening and feeling their ministry with us. The healing ministry of the church reaches beyond age. When we are truly one in Christ we are no longer separated by our differences. We all share a common ground of our humanity. We are mortal and our lives are precious. Sharing and caring for each other is the most beautiful gift we can give. May God help all of us to "bear one another's burdens, and so fulfill the law of Christ" (Galatians 6:2, RSV).

Scriptural Resources

From a Biblical perspective the old are recognized as being equal to the young in some vital ways. The old are to "bring forth fruit in old age, they are ever full of sap and green" (Psalm 92:14, RSV). They may enjoy life as the young, "The young men and the old shall be merry" (Jeremiah 31:13, RSV).

The Bible acknowledges the wisdom that comes through life's experiences. This wisdom is recognized when it is grounded in the fear and the reverence of the Lord (Deuteronomy 30:20).

In both the Old and New Testament the role of the sage, the fathers, the elders suggest the legacy of old people. There is enormous esteem for wisdom, mostly among old people in the Scripture. Writing on the contributions of older people in the Bible, Clements puts it bluntly,

> The phenomenon of this literature is unparalleled in its time. Its contents reveal an amazing degree of mental vitality, and to this day one who does not appreciate it is a fool in the biblical sense.[11]

The role of the elders as the council at the gates in the Old Testament, the wise sage, and the elders in the New Testament Church must not lend one to the conclusion that there was not an indispensable role for women. Although age is not usually mentioned one could conclude they were not all that young. They were advisors to kings (II Chronicles 23:3). They were wise women that are mentioned in II Samuel 14:2; 20:16. In the New Testament the essential role of the grandmother of the evangelist Timothy commands attention in II Timothy 1:5, KJV.

> When I call to remembrance the unfeigned faith that is in thee, which dwelt first in thy grandmother Lois, and thy mother Eunice; and I am persuaded that in thee also.

---

11. Ralf Knierim "Age and Aging in the Old Testament" in *Ministry With Aging*, p. 35.

Older women in the church were told that "they must set a high standard, and school the younger women to be loving wives and mothers, temperate, chaste, and kind, busy at home, repecting the authority of their husbands" (Titus 2:4-5). The consistent witness of the mother and grandmother can never be underestimated in the training of great leaders in the church. Today, the admonition in the pastorals describing the ministry of older women to younger women is largely forgotten. When the single women were forced to care for their households, the role of an older woman could never be more important.

As one grows older there is increasing awareness of priorities. The older person reaches the time when a declining energy level forces decisions as to what is most important. Relationships are meaningful. As the Apostle Paul called for Timothy to be present with him in what may have been the last winter of his life, the patriarchs set their house in order (II Samuel 17:23; II Kings 20:1). Surely a modern counter-part is the drawing of a will. What is often lacking is the fitting charge to the children found in the Old Testament, "When Jacob finished charging his sons, he drew up his feet into the bed, and breathed his last, and was gathered to his people" (Genesis 49:33). Paul frequently charged Timothy his son in the Gospel. Perhaps one of his best known charges would be found in II Timothy 4:1, 2, 4, 5, KJV:

> I charge thee therefore before God, and the Lord Jesus Christ, who shall judge the quick and the dead at his appearing and his kingdom; Preach the word; be instant in season, out of season; reprove, rebuke, exhort with all longsuffering and doctrine. . . . And they shall turn away their ears from the truth, and shall be turned unto fables. But watch thou in all things, endure afflictions, do the work of an evangelist, make full proof of thy ministry.

152

This charge ties into Paul's reflection on his own life and his death and subsequent reward. In the following verse is a hopeful reunion and personal farewell to Timothy in evidence.

> For I am now ready to be offered, and the time of my departure is at hand. I have fought a good fight, I have finished my course, I have kept the faith: Henceforth there is laid up for me a crown of righteousness, which the Lord, the righteous judge, shall give me at that day: and not to me only, but unto all them also that love his appearing. Do thy diligence to come shortly unto me (II Timothy 4:6-9, KJV).

The elderly need contact with their colleagues, with their sons and daughters in the Gospel just as the Apostle Paul. Naturally they have a special place in their hearts for their sons and daughters in the flesh. The Biblical picture of the recognition and honor due to one's parents is vividly clear. "Hearken unto thy father that begat thee, and despise not thy mother when she is old" (Proverbs 23:22, KJV). The Lord sets forth the admonition that parents be honored in the context of the Ten Commandments. "Honor thy father and mother" (Exodus 20:12). Each child must care for his own parents as indicated in the pastorals. "If anyone does not provide for his relatives, and especially for his immediate family, he has denied the faith and is worse than an unbeliever" (I Timothy 5:8, NIV).

The care of the church "the household of God" (Ephesians 2:19) is vital. However, the church can not be a substitute for one's own family. The care of the immediate family along with the church can provide a vital key to a longer and happier life. Those whose belonging needs are met by these available caring networks will live longer and more meaningfully. The church's proclamation of the message of love and hope prevents a sense of isolation and helps to maintain a belief system. Specifically the Scripture challenges the aged to be "faithful unto death" (Revelation 2:10).

Presently in society much emphases is placed upon continued education for the elderly. Many colleges and universities encourage older people to become involved in their educational programs. Life can be a continual growth experience for the older person spiritually. As a person grows older he experiences a number of losses: physical health, loved ones, friends who die, loss of position, loss of financial resources, but these are not the final and ultimate loss. The Christian may look forward to an ultimate gain. The Apostle Paul exclaimed "for me to live is Christ and to die is gain." The Christian faith helps to mobilize his resources and point him toward a growth opportunity in earthly life in spite of losses experienced. Peter insisted that Christians recognized a "lively" or "living hope" based on the resurrection of Jesus Christ. Hope as taught in I Peter focuses on the present trials of this earthly existence as well as the transcendent hope in the next world. These trials provide occasion to grow.

> Blessed be the God and Father of our Lord Jesus Christ, which according to his abundant mercy hath begotten us again unto a lively hope by the resurrection of Jesus Christ from the dead, To an inheritance incorruptible, and undefiled, and that fadeth not away, reserved in heaven for you, Who are kept by the power of God through faith unto salvation ready to be revealed in the last time. Wherein ye greatly rejoice, though now for a season, if need be, ye are in heaviness through manifold temptations: That the trial of your faith, being much more precious than of gold . . . might be found unto praise and honour and glory at the appearing of Jesus Christ (I Peter 1:3-7, KJV).

The Apostle Paul also accents how afflictions do not cause a loss of heart.

We are troubled on every side, yet not distressed; we are perplexed, but not in despair; Persecuted, but not forsaken; cast down, but not destroyed;

. . . .

For which cause we faint not; but though our outward man perish, yet the inward man is renewed day by day (II Corinthians 4:8, 9, 16, KJV).

Through the proclamation of the Word, through the minister and other teachers and caretakers who are present with the older person, and through personal Bible study, he or she can renew support. This strength from the Word comes at the time when physical strength is diminishing, possessions are shrinking, and various losses are accumulating. God provides renewal in the midst of the greatest trials this physical existence can accumulate. This source of strength is well expressed by the ancient Hebrew poet in Psalms 46:1, 2, KJV.

God is our refuge and strength, a very present help in trouble. Therefore will not we fear, though the earth be removed, and though the mountains be carried into the midst of the sea.

As comfort for every person in life's ultimate trials, what passage could provide more than the Twenty-third Psalm.

He restoreth my soul: he leadeth me in the paths of righteousness for his name's sake. Yea, though I walk through the valley of the shadow of death, I will fear no evil: for thou art with me; thy rod and thy staff they comfort me. Thou preparest a table before me in the presence of mine enemies: thou anointest my head with oil; my cup runneth over.

155

Surely goodness and mercy shall follow me all the days of my life: and I will dwell in the house of the Lord forever (Psalm 23:3-6, KJV).

DISCUSSION QUESTIONS: *Ministering Among The Aging*

1. How does the attitude of the Scripture toward aging contrast with the view of contemporary society?
2. Discuss the realistic approach of the Scripture toward aging.
3. What distinction is made between ministering to the aging and ministering with the aging?
4. What suggestions are made concerning ways to minister "to the aging"? "With the aging"? Can you add some of your own suggestions of ways to minister among the aging? How can your class or you as an individual implement this ministry?
5. What is being accomplished in the area of services to the aging in your community
    A. among the community agencies?
    B. among the churches in your area?
6. Schedule a visit to a rest home, or visit a Senior Citizens program or interview the director of the Council on Aging, or a minister to Senior Citizens in a local church.
7. What can your church, club or other organization do to help when an older person who has no family help is incapacitated?
8. As Christians, what is the appropriate stand on issues on the state, national and community level that involves the rights of older citizens? Justify your approach from a Scriptural perspective.
9. How important is the role of motivation when it comes to ministry among the elderly? Do you feel you have

problems in this regard? Under what circumstances? (Perhaps others could share how they have been able to deal with these feelings.)

10. What responsibilities do the elderly have toward mintry? Do you agree with Sam Stone's statement of the responsibility of the aging?

11. What Scriptural resources do you find especially helpful? Can you think of others that are relevant for you?

Chapter Ten

MINISTERING WITH THE WIDOWED

The Church's Role in the New Testament and Today

The roots of the church's ministry to the widowed reaches back into the earliest history of the primitive church recorded in the Acts of the Apostles. That ministry grew out of neglect similar to the accounts of survivors in the twentieth century.

> In those days when the number of disciples was increasing, the Grecian Jews among them complained against those of the Aramaic-speaking community because their widows were being overlooked in the daily distribution of food. So the Twelve gathered all the disciples together and said, "It would not be right for us to neglect the ministry of the word of God in order to wait on tables. Brothers, choose seven men from among you who are known to be full of the Spirit and wisdom. We will turn this responsibility over to them and will give our attention to prayer and the ministry of the word" (Acts 6:1-4, NIV).

This account from Acts sounds like several situations I have experienced in my ministry. This is what one widowed person related:

> After the funeral no one from my church came to visit me. I longed to share with someone my intense grief which at times nearly overwhelmed me. I felt the need for personal spiritual support. I tried on several occasions to see someone from the church but they appeared to avoid talking with me in any depth. I attempted on three distinct occasions to have the minister call on me. I asked if he would come or send someone from the church. No one came. I finally gave up.

The only difference between this modern widow and the widows of the first century is that the one managed to raise a bigger ruckus. The old cliché applies, "The squeaking wheel gets the grease." Of course, some of our modern counterparts manage to be heard when they are unhappy and their complaints may be met. Most of them, I suspect, live and die never receiving a helpful ministry. This is a sad commentary. The widowed often represent those that have given a life of service to Christ and His Church.

It is my contention that some of the neglect of the widowed is due to a lack of awareness. We do not appreciate the needs and ways in which the church should minister. This was the case in my own congregation in 1973 before a recently bereaved widow changed the focus of my ministry. She came up to me and said, "What we should have is a club for the widowed in our church." Her insistence, coupled with my interest in a ministry to the bereaved, provided the incentive for our work among the widowed. The Lord blessed that ministry during the next two years in ways I never dreamed possible. If someone would have claimed we were neglecting the widowed prior to the launching of that work I would have been quite offended. We were ministering as fully as we knew how. I thought at the time we were doing quite a bit. We made a big deal of our Christmas baskets to the shut-ins. I did try to squeeze a pastoral call in once in awhile between hospital calls, funerals, weddings, and all my other tasks. We grew in our concept of ministry with the widowed so much. Now as I look back it seems in comparison we were doing nothing at all.

Elsewhere I have shared specific programs employed among the widowed. See (*Lookout*, April 17, 1977 and *Lookout*, September 20, 1981). The direction this work has taken will be shared later in this chapter.

The Need for a Ministry among the Widowed

The need for a ministry among the widowed clamors for our attention. The vastness of this segment of our population produces a wide scope of consequences for the family and the ministry of the church. In sheer multitudes the widowed population in the United States alone is enormous. Presently, a broader view of the ministry to both widows and widowers will be explored. The number of widowers is well over two million while the number of widows soars to nearly ten million.[1] Obviously, this has to represent a significant proportion of our churches' membership. This widowed population shares basic needs. The specific situation will vary from person to person. Some are wealthy while others are destitute. Some possess internal resources while others are lacking desperately. Some have a meaningful religious faith while others have none. What we have gathered comes from serious sources that have attempted to assess this great number among our population. For our purpose in this chapter we shall take a look at the sociological situation and the psychological pain they generally experience. After assessing these important factors we shall suggest ways we can more effectively minister among the widowed.

The Sociological Situation of the Widowed

By sociological situation we mean to include the wide range of adjustment problems besides the grief reaction, which will be treated later under the psychological factors. At first glance it might be a temptation to concentrate on

---

1. U.S., Department of Commerce, Bureau of Census, *Statistical Abstracts of the United States*, 1971.

the grief of the widowed and to underestimate the sociological problems. Evidence suggests that the adjustments under the sociological factors may be even more devastating than the task of working through the grief itself.

Let us illustrate the impact of adjustment to the radical change of losing a mate with a brief observation from married life. Our mate strengthens our lives as he or she fulfills certain roles. She may be a housekeeper and a provider of money and services. Our mate is our therapist who listens and helps us ventilate our feelings about the rough day in the kitchen or in the office. Our mate provides affection and a sexual partner, a liaison with the community, and assistance in caring for our children. The spouse provides access to another family so that we benefit from an additional family support system beyond our own kin. If our mate provides these roles, it follows that the death of a spouse will result in the loss of the source that fulfills many of our most fundamental needs.

Carol D. Harvey and Howard M. Bahr in an article in the *Journal of Marriage and Family* entitled "Widowhood, Morale, and Affiliation" summarize the loss of these socialization roles as requiring significant adjustment. They state, "The greater the number of role changes necessary, the more difficult the adjustment to widowhood."[2]

In most cases one may safely say that most of the systems that have maintained life disintegrate. Life may very well revolve around the partner socially, emotionally, and especially in the case of the widow, economically. Due to the mobility of society today members of the family may not

_____

2. Hugh Carter and Paul Glick, *Marriage and Divorce: A Social and Economic Study* (Cambridge: Harvard University Press, 1970).

161

be near to provide care. If the widowed person is older, relatives may be deceased or perhaps there are no children and few, if any, brothers or sisters.

The widowed are often lonely and neglected. With all of our sophistication in this technological age the plight of the widowed has changed little from the world of the New Testament. Specifically, the widows in Acts six appear to have suffered loneliness and poverty. John Bowbly in the introduction to Peter Marris' monumental research conducted among London widows stated concerning their poverty, "In our present Western civilization to be widowed is to be twice stricken: both grief and poverty are the widow's lot."[3] The widower may possibly be better off financially as the basic provider of the family unit if he loses his wife prior to retirement. But lest we jump to unfounded conclusions concerning a more favorable circumstance for the widower, we need to hear a summary of the best research on the subject:

> Among the research findings relevant to the present study is the work of Tounsend (1957) who reported that loss of a marital partner was less traumatic for women than for men . . . Berardo (1967) reports that following widowhood frequency of interaction with kin and friendship groups declines, especially for widowers. Both add that widowers have fewer close friends than widows . . . In sum, the evidence suggests that widowers have a harder time than widows, establishing and maintaining relationships with both kin and social organizations, but that in comparison to their married counterparts both widows and widowers tend to experience attenuation of social relationships.[4]

3. Carol D. Harvey and Howard M. Bahr, "Widowhood, Morale, and Affiliation," *Journal of Marriage and the Family* 36 (1974):99.

4. Peter Marris, *Widows and Their Families* (London: Routledge and Kagan Paul, 1958), p. ix.

Helena Lopata also recognizes the impact of widowhood on men.

> The support systems of men also undergo disorganization
> with the death of their wives, particularly in our "person-
> oriented" form of marriage and our focus upon the nuclear
> family in its own housing unit. In fact, several social scientists
> (Berardo, 1968, 1970; Bernard, 1973) find that widowers
> exhibit more severe symptoms of disorganization than do
> widows. They have higher rates of suicide, physical illness,
> mental illness requiring treatment, alcoholism, automobile
> and work-related accidents, etc. *U.S. News and World
> Report* documented these facts in 1974.[5]

In spite of the present knowledge of the impact upon
men, most of the research has centered on women. This is
probably due to the following reasons: (1) there are more
widows, (2) women live longer and usually marry younger
partners, (3) they are more accessible for research, and
(4) men are more likely to remarry. It follows then that
most congregations would also have more women who
are widowed.

The life of the widow revolves around her husband socially, economically, and emotionally. Poverty is a main characteristic of the widow. The widow bereaved beneath the
age of 60 receives no assistance unless she has children
under the age of eighteen; then Social Security Insurance
covers her children. The younger widow will generally be
forced into the labor market. Often she is inadequately prepared since she suffers from a lack of training. The educated
woman or the woman with specific job skills has a better
opportunity. Poverty also affects other aspects of life such

---

5. Helena Lopata, *Women as Widows* (New York: Elsevier, 1979).

as socializing and health care. In a situation where she already feels sorry for herself, she must slip into a lower stage of society, thus increasing her frustration. She may be forced to sell her home and move to a less desirable neighborhood.[6] Inability to drive, failing health and difficulty in making decisions may plague her. The availability of family and friends may radically alter the negative picture. However, at best being a widow is hard, at worst it is almost intolerable.

As restructured as their lives may be, many are very pleased with their independence and are able to build meaningful lives.

The influence of economic problems may be the single most devastating problem facing the widowed that contributes to low morale and lack of socialization.

> The present analysis, drawn from a variety of national settings and from samples larger than in typical studies of the effects of widowhood, indicate that the negative impact sometimes attributed to widowhood derives not from widowhood status but rather from socioeconomic status. The widowed have appeared to have more negative attributes than the married, and they have appeared less affiliated for the same reason.[7]

Helena Lopata contends that in contemporary society a person's support systems are embedded at birth as one is born into a family.[8] When a person marries and establishes his own family, the support system is locked in again surrounding his new family. Whenever this system is altered, such as with retirement, some trauma is usually experienced.

---

6. Harvey and Bahr, "Widowhood, Morale, and Affiliation," p. 99.
7. *Ibid.*, p. 104-106.
8. Lopata, *Women as Widows*, p. 5.

The death of a spouse provides the occasion for the most dramatic change in the support system of an individual. This person experiences stress of the greatest magnitude.[9]

Lopata observes that

> Problems with support exchanges can arise if the person is seen by associates as somehow different or unable to participate "normally" in conventional interaction. This is especially likely to occur in the case of divorced or widowed women or men in a society such as ours, which favors the marital state as the norm of all adults.[10]

Unfortunately the church has often failed to counter this social phenomena. The support the church provides, such as a nucleus of former friends who are presently widowed, usually happens apart from any organized effort.

The Grief Reaction of the Widowed

Having set forth the problems of adjustment confronting the widowed, we now come to the psychological factors. We have observed that in the midst of grief the widowed must cope with a multitude of changes in life style. This alone may produce a greater crisis than grief itself.[11] But our purpose now is to briefly describe the grief reaction of the bereaved mate.

---

9. *The Social Readjustment Rating Scale (SRRS)* which measures the impact of stress placing the death of a spouse on the top of the scale. See James C. Coleman, James N. Butcher and Robert C. Carson, *Abnormal Psychology and Modern Life*, 6th ed., (Glenview: Scott, Foresman and Company, 1980), p. 110 for the scale and for explanation of the impact of stress. The scale is displayed on page 5 of this present book.

10. Lopata, *Women as Widows*, p. 5.

11. Alvin Toffler, *Future Shock* (New York: Random House, 1970), p. 333.

The sociological adjustments are staggering but the first blow the widowed endures is grief itself. Failure to come to grips with this smothers out the possibility of handling the myriad of details in everyday life. Progress must be made on the major crisis of grief. To expect that one recover from grief and calmly handle the other problems is presumptuous. A cliché often voiced among the widowed insists that "you never really get over it." Even when one recovers from the grief there will be times when painful memories may reoccur.

It is now our task to attempt to describe briefly and as clearly as possible what the experience of grief is like. The first stage in the experience of grief is that of shock. God was merciful in the way he provided a built-in anesthesia for both physical and mental pain. This is why a person who receives a physical injury in an accident may not experience pain initally and why one who suffers a psychological loss may not realize the force of that blow immediately. This accounts for the reason one may see the widowed greeting guests at the funeral home almost as though nothing had happened. The bereaved person often experiences initial shock before it wears off and the fuller reality hits. During this period the person may exclaim, "I just can't believe this has happened!" They can't believe it and that denial acts as a cushion from the blow for awhile. The duration of time one may experience shock varies greatly from individual to individual. One thing is fairly certain: intense pain follows.

The pain that accompanies grief is an acute combination of physical and mental anguish, if indeed they can be separated. Sarah Morris, a widow with a doctorate in psychology, writing out of her own grief states, "Grief is among the deepest pains that can be experienced. . . .[12] Those who have endured

---

12. Sarah Morris, *Grief and How to Live With It* (New York: Gossert and Dunlap, 1972), p. 8.

it have difficulty expressing the intensity of the suffering. Robert P. Hansen, a minister who lost his wife, writes soon after her death:

> I can tell you that no matter how much you anticipate death, it always has a finality about it that you never realize. I have seen death come many times. But when it takes a part of you—I am at a loss for words to describe it. I remember recalling the words of St. Paul when he speaks of death as having a sting, but I would describe it as giving you a knockout blow in the pit of the stomach.[13]

The Churches' Spiritual Ministry among the Widowed

We have sketched briefly the extent of the situation the widowed face both sociologically and psychologically. The gravity of their plight is accented by the serious health deterioration that may result when their needs are not met. The question that remains is what can the church do to minister among the widowed. The answer appears rather obvious when we allow Acts six to speak to us.

First, the early church recognized their needs. This is where it all began for the Apostles and where it must begin with us. We must become aware of their predicament. Those ministering among the widowed must be aware of these needs. If God's word is to be helpful it must reach the real crisis. It is possible to rush in with the panacea of the Gospel without sensing either the extent of the situation or the specific solutions. If the church is to minister in a helpful way she must respond to practical or sociological factors

---

13. Robert P. Hansen, "In the Company of Heaven," *The Lutheran Standard* 13, (November, 1973):5.

such as poverty and loneliness that strike the widowed. Some awareness of where the survivor is psychologically helps to clarify the extent of the grief.

Second, the church must become aware of the grief process and how to minister in the midst of that process. Remember the bereaved will probably experience shock and then pain both physically and mentally or psychologically. After shock and pain, they will hopefully experience recovery or healing. There is a specific ministry the church can render in each of these times. Now let us take a look more closely at that ministry.

The criteria of the ministry may be summed up in the concept of love. We should ask ourselves at each stage in the grief pattern—what is the most loving thing that I can do—and then do it. Under each stage I will suggest ways the church family may minister. Each of these suggestions are things that the church where I ministered did.

During the initial time of shock the most loving thing to do is to be supportive. If possible be present at the time of death. This is especially vital if death strikes unexpectedly. A deacon in our congregation had a heart attack and died while he was waiting for a ride to work. He was two city blocks from his home. The policeman on duty happened to be a member of our congregation. He called me. I went by and picked up a widow who was a member of our widows' group. We all met at the bereaved woman's home at about the same time. During that time of shock we sat in silence. I recall her first words as she turned to the widow who went with me and said, "Blanche, I guess you went through this same thing." I have always felt that her presence was more significant than mine in that she had survived a similar experience. Her long-time friend was symbolic of the fact that life could go on at a time when she was wondering,

"Where do I go from here?" Also, this member of the widows' group could remain until other friends and relatives were on the scene. The minister's schedule may not permit him to remain for an extended period nor may it be appropriate. In the case of a bereaved man we had an elder who was familiar with the needs of the bereaved; his company allowed him considerable freedom to minister in this way. Support may consist of making phone calls to relatives and assisting with various details. (Some people would rather do many of these things themselves, however.) Merely being present and ministering appropriately to the individual situation is the key.

Encourage the congregation to visit the funeral home. Provision for a meal for the family of the bereaved immediately after the funeral is a beautiful gesture. It relieves the widowed of the pressure of making some provision for what could be a large delegation of relatives. In a relaxed atmosphere they can all remain together and find support in each other.

Whatever provides support during this initial period of shock is appropriate and is the most loving thing to do.

In the second stage of grief where the widowed person is suffering that pain we previously described, the most loving thing to do is to assist in working through the pain, the grief work. The breaved needs a sounding board for complaints, gripes and that aching sense of loss that no one else wants to hear. The bereaved person needs an ear to hear and shoulder to lean on. Once again we would stress the appropriateness of another caretaker, ideally a widow or a widower who understands and at the same time stands as the towering strength of survival. Quietly and effectively faith and hope come alive through this kind of a witness. In my experience there is no substitute for the one-on-one ministry. (Although we maintained a support group I will say more about it later.) Over and over again the importance of the personal touch has been demonstrated. He or she needs a friend, not just a counselor; someone whose ministry is not limited to the therapy hour or a pastoral call.

This leads us to the final stage of healing or recovery. The sociological factors, such as loss of financial stability, social status, discrimination, isolation and loneliness, linger a long time after significant recovery is realized. The church's ministry during this extended period hopefully will not be neglected. As with the early church it may involve financial administration to their needs. The Scripture makes it implicit that the first providers are to be the family. The church is to care for those who have no one else to help them (I Timothy 5:3-5). Certainly they should be included in the regular pastoral ministry of the congregation. Here again that sharing of one person with another is crucial. Relationships can be established at the deepest levels of human existence that will transcend all earthly ties and reach to eternity.

Thirdly, the church must come to appreciate the unique role of widows in the church. The Bible gives suggestions concerning a special ministry by the widows.

> No widow may be put on the list of widows unless she is over sixty, has been faithful to her husband, and is well-known for her good deeds, such as bringing up children, showing hospitality, washing the feet of the saints, helping those in trouble and devoting herself to all kinds of good deeds.

> As for younger widows, do not put them on such a list. For when their sensual desires overcome their dedication to Christ, they want to marry. Thus they bring judgment on

themselves, because they have broken their first pledge. Besides, they get into the habit of being idle and going about from house to house. And not only do they become idlers, but also gossips and busybodies, saying things they ought not to. So I counsel younger widows to marry, to have children, to manage their homes and to give the enemy no opportunity for slander. Some have in fact already turned away to follow Satan (I Timothy 5:9-15, NIV).

They are given certain credentials to qualify them for this ministry similar to those for elders and deacons. We have too long overlooked this unique and practical ministry they may perform toward each other.

One of the beautiful benefits of another caretaker, such as a widow or widower is the satisfaction that person receives from helping a friend. If the caretaker is widowed, he or she receives the added benefit of a friend. Being widowed that caretaker needs companionship too and finds it in helping someone else through an experience that only one who has endured can fully appreciate. However, they need and find strength in each other.

Specific Suggestions for Ministering:
A Group for the Widowed

During the past ten years I have had the opportunity to help five groups begin a special ministry among the widowed. These groups have been reported on in detail elsewhere, but a general outline of their ministry will be presented here. The focus of these various groups in five different settings may be viewed as they cluster around four concepts: therapy, tasks, socializing outlets, and spiritual development.

The therapy in these groups basically evolves from the frequent contacts and the planned meetings although few specific therapy sessions are held. The atmosphere which permits sharing is provided. Often, some meetings have found the members sharing how each one handles his life since the death of his mate. But most of the support comes as a result of one-on-one contact. The subject is opened up as being permissible to discuss. One-on-one pairing spontaneously seems to provide considerable support.

The groups vary as widely as the tasks that interest them. They range from hospital and pastoral calls and even evangelistic calls on prospects to planning a dinner for the church officers. The task orientation distinguishes these groups from other social gatherings. They provide a chance to serve Christ and His Church.

Socializing becomes important when one lives alone as most widowed people do. A chance to fellowship together and participate in social events provides a vital role in the life of each of these five groups.

Last but certainly not least, the spiritual discussion gives a depth of meaning to each group. Some have their own devotional talks while others invite guest speakers to their meetings. Most of all each meets in the context of the church. The church nurtures the groups in providing encouragement from the church board but most of all provides the context for the proclamation of the hope and challenge for daily life that inspires each individual in his own life.

Some of the groups are limited to widows, others include the widowers in their meetings. Some consider their group as a singles groups to serve Christ, and include all singles. Each is a little different in its basic thrust but each includes some aspects of therapy tasks, socializing, and spiritual growth.

In summary we have traced the obligation of the church and especially the church leaders to follow the precedent of the New Testament Church and to become more involved in a ministry among the widowed. The leadership should establish priorities insisting, "This is a vital part of the church's ministry." Once they confirm that initiative the work but remains to the creativity within the local congregation to accomplish it. As suggested previously the responsibility does not lie solely with the leadership. Those whose gifts are most evident should be employed following the New Testament concept of "bearing one another's burdens." We are calling for special attention to a neglected ministry but we would bear in mind that each body of believers that experiences the proclamation of the Gospel heralds the healing message of the faith. The blessings the widowed receive in various services of the household of faith can never be fully appreciated. The message of "faith, hope and love" gives them stability when everything else is changing. In my experience in working with the bereaved this was the first and most important finding. However, if the proclamation is real, the church will hear and act upon what James says about true religion, "The Christian who is pure and without fault, from God the Father's point of view, is the one who takes care of orphans and widows, and who remains true to the Lord—not soiled and dirtied by his contacts with the world" (James 1:27, TLB).

DISCUSSION QUESTIONS: *Ministering With The Widowed*

1. What evidence points up the neglect of the widowed both in the New Testament and in the present day? Do you feel this assessment fits the church where you worship? If it is not an accurate picture of your congregation, how is it different and what approach does your church employ to meet the need of the widowed?

2. What is the extent of the problem in today's society? What are the basic problems of the widowed? What adjustment problems are unique to widow's and to widowers?
3. Do you agree that the sociological problems are greater than the psychological problems? Explain your answer.
4. In what specific ways can the church help? Which ways are typical of the way the congregation where you worship helps? Which ways may be implemented.
5. Name and describe the stages a person goes through when he loses a loved one. How may a helping person assist during each of these stages?
6. Describe the specific ministry among the widowed? What three facets of ministry are set forth?

Chapter Eleven

DEVELOPING DISCIPLINE IN CHILDREN

Scriptural Illustration

Eli's sons were wicked men; they had no regard for the Lord. Now it was the practice of the priests with the people that whenever anyone offered a sacrifice and while the meat was being boiled, the servant of the priest would come with a three-pronged fork in his hand. He would plunge it into the pan or kettle or caldron or pot, and the priest would take for himself whatever the fork brought up. This is how they treated all the Israelites who came to Shiloh. But even before the fat was burned, the servant of the priest would come and say to the man who was sacrificing, "Give the priest some meat to roast; he won't accept boiled meat from you, but only raw."

If the man said to him, "Let the fat be burned up first, and then take whatever you want," the servant would answer, "No, hand it over now; if you don't, I'll take it by force."

This sin of the young men was very great in the Lord's sight, for they were treating the Lord's offering with contempt.

. . . .

Now Eli, who was very old, heard about everything his sons were doing to all Israel and how they slept with the women who served at the entrance to the Tent of Meeting. So he said to them, "Why do you do such things? I hear from all the people about these wicked deeds of yours. No, my sons; it is not a good report that I hear spreading among the Lord's people" (I Samuel 2:12-17, 22-24, NIV).

When Samuel grew old, he appointed his sons as judges for Israel. The name of his firstborn was Joel and the name of his second was Abijah, and they served at Beersheba. But his sons did not walk in his ways. They turned aside after dishonest gain and accepted bribes and perverted justice (I Samuel 8:1-3, NIV).

175

Few Scriptures could strike a more sensitive chord in a parent's heart than this illustration. One would be hard pressed for a finer heritage than that found in both Eli and Samuel. It is this awareness of their greatness in the Biblical record that frightens any parent who strives to rear children. The failure of these great men as parents blemishes otherwise admirable characters and outstanding ministries. A closer examination of the Biblical record raises some provocative lessons for parents.

Lessons from Eli's and Samuel's Life

Eli was the first person to combine the two offices of high priest and judge. He had a long and outstanding service as judge of Israel for forty years. His failure to discipline his sons became a black mark on his magnificent service to Jehovah. The lessons to be observed from Eli's failure as a parent challenge any parent.

However, one cannot help but admire the unique contribution of Eli to the life of Samuel. Samuel was handed over to Eli's care. His childhood was spent within the Israelite Shrine. The Scriptures state:

> Then Elkanah went home to Ramah, but the boy ministered before the Lord under Eli the priest (I Samuel 2:11, NIV).

Although his mother would not have had a continual daily role in his training, the impact of her vow to the Lord to dedicate her son to the service of the sanctuary would have been perpetuated during his boyhood years. It would be hard to imagine a more emphatic reminder of his solemn duty than the act of Hannah's vow. This constant reminder of his destiny, Eli's tutorage, and the practical experience blended together to provide a maximum background for Samuel.

176

The favor of God upon Samuel is evidenced by his selection by the Lord to succeed to the priestly office. The sons of Eli who would have been priests proved unworthy and so God's purposes are furthered instead through Samuel. Samuel was also recognized as a prophet. Samuel was likened unto a second Moses as he exhorted the people of God to turn from their adulterous practices and return to the Lord. Samuel is depicted as a judge. In the course of time, he quite naturally associated his sons in the office of judge. At this point, the story repeats itself as his sons, like the sons of Eli, failed to "walk in the ways" of their father. This is one reason why the people desired a king. Samuel is not in favor of their request but complies with the divine command. He takes steps to grant their request.

There are several lessons to be learned from the lives of these two great men of God. Lives of great servants of the Lord teach by their weaknesses as well as strengths. These lessons from such noteworthy individuals command the attention of every parent to the awesome responsibility of parenthood.

1. *Early training prepares the child for the call of God.*

When God called, Samuel was trained and ready to respond. Eli set the stage for Samuel's call through the training which enabled Samuel to understand the significance of that ministry. Although Samuel did not comprehend the precise moment of the call and demanded the clarification of his mentor, Eli, years of on-the-job training preceded that strategic occasion in his career.

Of course, if Samuel had practiced religion as a matter of mere habit, he would never have been prepared. Samuel had long before opened his heart in devotion and service. Adequate background is no absolute guarantee that one will develop into a faithful servant, but it lays foundation. This training in the home was recognized by the Apostle Paul as an essential factor in Timothy's ministry.

> I have been reminded of your sincere faith, which first lived in your grandmother Lois and in your mother Eunice and I am persuaded, now lives in you also (II Timothy 1:5, NIV).

With Timothy one recognized the role of a mother and grandmother. They provided a model of a faithful life and a profound appreciation for the word of God that was such an integral part of Timothy's life. Paul writing to Timothy makes the role of Timothy's background clear.

> But as for you, continue in what you have learned and have become convinced of, because you know those from whom you learned it, and how from infancy you have known the Holy Scriptures, which are able to make you wise for salvation through faith in Christ Jesus. All Scripture is God-breathed and is useful for teaching, rebuking, correcting and training in righteousness, so that the man of God may be thoroughly equipped for every good work (II Timothy 3:14-17, NIV).

Since Timothy's father was a Gentile he lacked a male role model in his early life. However, his mother and grandmother more than compensated for this lack in their devotion to his early training. Samuel, of course, had a more than adequate mentor in Eli. It is impossible to know the precise role of his mother. Probably, she was supportive but Eli provided the basic impetus. Samuel's role as a priest took him out of the immediate context of his home. Ideally, both mother and father would be available to contribute to the training of their children for Christian service.

One might speculate that being an only child Samuel was "babied" and shown special affection. The role of Eli's wife toward Eli's sons is missing in the Scriptural account.

Eli was a kind and impartial man in his dealings with people and it seems unlikely he was anything else but fair to his children.

The record indicates quite clearly that Eli provided his sons opportunities for great ministries. Samuel claimed this ministry in its finest tradition whereas Hophni and Phinehas, Eli's sons, defamed their office. The responsibility of the priestly office was appropriate for Samuel while inappropriate for Eli's sons who abused their positon.

2. *Chidren born in the same house often respond in different ways to their opportunites.*

The man that trained Samuel also produced Phinehas and Hophni. The contrast between these children is clearly revealed.

> This sin of the young men was very great in the Lord's sight, for they were treating the Lord's offering with contempt.
> But Samuel was ministering before the Lord—a boy wearing a linen ephod (I Samuel 2:17-18, NIV).

There are many unanswered questions concerning their background. Was Samuel favored in ways that Phinehas and Hophni were not, even though Phinehas and Hophni were natural children and Samuel was in a special trust from God? If he was favored in some way, was this because he responded to ministry in a way Phinehas and Hophni did not? In other words, parents sometimes treat children differently because each child is unique. One child may be lovable while another more difficult.

179

3. *The curse of clerical favors.*

The minister is usually looked up to by most people. The community often provides them certain privileges. Ministers and their families, although seldom well-heeled financially, nevertheless receive special considerations. A problem develops when one expects special favors. Hophni and Phinehas looked for special consideration; they expected the prime cut of meat.

> Eli's sons were wicked men; they had no regard for the Lord. Now it was the practice of the priests with the people that whenever anyone offered a sacrifice and while the meat was being boiled, the servant of the priest would come with a three-pronged fork in his hand. He would plunge it into the pan or kettle or caldron or pot, and the priest would take for himself whatever the fork brought up. This is how they treated all the Israelites who came to Shiloh. But even before the fat was burned, the servant of the priest would come and say to the man who was sacrificing, "Give the priest some meat to roast; he won't accept boiled meat from you, but only raw."
>
> If the man said to him, "Let the fat be burned up first, and then take whatever you want," the servant would then answer, "No, hand it over now; if you don't, I'll take it by force."
>
> This sin of the young men was very great in the Lord's sight, for they were treating the Lord's offering with contempt (I Samuel 2:12-17, NIV).

This practice has always been condemned. It was expected that the best meat was to be sacrificed to God. The sons of Eli refused to take potluck and instead sought the choice cuts of meat. They were determined to take advantage of their high office. This greatly displeased the Lord.

180

Not only did they expect a favor, they were prepared to take it by force. This overbearing characteristic is more in keeping with common criminals than a priest.

4. *Hophni and Phinehas failed to respect the discipline of their vocation.*

John C. Schroeder in the *Interpreter's Bible* comments:

When men are reluctant to accept the disciplines imposed by the tasks of their vocation, they soon reject all discipline. Every conceivable vocation makes its demands upon those who follow it. When they are recognized, they give life order, and the order permeates all experience. Faithfully to observe the conditions which a task imposes enables a man to discipline himself. To believe that one is immune from some responsibilities is to persuade oneself that one has none.[1]

5. *Hophni and Phinehas failed to exercise discipline in other areas of their personal life.*

The Scriptures indicate the further immorality of Eli's sons.

Now Eli, who was very old, heard about everything his sons were doing to all Israel and how they slept with the women who served at the entrance to the Tent of Meeting (I Samuel 2:22, NIV).

Once again they flaunted their favored position and disgraced their office in order to satisfy their selfish needs. The RSV translates I Samuel 2:12:

Now the sons of Eli were worthless men; they had no regard for the Lord.

The sons of Eli were unsuited for their vocation as High Priest.

---

1. Buttrick, George Arthur, ed. *The Interpreter's Bible Commentary* (Nashville: Abingdon-Cokesbury Press, 1953), Vol. 2: I Samuel, by George B. Caird, p. 888.

6. *Not every son is suited to follow in the footsteps of his father.*

This is true in business, industry, law, medicine, and certainly in the ministry. Although God set up the priestly order and it would be expected a son would follow his father, a more observant parent might have realized Hophni and Phinehas had disqualified themselves from the position.

7. *God judged Eli for his failure to discipline his sons.*

This judgment is forceful.

> Why do you scorn my sacrifice and offering that I presribed for my dwelling? Why do you honor your sons more than me by fattening yourselves on the choice parts of every offering made by my people Israel?
>
> Therefore the Lord, the God of Israel, declares: "I promised that your house and your father's house would minister before me forever." But now the Lord declares: "Far be it from me! Those who honor me I will honor, but those who despise me will be disdained. The time is coming when I will cut short your strength and the strength of your father's house, so that there will not be an old man in your family line.
>
> . . . .
>
> And what happens to your two sons, Hophni and Phinehas, will be a sign to you—they will both die on the same day. I will raise up for myself a faithful priest, who will do according to what is in my heart and mind. I will firmly establish his house, and he will minister before my anointed one always (I Samuel 2:29-31, 34-35, NIV).

At first this judgment seems cruel. Eli was a faithful priest and seemed to be a responsible parent. He did voice his disapproval of his son's actions. By word and his example he opposed their abuse of the priestly office.

On the other hand, there is a difference between sentimentality and firm discipline. Firm action should have been taken in light of their sins. However, discipline reaches further back into their lives. He certainly must have failed to discipline them in their younger years. He failed to demand accountability from them in the discharge of their office. Eli was a good man but a weak one. He failed to exercise oversight in their early training. Eli was satisfied with the privileges of the position rather than the specific exercise of excellence demanded by the position. Schroeder's words are suggestive of a possibility for all parents to guard against.

> . . . there is always a difference between sentimentality in the handling of children and the sound preparation which is necessary for a life of service. So often the home is nothing but a cell of soft selfishness. Children do not learn within it the meaning of sacrifice and devotion and service. Parents in their struggle to make their children better off fail to make them better. Unconsciously they betray their own true ambitions. Anyone connected with education quickly recognizes how many children are spoiled by their parents' inverted pride. Materialistic standards of success control too many parental hopes, and consequently bring ruin upon distinguished family traditions.[2]

8. *Mistakes of parents often abound in their sons and daughters.*

Perhaps the most ironic feature of this entire passage may be found in Samuel's failure to heed the lessons of Eli since he also failed to discipline his sons. Any student of human nature can easily observe how often this story repeats itself. Parents leave many vital messages which serve

---

2. *Ibid.*, p. 890.

children well. Unfortunately, the tendency is to learn from their weaknesses as well as their strengths. Samuel models Eli's example as a father and also blunders with his own children. He also makes his sons judges. As with Eli, Samuel was a distinguished leader and wise man but he failed to disengage himself from the pattern of his mentor. As an old man and perhaps desiring to leave a significant legacy to his sons, he makes them judges. Instead of learning a lesson from Eli's experience, he repeats his error. Unfortunately this scene is often repeated as children follow the destructive tendencies of parents or guardians as well as their life-sustaining and creative features.

9. *Parents have blind spots when it comes to their children.*

Samuel was a great champion of Israel and a distinguished judge. He was an impersonal umpire whose wisdom dispensed justice in an impeccable manner. However, with his sons he had a blind spot. Perhaps in his later years, intent to leave them a gift of great honor, prestige and service, he went against his better judgment.

10. *Parents sometimes pressure their children into positions for which they are unfit.*

When this happens children often rebel against doing that which they do not desire to do. Parents that exercise these pressures invite rebellion. At times the pressure emerges from the parent's overselfish pride. This attitude that forces subjection is extremely manipulative and often backfires on the parent. Parents must discover that each child is an individual with gifts and potentialities to develop in ways that may be very different from their own capabilities.

184

Joel and Abijah might have been good men had they been farmers or craftsmen. When Samuel made them "judges over Israel," they may have so hated it that they corrupted the office.[3]

Parent's Struggle with Discipline

Every parent can identify with the plight of Eli and Samuel. A parent sees his children from a unique perspective. He or she is usually prejudiced. This is often quite evident to other people. It is healthy that someone views them with favor and gives every benefit of doubt and is always in the child's corner.

However, the other side of this prejudice is that it may be a liability when parents fail to observe obvious negative trends in the lives of their children. When an otherwise healthy prejudice provides such heavy insulation that parents are blind to his sins, this is a serious deterrent to the child's development. Children need their parents approval and disapproval. If parents are unable to see or hear evil regarding their children, their prodigy have lost a valuable monitor on their moral development. Although any parent can identify with the plight of Eli and Samuel, a Christian parent cannot condone it. Every parent recognizes the struggle with discipline. What parent cannot recall his parent's words, "This hurts me as much as it hurts you," and vividly remembers how utterly ridiculous it sounded at the time. However, as a parent, he hears those same words echoing from his own lips. When it comes to pain, a parent would far rather that pain be inflicted on him. But it is true that discipline in form of punishment must be administered for the child's own good.

3. Ibid., p. 918.

It hurts the father to do it, but he recognizes that the pain he suffers for a short time is best for his child in the long run. The writer of Hebrews certainly catches the temper of the emotion and the clarity of the wisdom of discipline.

> And you have forgotten that word of encouragement that addresses you as sons: "My son, do not make light of the Lord's discipline, and do not lose heart when he rebukes you, because the Lord disciplines those he loves, and he punishes everyone he accepts as a son."
>
> Endure hardship as discipline; God is treating you as sons. For what son is not disciplined by his father? If you are not disciplined (and everyone undergoes discipline), then you are illegitimate children and not true sons. Moreover, we have all had human fathers who disciplined us and we respected them for it. How much more should we submit to the Father of our spirits and live! Our fathers disciplined us for a little while as they thought best; but God disciplines us for our good, that we may share in his holiness. No discipline seems pleasant at the time, but painful. Later on, however, it produces a harvest of righteousness and peace for those who have been trained by it (Hebrews 12:5-11, NIV).

Therefore, although discipline is painful, it is necessary. Most parents recognize discipline is important but frequently raise questions as to the form it should take. In speaking before a number of different groups on personal problems, the areas of greatest concern revolve around an appropriate way to discipline.

The Problem with Discipline in Contemporary Society

A glance at the world is sufficient to acknowledge that the sons of Eli are obvious today; lawlessness is rampant. Parents are often fearful their children will be rebellious.

186

They worry about how to guide them. Parents are often confused on the subject of discipline. Much has been said on the subject of discipline through the media of radio, T.V., movies, and in books. Parents are searching for answers and T.V. talk shows and popular paperback books attempt to fill the bill. Psychologists have rushed into this vacuum with various models. To the parent looking for a quick cure to this morning's problems with Johnny or Suzie, it is a baffling array of help. Some psychologists are honest enough to warn parents against any textbook approach. The subject is far too complicated and far too vital to entrust to any one new fad to come down the pike. Christians, of course, are uncomfortable with accepting the most recent book when they realize the Book of Books has something to say on the subject. However, unable to sort through the Scripture and measure these recent trends there is a temptation to jump on to a particular approach that appears to have adequate enforcement. An understanding of the various trends is necessary to make a personal judgment as to the appropriateness of a particular approach.

Present Trends in Discipline

The present trend appears to be in the direction of stricter guidance than in the more recent past, but not as extremely stern as in the early days of our country's history. In the early days "the father knows best" school was in vogue. In this approach parents made their will known to their children and enforced it in no uncertain terms. In the 1930's and 40's psychoanalytic theories presaged a shift to a permissiveness, or a belief that the child knows everything and the parent knows nothing. Parents were convinced by Freudian theory that they could severely harm their children in the early stages of development as they dealt with such sensitive stages as weaning and toilet training, and they went to the extreme of letting children set their own pace for feeding and toilet training. Presently, under the heavy influence of Carl Rogers' basic emphases upon listening skills as demonstrated in Parent Effectiveness Training[4] and the dominance of behavior modification in such writers as Skinner, Bandura and Krasner the pendulum has settled on a style midway between the extremes of permissiveness and restrictiveness.

The present mold of parenting is generally called authoritative.[5] It avoids the extreme harshness of the parent who forces absolute control while it also circumvents the trap of letting the child "call the shots" in the permissive style. Research indicates that exclusively "restrictive and permissive styles of parenting are . . . equally destructive. . . ."[6] Speaking of these parents in this mediating position Howard Gardner sums it up in these words:

> They are careful to introduce a calm and comfortable tone into interactions and deliberations. Yet, while being warm, conscientious, and supportive, they exert clear controls over their children's behavior and expect the child to behave as maturely as possible.[7]

---

4. Thomas Gordon, *P.E.T.: Parent Effectiveness Training* (New York: Peter H. Wyden, 1974).

5. Diane E. Papalia and Sally Wendkos Olds, *Human Development* (New York: McGraw-Hill, 1981), p. 242; Arthur J. Jersild, Judith S. Brook, David W. Brook, *The Psychology of Adolescence* (New York: MacMillan, 1978), pp. 318-321.

6. Howard Gardner, *Developmental Psychology* (Boston: Little, Brown and Company, 1978), p. 299.

7. *Ibid.*, p. 301.

Most of the present authorities honor a mediating positon between always leaving decisions up to the child and always dictating absolutely the decisions the child is to act upon. The authoritative style provides the child with opportunites to have input into decisions but the final authority unquestionably lies with the parent.

The Value and Limitations of Psychological Theories

A psychological approach shifts as leaders in the field dominate the thought. Therefore, one must be cautious in total adherence to a particular theorist. For example, the crude style may be found among some behaviorists such as John B. Watson's attempt to produce a conditioned fear in a child. Watson never made any attempt to decondition the child's fear.[8] Few parents would be comfortable in entrusting a parenting style to such an insensitive person as this. By the same token Skinner's apparatus box, where he kept his own child for a period of time, hardly endears him to the typical parent.[9] However, when a behavioral approach is tempered by behaviorists such as Gerald R. Patterson,[10] or by a renowned Christian psychologist such as James Dobson,[11] then it can be worth serious attention. There is something to be said for learning to reinforce appropriate behavior and learning to curtail negative behavior. Psychologists can be helpful in this regard. For example, Gerald

8. Raymond E. Fancher, *Pioneers of Psychology* (New York: W. W. Norton & Company, 1979), pp. 328-332.

9. B. F. Skinner, "Baby in a Box" in *Readings in Developmental Psychology*, ed. Judith Gardner (Boston: Little, Brown and Company, 1978), pp. 98-104.

10 Gerald R. Patterson, *Families* (Champaign: Research Press, 1971).

11. James Dobson, *Dare To Discipline* (Wheaton: Tyndale House, 1970).

Patterson provides helpful down-to-earth tips on reinforcing positive behavior. He also applies specific procedures for dealing with noncompliance which are fair and firm. It helps avoid that emotional upheaval that sets most parents up for blowing their stack when falling into the pattern of hasseling their kids into doing something. James Dobson's approach also warns parents against being pushed too far and then engaging in inappropriate screaming and yelling or uncontrolled beatings. Patterson suggests a careful record or data card where over a period of a week the name and dates are provided and a day by day record is kept of noncompliance and a procedure for reinforcing positive behavior is set up. The idea of record keeping and stressing positive behavior is helpful. In discussing discipline, it is a mistake to think of molding behavior by merely punishing the negative actions. Psychologists have long accented that what really changes behavior is positive reinforcement or a system of rewards. Parents need to become effective listeners and celebrate with a child whom they love through positive actions. Unfortunately parents who experience difficulty with a child often tend to key into the negative actions and not pick up the very positive changes that are taking place. Sometimes they may be so angry for all the times the child has disobeyed that they are not open to the occasions when he does follow through. The child consistently forgets his homework and gets poor grades. Mom and Dad have been disappointed so often that they cannot get excited as the behavior begins to change. They fail to acknowledge the times he brings home acceptable daily assignments and hold off any encouragement until the report card comes out. The child obviously needs the encouragement each step along the way. The encouragement strengthens his confidence in himself, feeds his shattered ego and firms up his endurance for work which after long bouts of failure is a real chore.

Bruce Narramore suggests each parent check his approach to certain discipline problems. His workbook *A Guide To Child Rearing* provides a number of typical situations a parent will encounter and a multiple choice means of scoring how each problem would be handled by the parent. This approach brings theory to the level of dealing with specific situations every parent must handle nearly every day.[12]

Scriptural Guidelines to Discipline

Discipline defined. Discipline has a wider meaning than mere punishment. "Discipline" is proper instruction which belongs to the scholar. In common vernacular we speak of any scholarly pursuit as a discipline. The discipline of a child should include instruction. However, as we think of the discipline of the child, we probably think of some form of punishment. By the same token if we thought of any person who was to be disciplined we would naturally anticipate some form of punishment. The dual emphases of this word can be seen in Proverbs 3:11, 12:

> My son, do not dispise the Lord's discipline and do not resent his rebuke, because the Lord disciplines those he loves, as a father the son he delights in (NIV).

If you have a footnote on verse 12 in the New International Version, you will observe that the Septuagint reads "and he punishes." The context of Proverbs 3 definitely stresses instruction as well as discipline in the form of rebuke

---

12. Bruce Narramore, *A Guide to Child Rearing* (Grand Rapids: Zondervan Publishing, 1972).

and some other form of punishment. The concept clearly stresses corrective training in Job 36:10.

> He makes them listen to correction and commands them to repent of their evil (NIV).

Charles Matthews defines discipline as "training and correction designed to bring about obedience and respect for authority."[13]

Discipline in relationship to punishment. The fact that discipline may require physical punishment is clearly stated in the Scriptures:

> The rod of correction imparts wisdom, but a child left to itself disgraces his mother (Proverbs 29:15, NIV).
> Discipline your son, and he will give you peace; he will bring delight to your soul (Proverbs 29:17, NIV).
> A fool spurns his father's discipline, but whoever heeds correction shows prudence (Proverbs 15:5, NIV).
> Do not withhold discipline from a child; if you punish him with the rod, he will not die (Proverbs 23:13, NIV).
> Discipline your son, for in that there is hope; do not be a willing party to his death (Proverbs 19:18, NIV).

Many parents who spank do so because it was done to them. In a crisis they revert to the only methods they know. Children have a way of pushing parents to the brink. Unfortunately, what may be an effective form of correction is reduced to an inappropriate emotional release. A parent who administers punishment out of proportion to the child's misdeeds may be guilty of displacing anger on the child. A parent who finds himself using a child as a scapegoat for his own tensions should strongly evaluate what is happening and not hesitate to seek counseling if unable to curb these tendencies. Most parents who spank can probably recall

---

13. Charles Matthews, *The Christian Home* (Cincinnati: Standard Publishing, n.d.), p. 34.

times when they did so out of frustration. When you do spank your child, it should be in an effort to teach the child something. The child needs to know the guidelines where they have gone wrong and why you are punishing them. Most of all, love needs to be conveyed. A parent who exercises this kind of constraint is unlikely to be reacting out of anger and revenge.

Consistent willful disobedience may demand a spanking when other forms of discipline have been employed. Accidents and carelessness due to immaturity should not be punished by a spanking. When a child leaves his best glove out in the rain or misplaces a valuable tool, these are acts of immaturity, not willful disobedience. Some other forms of discipline such as earning money to pay for it would be better. When a child deliberately and willfully challenges authority, it is time to answer emphatically that you are in charge as a parent. Disrespect must not be tolerated.

Relationship of Discipline to Respect of God. All order and authority resides in God.

> He is the image of the invisible God, the firstborn over all creation. For by him all things were created: things in heaven and on earth, visible and invisible, whether thrones or powers or rulers or authorities; all things were created by him and for him. He is before all things, and in him all things hold together (Colossians 1:15-17, NIV).

A vital lesson for every person to learn is respect for God (Proverbs 9:10) and respect for law and order.

> Everyone must submit himself to the governing authorities, for there is no authority except that which God has established. The authorities that exist have been established by God. Consequently, he who rebels against the authority is rebelling against what God has instituted, and those who do so will bring judgment on themselves. For rulers hold no

terror for those who do right, but for those who do wrong. Do you want to be free from fear of the one in authority? Then do what is right and he will commend you. For he is God's servant to do you good. But if you do wrong, be afraid, for he does not bear the sword for nothing. He is God's servant, an agent of wrath to bring punishment on the wrong-doer. Therefore, it is necessary to submit to the authorities, not only because of possible punishment but also because of conscience (Romans 13:1-5, NIV).

A child who will disregard the authority of his parents will disregard other sources of authority in society. A child who will degrade the authority of his parents will likely disrespect God in his life. The Jewish home was built upon the foundation of the fear or respect of God.

These are the commands, decrees and laws the Lord your God directed me to teach you to observe in the land that you are crossing the Jordan to possess, so that you, your children and their children after them may fear the Lord your God as long as you live by keeping all his decrees and commands that I give you, and so that you may enjoy long life. Hear, O Israel, and be careful to obey so that it may go well with you and that you may increase greatly in a land flowing with milk and honey, just as the Lord, the God of your fathers, promised you.

Hear, O Israel: The Lord our God, the Lord is one. Love the Lord your God with all your heart and with all your soul and with all your strength. These commandments that I give you today are to be upon your hearts. Impress them on your children. Talk about them when you sit at home and when you walk along the road, when you lie down and when you get up. Tie them as symbols on your hands and bind them on your foreheads (Deuteronomy 6:1-8, NIV).

Paul likewise admonishes the exercise of discipline based on the premise that respect of parents is vitally associated with reverence for the Lord and His Word.

194

Children, obey your parents in the Lord for this is right. "Honor your father and mother"—which is the first commandment with a promise—"that it may go well with you and that you may enjoy long life on the earth." Fathers, do not exasperate your children; instead, bring them up in the training and instruction of the Lord (Ephesians 6:1-4, NIV).

The Apostle clearly cautions against abusive discipline in Ephesians 6:1-4 when he warns against "exasperating your child."

Relationship to Conscience Development. Discipline helps a child develop guidelines to govern his future life. On the other hand, cruel and excessive punishment that is unreasonable and lacking any rhyme or reason can destroy conscience development. Psychologists have long insisted that indiscriminate cruel treatment such as acts of child abuse contribute to psychopathic or anti-social behavior. When a child cannot understand the beatings that are applied excessively and inconsistently, he endures it and lives for a chance to show revenge. The child who has never known love and only extreme battering presents a severe threat to society.

Charles Matthews describes the role of discipline in conscience development:

A child receives discipline so that he will not need to be ruled by either fear or force but will become a self-respecting, self-governing individual. Discipline helps a child develop an inner drive that leads him to act on the basis of what he feels he ought to do. As conscience is developed and the reasoning powers of maturity become active, the need for discipline will decrease.[14]

---

14. *Ibid.*

Discipline in Relationship to the Uniqueness of the Individual Child. Every child is different. A glance is adequate for one child while a thorough spanking may be required for another. As Matthews insists: "It requires correct diagnosis and then the administration of the right medicine to the right patient at the right time."[15]

Discipline in Relationship to the Age of the Child. When considering discipline the age of the child is an extremely important consideration. I remember an occasion when our oldest child ran across the street to play in the city park. She was nearly run over by a passing truck. At the time she was eighteen months old. It would have been ridiculous to sit down and reason with her concerning the dangers involved in crossing the street. The most effective procedure was to spank her. At eighteen months she did not have the reasoning capacity to understand the dangers. At the same time, when she was fifteen I cannot imagine an occasion in which that would have been appropriate.

The other form of discipline, the reproof, is far more appropriate for an adolescent daughter than a spanking. Taking privileges away is better. If firm discipline is administered in the early years reasoning should be adequate in adolescence. When discipline is required, deprivation of privileges gives the child a chance to think through his inappropriate action. Deprivation of things or privileges should not be to such excess as to endanger the child's physical or emotional well being. The value of reproof as discipline must not be forgotten (Proverbs 29:15).

Discipline in Relationship to Consistency on the Part of Both Parents. I shall never forget a client who related that

---

15. *Ibid.*, p. 35.

when he was a child he hated to see his father coming because his mother used to always threaten him with the admonition he was going to get it when his father got home.

If a child needs discipline, he needs it right then, not three hours later. The average attention span of an elementary child is quite short. By the time dad gets home he has forgotten what he has done that is wrong. In Ecclesiastes 8:11 we read:

> When the sentence for a crime is not quickly carried out, the hearts of the people are filled with schemes to do wrong (NIV).

Parents need to come to some agreement on the most effective discipline. It is natural that due to their different backgrounds and temperaments they would view the form of discipline differently at times. This provides a check and balance as to procedure but they should not openly disagree in front of the child. A child will be quick to seize this lack of decisiveness and will frequently attempt to divide the parents.

Discipline in Relationship to Parental Example. The old adage "do as I say and not as I do" simply does not work with children. An undisciplined parent cannot effectively teach discipline. Discipline affects everything a parent does and says in the course of his daily life. Few inadequacies in a parent's life will not be seen by a child. The parent who sets high goals for his or her own Christian life will have a child who will be more inclined to accept high parental expectations.

Discipline in Relationship to Flexibility. Every child is unique and situations are different. The parent who resorts to only one form of discipline such as yelling or spanking is in a rut which is usually ineffective. A parent should employ a number of approaches which are appropriate to the offense. Reproof is usually adequate. Most children want to meet a parent's approval. A child will often respond to this response and when the child does acknowledge the correction the matter should be dropped. Yelling and screaming and a lengthy, highly emotional dressing down provokes the child to defend his or her shattered ego. Arguments and emotional confrontation often follow such loss of control by parents. Children also have to deal with their anger. Excessive harassment leaves the child at his or her wits end as how to cope with it.

Deprivation of privileges is one of the best forms of discipline. Children will often prefer a whipping to undergoing a day without their favorite T.V. programs, or going to a friend's house. This method provides children with opportunity to think through their behavior. If the boundaries have been clearly set up previously children realize they caused the break in their usual routine. The lesson that emerges is that they knew the rules and they broke them and they must pay the consequence. Children can easily see that appropriate behavior results in a happier relationship in which they are able to enjoy their favorite activities.

Corporal punishment should not be the first line of discipline. It should be employed when others fail and when a child disrespects his parents. Parents must be cautious that in their confrontations with their children they do not so conduct themselves as to provoke disrespect such as uncontrollable aggressive actions (Ephesians 6:4).

Children need boundaries. As a child grows older, it becomes increasingly important for there to be flexibility regarding rules and regulations. There are exceptions to a 12:00 arrival time for a teenager on a date if a very special occasion does not end until 11:30 and he is going out to eat afterward. These exceptions need to be negotiated to mutual satisfaction of all involved, if possible. However, as long as children are in the family household, a final judgment must be made by the parent and be respected by the child.

In addition to boundaries as to rules and regulations, boundaries need to be kept by children and parents in how they treat each other. Children in the process of their emotional development test the limits. They exercise their growing independence. There will be times of confrontation. Children generally feel they are more capable and mature than parents view them. Parents often recognize the potential consequence of immature judgment on the part of their children and want to protect them from unnecessary hurt. However, they also may be overprotective. Children will test the limits increasingly as they grow older. These occasions may become arguments. It is not necessary that a parent be so rigid as to never permit an emotional confrontation. A parent has a right to expect respect, and abusive language is out of bounds. Likewise inappropriate language is out of bounds for the parent. In a permissive atmosphere this confrontation is unlikely to occur because the child has few limits. Few occasions arise where the boundaries are tested. In an authoritarian approach the parent is the unquestioned authority, whose word is absolute and the rules never bend and negotiation is hopeless. Some children will be repressive in light of rigidity and harsh punishment while others will rebel. The rebellion may invoke serious acting out. The rebellion may only come when children are old enough to physically intimidate their parents as the parents have their children. In an authoritative approach confrontation is occasionally inevitable but children can grow in the experience of dealing with their growing independence and even their angry feelings. When either parents or children overstep the boundaries of propriety and fight unfairly and hurt each other an apology is in order. Parents need to learn that children learn from what parents apologize for as well as what they positively affirm. It takes discipline to apologize when one is due another person. These are also lessons parents in their imperfections with their children can model.

Obviously, no parent is perfect. The parents who convey openly their love and respect for their children will be more effective. No method is perfect or no parent has perfect judgment. The child who knows he is loved will be much more inclined to profit from appropriate discipline and to survive unscathed from the parents' inadequacies of manner and procedure in teaching discipline.

DISCUSSION QUESTIONS: *Developing Discipline In Children*

1. Why is the illustration of Eli and Samuel so frightening for a parent who strives to rear children in the Lord?
2. Which of the lessons from the experiences of Eli and Samuel do you feel are most meaningful to you personally? Explain why?
3. Do you agree that establishing an approach to discipline is a struggle for most parents? Defend your answer.
4. What is the thrust of Hebrews 12:5-11?
5. What is the focus of the present trend among psychologists concerning discipline. Explain PET and behavior modification.
6. What caution should parents take in following psychologists?

7. What does the Scripture say about spanking? What guidelines must one exercise in this regard?
8. How would you define discipline? What is the relationship of discipline to punishment, conscience development, and the uniqueness of the child? How important is consistency? In what ways does flexibility enter into the subject of discipline?
9. If you had to choose one aspect that is most important in disciplining a child, in fact, the one ingredient most indispensable in child rearing, what would you select?
10. Has this chapter helped to expand your knowledge of the Biblical and psychological perspectives of this subject? If so, how has it been helpful? If it has disagreed with your approach or solidified your present position and procedure concerning discipline, indicate how this is the situation?
11. Apply the insights of the chapter to particular problems many parents have. Focus on a selective age level and apply the chapter to certain developmental stages.
12. If you have access to a group setting where parents share and support each other, each person could share some of his struggles with the discipline of his children. Go around the circle, share understanding and use the chapter to bring Scriptural insight to bear upon the problems.
13. What additional resources have you read recently that touch upon this topic? If you recently viewed a TV program or read an article in the newspaper related to this problem, react to that source in light of this chapter.

Chapter Twelve

COPING WITH ANGER

A Scriptural Illustration

". . . and Cain was very wroth, and his countenance fell. . . . and it came to pass, when they were in the field, that Cain rose up against Abel his brother and slew him" (Genesis 4:5, 8, KJV).

Throughout history the name of Cain has been associated with the crime of murder. It has been symbolic for this most violent act of aggression. However, there is no evidence that "Cain intended to commit murder."[1]

Walter Russell Bowie in *The Interpreter's Bible* suggests that Cain struck "Abel in the instinctive reflex of his anger, but who can say that he had any deliberate purpose to end his brother's life?"[2] The tragedy of that first murder is repeated often in society today. But beyond that threat which is real enough in these times, a lesson concerning the ungoverned unleashing of anger provides instruction for everyone. So often we say those things in a rage of anger that are hard, if not impossible, to erase when tempers subside. Headlines confirm that murder happens all around us but a deeper lesson resides even nearer where we all live.

Jesus warned of the destructiveness of harboring hatred.

You have heard that it was said to the people long ago, "Do not murder, and anyone who murders will be subject to judgment" (Matthew 5:21, NIV).

Hate must be snuffed out before the raging blaze of anger is released in all of its fury. Anger can be destructive in the

---

1. Walter Russell Bowie, "Genesis" in *The Interpreter's Bible*, Vol. 1, ed: George Arthur Buttrick (Nashville: Abingdon-Cokesbury Press, 1952), p. 516.

2. *Ibid.*, p. 517.

home and Paul certainly warns in Ephesians 6 that parents are not to incite anger in their children.

> Fathers, do not exasperate your children; instead bring them up in the training and instruction of the Lord (Ephesians 6:4, NIV).

It must also be asserted that husbands and wives and brothers and sisters and neighbors and friends and all those next of kin must not exasperate each other. Few problems have more influence on the world around us and immediate community of our homes than the subject of coping with anger.

Relevance to Contemporary Society

Incidents of aggression are alarmingly high and appear to be on the rise. It seems impossible to pick up a newspaper or watch the evening news without being confronted with some act of cruelty. With the proliferation of nuclear weapons to countries that are especially involved in acts of terrorism toward each other and the conflict among the super powers, the survival of the entire human race is indeed threatened.

Few subjects loom such an imposing challenge to political leaders, law enforcement officers, psychologists and the entire Christian community than the control of violence.

Of course, the ramifications of this problem hit much closer to home than the threat of nuclear holocaust and crime in the streets. To most people, the control of aggression on a global scale or even community acts of violence are not the underlying concern. The basic issue is coping with feelings of anger in the immediate community of home and work.

Scope of the Chapter

Before addressing the practical issues of how to deal with anger and the Scriptural resources available, attention must turn to attempts to determine the factors that precipitate aggression and violence.

Factors Responsible for Aggression

A number of attempts have been made to determine the causes of violence.[3] A cursory review of some of the more familiar explanations will be explored.

Instinctive Urges. Many social scientists have focused on instinctive urges as an explanation for aggressive behavior. To be quite blunt, they have insisted man is aggressive because it is his nature to be this way. Sigmund Freud was a proponent of this concept. He believed man posssessed a death wish which either turned inward causing depression or even suicide or would be directed outward manifesting itself in hostility. According to Freud, pressure builds up in this system and must be sublimated—directed to other acceptable outlets. This pressure needs to be drained off.

This approach relates to the evolutionary concept of the survival of the fittest. The argument contends that as animals are instinctively violent, man is also aggressive. In fact, the contention is that he must be such to survive.

As one observes animals one can see this is true but so also are more docile aspects of animal life.[4] In fact, animals even share food and help each other.

---

3. Robert A. Baron, Donn Byrne and Barry Kantowitz, *Psychology: Understanding Behavior* (Philadelphia: W. B. Saunders Company, 1979), pp. 415-425.

4. Elliot Aronson, *The Social Animal* (San Francisco: W. H. Freeman and Company, 1980), p. 167.

A friend of mine reluctantly adopted a stray dog that kept hanging around. The family appropriately dubbed him "Hobo." After he was taken in and provided food, Hobo wanted to introduce another dog to the handout he had found. The friends of mine did not want one dog—to say nothing of two. They drove the newest beggar off. What they discovered was that Hobo was taking a portion of his food to his friend. In order to eliminate this, they cut back on Hobo's portions. However, they traced him and he still shared with his friend. Hobo began to look bad. Over a period of time he became sick. What was happening, quite simply, was that Hobo was gradually starving to death. Neither dog would survive under this arrangement. Recognizing how much Hobo cared for his friend, they determined to provide for both of them. They now have two dogs—Hobo and the companion of Hobo they named "Hobo's Friend."

The above account is an actual observation but it may not be considered very scientific. However, behavior scientists have observed similar kinds of sharing among animals enough that many have abandoned the survival of the fittest notion and the premise that animals are instinctively aggressive.

One may be hard pressed to maintain this position of instinctive aggression regarding animals. The important point to recognize is that man is different from animals. The trend has shifted to a recognition that aggression in human beings is a learned behavior that is intricately more complex than in animals. As a behavior it can be readily changed.

Frustration. Although frustration does not always lead to aggression, it must be acknowledged that it has a role in acts of aggression. Research among children and among

205

deprived people, who see what others possess, suggests that frustration can lead to aggression.[5]

Verbal Attack or Physical Attack. Many psychologists insist that physical or verbal attacks are a very powerful influence to ignite violence. Common sense tells us this is a factor.

Aggressive Models. The exposure to violent models influences aggression. Psychologists are generally concerned about the type of modeling provided children by the violent programs on T.V.[6] Children who are reared in homes where they are exposed to violent interchanges in the family are likely to practice the same behavior in their own homes.

Biblical Perspective

In light of present knowledge concerning the factors that result in aggression, a Biblical injunction appears to be extremely appropriate.

Jesus addressed himself both to murder and the origin of this violent act.

> You have heard that it was said to the people long ago, "Do not murder, and anyone who murders will be subject to judgment." But I tell you that anyone who is angry with his brother will be subject to judgment. Again, anyone who says to his brother, "Raca," is answerable to the Sanhedrin. But anyone who says, "You fool!" will be in danger of the fire of hell (Matthew 5:21-22, NIV).

The Old Testament law as with modern law is concerned with the act, but the new law regards that contemptuous

---

5. *Ibid.*, pp. 180-181.
6. *Ibid.*, pp. 175-178.

sneer as worthy of the penalty of the court. Jesus insists that we dare not merely give attention to the end of the process, but must be concerned with the motive and thought. How we feel and how we express ourselves to our fellow-man comes under the severest judgment. Praise God for grace or none of us would escape divine wrath. Earthly courts have a hard enough time determining acts that are criminal. The Lord does not have the problem of incomplete knowledge. God has pity on the person we put down, take advantage of, manipulate, or intimidate by word or deed. He likewise takes pity on us when we are treated unfairly. He holds all people responsible for their treatment of their brothers. He takes pity on every person because he is potentially His child. Whatever is done against another of His children is done against His loving heart.

The importance of coming to grips with what is done in anger is set forth vividly in the next verses in Matthew 5.

> Therefore, if you are offering your gift at the altar and there remember that your brother has something against you, leave your gift there in front of the altar. First go and be reconciled to your brother; then come and offer your gift.
> Settle matters quickly with your adversary who is taking you to court. Do it while you are still with him on the way, or he may hand you over to the judge, and the judge may hand you over to the officer, and you may be thrown into prison. I tell you the truth, you will not get out until you have paid the last penny (Matthew 5:23-26, NIV).

God sees the heart and if a heart is filled with grudges there is no way it can be ready to be offered in adoration to God. This new law demands the inmost searching of grudges at the root of a potential murder. Cain's grudge was first in his heart before the abominable act of murder.

207

The challenge here is to cleanse that heart. Get right with the other person—then get right with God.

Jesus clearly insists that we agree quickly with the adversary. If this is done, it pleases God that we make amends for our wrongs and enables us to cope with the anger at the time. Anger is most destructive when we "sit on it" and let it build up. All kinds of negative things can happen as a result of delaying the reconciliation. When anger is inernalized, it may: (1) result in depression, (2) further alienate us from the brother, (3) boils beneath the surface to come out in displacement on the other people around us who are altogether unrelated to the instigators of the feelings, or (4) rush out in uncontrollable rage at some unguarded moment.

The admonishment of the Lord fits well with the Apostle Paul's words in Ephesians 4:26, 27.

> "In your anger do not sin": Do not let the sun go down while you are still angry, and do not give the devil a foothold (NIV).

These words of Paul warn that if we nurse our anger and let it burn inside for a period of time instead of snuffing it out before we go to bed at night, it is sinful. This Scripture acknowledges anger is sinful when we permit it to fester. Naturally, there are causes that are right and concerning which we might legitimately be angered. Jesus was capable of anger as Mark 3:1-5 plainly records.

> Another time he went into the synagogue, and a man with a shriveled hand was there. Some of them were looking for a reason to accuse Jesus, so they watched him closely to see if he would heal him on the Sabbath. Jesus said to the man with the shriveled hand, "Stand up in front of everyone."

Then Jesus asked them, "Which is lawful on the Sabbath: to do good or to do evil, to save life or to kill?" But they remained silent.

He looked around at them in anger and, deeply distressed at their stubborn hearts, said to the man, "Stretch out your hand." He stretched it out, and his hand was completely restored (NIV).

Jesus was clearly angry on this occasion. Anger may be provoked out of hatred for sin. However, the problem most people face is how to control the occasions when anger is experienced whether the cause be righteous or not. Even when anger is justified, it may get out of control and result in sin. Many times we become confused, tend to see our side of things, and equate our anger with righteous indignation whereas it may be quite removed from a righteous cause. When angry it is difficult to view things objectively.

There is a need to be firm in our convictions concerning a righteous cause. Vernon Grounds puts the challenge succinctly, "Thus one of the toughest tasks is to learn under the tutelage of the Holy Spirit to hate the right things for the right motives at the right time and to the right degree."[7]

Once again we come back to Paul's injunction: "be ye angry and sin not" (Ephesians 4:26, 27, KJV). When the adrenalin is released, how do we control it?

Jesus is very specific in this regard and lays down a clear command.

You have heard that it was said, "Love your neighbor and hate your enemy." But I tell you, Love your enemies and pray for those who persecute you (Matthew 5:43, 44, NIV).

---

7. Vernon Ground, *Emotional Problems and the Gospel*, (Grand Rapids: Zondervan, 1976), pp. 60-61.

If we pray for a person, it will be hard to continue to view that person as an enemy. Vernon Ground insists:

And what happens if we obey our Lord's commandment, praying for an obnoxious person? Well, an individual may still hate us, but we can no longer view him as an enemy. We cannot prayerfully carry him into the presence of Jesus and still hate him. As we pray, we come to see him as a fellow-sinner and a fellow-sufferer and a fellow-struggler. We begin to feel a genuine compassion for him. We cannot prayerfully carry him into the presence of Jesus and still refuse him forgiveness or be indifferent to his needs, his weaknesses, his longings. Neither can we be indifferent to our Savior's desire that the obnoxious person as much as ourselves be happy and fulfilled in God's fellowship. We cannot prayerfully carry him into the presence of Jesus without standing there ourselves, rebuked for our lack of understanding and sympathy. Thus prayer helps us view even a self-defined enemy as a person whom God loves and can enable us to love.[8]

It is imperative that we also obey Romans 12:20, 21.

On the contrary: "If your enemy is hungry, feed him; if he is thirsty, give him something to drink. In doing this, you will heap burning coals on his head." Do not be overcome by evil, but overcome evil with good (NIV).

When we are seeking an opportunity to minister to a person, we are going to do everything we can to help. Whatever reaction that person has toward us, through prayer our heart will soften. As we pray for the other person we must also pray for the Holy Spirit to fill us so that we can control our anger.

---

8. *Ibid.*, p. 63.

Toward the Control of Anger

Prayer intervenes at the origin of violence—the thought process. This internalized process and specific behavior provides a basic foundation for coming to grips with this problem. Are there other approaches? Certainly many are in vogue today. Some are helpful, some are not.

1. *Punishment.* One of the most common ways of dealing with aggressive acts of violence is punishment. Probably the average citizen would choose this as the first example of a method of treating aggression. However, the flooding of penal institutions and the high incidence of repeaters confirm the questionableness of this approach.

On a more practical scale evidence of aggression on children confirms that aggressive parents raise violent children. To teach a child not to fight by "knocking his block off" or excessive spanking tends to confirm the very behavior the parent attempts to curtail. Children model the overall patterns of parents. A harsh, punitive, unreasonable parent tends to embitter the child and at the same time models excessively aggressive behavior. On the other hand a warm, caring parent who occasionally spanks the child will not as negatively affect the child.

2. *Catharsis.* Until quite recently psychologists assumed that the best way to deal with anger was to get it off your chest, blow off some steam, hit a punching bag, kick a tin can or beat the stuffing out of a pillow.

Although this method has been widely employed there is little researched evidence to prove that it actually helps reduce aggression. In fact, there is growing evidence that opportunities to aggress against someone will actually increase instead of decreasing it. What seems to happen is that having aggressed once against a person we apparently need to go one step further to justify ourselves. There does appear

211

to be some relief of tension but this catharsis does not reduce aggression. The reason for this may be that catharsis deals with the problem physically in reducing tension, but it does not deal with how we think as well as how we feel.

3. *Desensitizing Anger with Humor and Prayer.* At the present time the most promising technique is based upon the assumption that a person is incapable of engaging in two incompatible responses at once.[9] It is impossible to listen to a lecture and laugh at a classmate's joke. Any condition that will serve to induce a response incompatible with anger or the actual violent act will be an extremely effective deterrent of this behavior. Humor, for example, can be effective in deterring aggression. A couple, family, or individual may be encouraged to stand outside themselves for awhile and see humor in some especially explosive situation. Hopefully later they may recall the humor in the way they actually look rather than the hostility.

I recall a family describing how hectic it was in the morning as six people tried to get into one bathroom and meet their appointments at 8:30 A.M. I had them describe and act it out. They began to laugh at how funny it was. It did not solve their problem but it defused a constantly explosive situation. The problem became more manageable and less threatening. When they got angry they remembered acting out a typical morning at their house and they would laugh instead of fight.

Probably most people recall situations when tensions were high and someone was able to insert a humorous line and the aggression was sharply reduced.

Humor is not the only effective tool. Any emotion incompatible with anger may be effective. Prayer or Bible reading

---

9. Robert A. Baron, *Psychology: Understanding Behavior,* pp. 423-424.

can ignite warm and accepting feelings of love and caring are positive factors that could prevent aggression. As with the use of humor, timing is crucial in this regard.

I recall at a rather large convention service a speaker systematically encouraged each person in the vast audience to take some person who was their enemy before the Lord and pray about it. After spending time with the Lord in prayer, the audience was asked to come up with a specific procedure of dealing with the problem. In addition, each person was then to share this experience and their plan or add their release from the burden of their hatred with the person next to them. In most cases, this was a total stranger. I felt much better personally and made serious inroads toward reconciling some personality conflicts with people in my life right then. As laughter and anger do not go together—neither do hatred and the loving experience of praying for our enemy. Our enemy ceases to be our enemy.

Understanding Different Temperaments

Some people have more difficulty dealing with anger because of their temperament. Styles of dealing with people may be learned from parents and peers. However, the observations of many parents that each of their children is different from birth has been acknowledged by psychologists.

1. *The Expressors.* This is the person who insists that he is going to be perfectly honest and when you hear this you want to take three steps backward. His anger appears to be close to the surface—he is explosive. These people speak first and ask questions later. In the Bible, Simon Peter, and the Sons of Thunder, James and John, characterize this style.

2. *The Repressors.* This is the person who is unaware of his anger. He sits on it for a period of time and then

explodes. Jonah's brooding over God's treatment of Ninevah or Elijah's self-pity because he was the last faithful servant come to mind as examples of this style. This style often leads to depression, displacement of angry feelings on innocent targets and psychosomatic illness as a result of the build-up of anger in our bodies.

3. *The Suppressors.* The person who thinks before he speaks, but indeed does express his feelings provides the healthiest example. The old motto, "count to ten before you speak," has some merit. It is necessary to give careful consideration to the advisability of sharing our feelings and how to express them so that our anger does not block our relationships or burn within us. In this regard the best description may be found in the reference to God as being slow to anger (Joel 2:13; Jonah 4:2). How appropriate the words of Ecclesiastes 7:9, "Be not hasty in thy spirit to be angry," as well as the challenge to a candidate for the office of an elder who is "not soon angry" (Titus 1:7).

Any person who finds himself either as an expressor or repressor must move in the direction of the mediating position. It is dangerous to assume that this is the way we are and not attempt to change the style of dealing with angry feelings. The tendency to excuse anger can readily be heard when people rationalize, "I have a bad temper." Sometimes they add "I'm a readhead" or "my mother was this way" or "I get this from my dad, he was a real hot head." Often a married couple must make important changes if their marriage is to survive. The expressive mate needs to exercise control and to be less caustic and destructive in reactions. The repressive person needs to become aware of his angry feelings, and express those feelings before they boil beneath the surface and erupt on unexpected occasions. If a person can recognize what temperament fits him and what adjustments need to be made, an important milestone has been achieved. Next, we would explore some specific procedures that can help a person of any temperament.

How to Deal with Anger

Often people say, "I know I'm angry. What can I do about it? Are there some guidelines that will help me?" Of course, this chapter provides Scriptural principles and insights but perhaps a rather brief formula would further enhance the practicability of this chapter.

Leo Madow's book, *Anger, How To Recognize And Cope With It,* describes a four step procedure to cope with anger.

1. *Recognize that you are angry.* As previously noted, the person who is repressive is unaware of his anger. When we are aware of our anger it is much less harmful. Many times in counseling with Christians I have observed that they are uncomfortable with the emotion of anger. They will admit to being disappointed or discouraged but are reluctant to own up to their anger. Christians are prone to feel guilty about their anger more than others. The harder the counselor tries to confront them, the more they may resist. Personally as a counselor, I will try to stay with "how people have let them down," "how they feel disappointed." By avoiding the term "anger," I can help them release the negative feelings without clamming up with a phrase like, "Oh, I'm not angry" or "I don't get angry."

The person who claims he is not angry and yet is depressed is probably disguising the anger which is in fact turning in on himself. Whenever a person becomes depressed, it is a good idea to ask the question "What am I angry about?"

On occasion I find in my own life that I cannot sleep. When I think back on some event I recall something that happened that made me angry. I think back on the day's activities and often I will come up with some clues as to what is keeping me awake. When I come across what is bothering me, I can feel the flush of anger.

Discovering that you are angry is an important first step. Sometimes the process of getting in touch with our angry feelings is detracted by thinking that it is not reasonable— I should not be angry. It is important to remember that anger is an emotion, it is not necessarily reasonable. An awareness that you feel the emotion legitimizes it. Sometimes people have difficulty coping with anger because they cannot find a legitimate reason to justify it.

Feelings of guilt or unreasonableness must not be permitted to block the process of getting in touch with your angry feelings. Recognizing that we are angry must take place on the emotional level as well as the intellectual level. To recognize you are angry means that you can feel it and accept it as fact.

2. *Identify the Source of the Anger.* The first step is to recognize you are angry and now you come to the second step—identifying the source of the anger. Let us say a person drops something heavy on my toe. The source is obvious. However, if this person drops something on my toe in the course of moving my furniture out on my request without any remuneration, reason tells me I cannot be angry. It was an accident and he has worked all day helping me move.

Whenever the source of our anger is difficult to trace down, there is a good chance that anger is directed toward some powerful person. An indication that we are dealing with anger toward a powerful source may be found when we are guilty of focusing anger on an inappropriate source or a scapegoat. Psychologists call this experience displacement. Most of us have the occasion to be angry at our boss at work and find that we take it out on our wife or children. We may be threatened by the thought of resentment towards a person that has a great deal of control over our lives, so when our child steps out of line a bit she gets the brunt of our anger. When anger is out of proportion to the offense, then it probably is an outlet for anger generated by an altogether different person. In order to deal with anger the real source must be identified. When anger is out of proportion to the offense this may indicate the source of anger is really someplace else.

3. *Understand Why You Are Angry.* Is your reason for being angry reasonable? If you are taking a class and the professor treats you unequally, this is a realistic reason. If you are angry because he will not give you special considerations, this is not realistic.

Sometimes we feel anger because we take things personally. The example Madow uses is a good one.

> A driver may cut in front of you in a traffic lane. You get furious at him, but why? It is important to recognize that he is not doing it to you personally; he would probably do it to anyone. You have a right to be angry at his careless driving, but if you take the incident personally it can release a great deal of resentment. You should say, "How can he do that stupid thing?"—which is realistic and appropriate—not "How can he do that stupid thing to me?"—which is unrealistic and infuriating.[10]

Anger that is unrealistic may involve all sorts of hidden feelings which are difficult to face and deal with.

4. *Deal with the Anger Realistically.* Dealing with the anger realistically is the fourth and final step. If we recognize

---

10. Leo Madow, *Anger: How to Recognize and Cope With It* (New York: Charles Scribner's Sons, 1972), p. 115.

we are angry, know the source and have discovered that the anger is realistic, then we are ready to deal with it realistically. If you are waiting in the cafeteria line and someone pushes ahead of you, it is reasonable to ask him to go back to the end of the line. However, it is not reasonable to hit him over the head or to swallow your anger.

A confrontation with the person may be the most appropriate way to deal with your anger. This is rather simple when the problem is clear cut. When anger is unrealistic, it is much more difficult to deal with. When the anger is within you, it may require considerable effort on your part to solve.

In marital counseling let us say that the husband is angry at his wife because she does not keep a clean house. On closer examination it is learned that his real complaint is that she parents him. In actuality he gives her a double message, parent me—take care of me. When she responds to this, his autonomous-independent side rears up and he puts her down. The husband in this illustration may not recognize what is happening with him. Marital therapy can help provide insight. When he realizes his wife is not his parent he will be able to handle his anger more effectively. He must also learn to accept the conflicting needs he has to be both independent and dependent. At the same time his wife may very well be exercising a parenting style she learned, perhaps as the first-born child who gave a lot of orders around the house, or from her mother who was dominant.

Assertiveness Versus Aggression: A Christian Perspective

One of the most frequent questions that arises among Christians is "How can I express my anger as a Christian? I use to have a very explosive temper. I am trying to overcome that. Are you suggesting that I regress to a non-Christian style of life?" This is an important question and deserves careful consideration.

Before proceeding with a Christian overlay of this theme, it is necessary to clarify some terms. The Christian is not justified in being aggressive as we shall define aggression. To be aggressive means that we have the intent to harm another person physically or emotionally. The vernacular uses aggression in a number of different ways and that may or may not be appropriate. At times aggression may be confused with another concept—assertiveness.

A salesman, for example, may be assertive rather than aggressive. If he is merely enthusiastic and thorough in his preparation and if he presents himself and the product in a straightforward way, he is assertive. If he pushes against your resistance, manipulates you, intimidates you, runs you down, is insensitive to you, and does not care about your feelings, he is aggressive.

The Christian is not justified in running rough shod over people without regard to their feelings. However, the Christian is called upon by the very nature of his position as the salt of the earth, in a tasteless, sickening world, to present himself and his message in such a way as to get his message across.

Misconceptions of a Christian Stance

Some Christians jump to the conclusion that a Christian is to be passive at all costs. In the common vernacular he is to be a "doormat" for anyone to trample on at all costs.

This view is contrary to an appropriate understanding of Scripture. Perhaps the most frequently cited reference in this regard may be found in Matthew 5:39-42. This passage is germane to our discussion and the reference reads:

But I say unto you, That ye resist not evil: but whosoever shall smite thee on thy right cheek, turn to him the other also. And if any man will sue thee at the law, and take away thy coat, let him have thy cloak also. And whosoever shall compel thee to go a mile, go with him twain. Give to him that asketh thee, and from him that would borrow of thee turn not thou away.

Ye have heard that it hath been said, Thou shalt love thy neighbor, and hate thine enemy. But I say unto you, Love your enemies, bless them that curse you, do good to them that hate you, and pray for them which despitefully use you, and persecute you; That ye may be the children of your Father which is in heaven: for he maketh his sun to rise on the evil and on the good, and sendeth rain on the just and on the unjust. For if ye love them which love you, what reward have ye? do not even the publicans the same? And if ye salute your brethren only, what do ye more than others? do not even the publicans so? Be ye therefore perfect, even as your Father which is in heaven is perfect (KJV).

For guidelines in interpreting this passage and for insights into this section on assertive behavior, I am richly indebted to Arthur C. May's article *Assertive Behavior In A New Testament Perspective, (Journal of Psychology and Theology,* Winter, 1980, Vol. 8, No. 4, pp. 288-292).

May contends that in interpreting Matthew 5:39-42, the following points must be kept in mind:

1. The purpose of the passage is to counteract the tendency among the Jews to seek revenge based on the Mosaic law and to enjoin them to follow His higher law.

2. Jesus challenges His disciples to give up rights and go the second mile but not out of psychological weakness.

3. The Scripture does not exclude certain exceptions such as the threat of serious personal injury to the Christian himself or discredit to the person who offends us.

Conceivably situations may arise in which yielding to the demands of another may place both the Christian being confronted and the other party in moral compromise. Obviously, Christians cannot passively permit anything to be done to them. A Christian must turn the other cheek whenever this can be done without moral compromise.

Occasions may arise when the principle of turning the other cheek may place the cause of Christ in jeopardy. As a representative of Christ and His cause, utter foolish compromise is not a credit to the Gospel.

Assertiveness must be done thoughtfully and appropriately. Jesus clearly teaches that there is a time to set aside personal preferences. All assertive behavior must flow out of the heart of love. Any treatment of a brother or sister must be approached in love as Paul maintains in I Timothy 5:1 which reads as follows:

> Rebuke not an elder, but intreat him as a father; and the younger men as brethren (KJV);

More specific guidelines are provided in May's application of the assertiveness approach. He provides Scriptural examples of the categorized assertive behavior of leading psychologists in assertiveness training.

1. *Basic Assertiveness.* In basic assertiveness, stress is placed upon simple facts. Here the example of John the Baptist when questioned by the Levites is in order. John said: "I am not the Christ." He goes on in this passage to further emphatically clarify the facts (John 1:19-23). Many of the "I" statements of Jesus may be considered examples of basic assertion (John 4:31f.). Paul's admonition is also relevant here (Acts 23:6).

2. *Empathic Assertion.* This type of assertion is characterized first by recognition of the other person's situation or feelings before making an assertion.

221

Examples of this procedure are amply illustrated in the Lord's admonition to the seven churches of Asia in Revelation (Revelation 2:1-6, 12-16, 19-25) and the preaching of Paul on Mars Hill (Acts 17:22-31). Paul celebrated the obedience of the Roman church prior to specific admonitions to Romans 16:19. These examples demonstrate empathy that was employed before assertion in preaching and writing. When Peter refused to let Jesus wash his feet, Jesus empathized with Peter, "What I do you do not realize now; but you shall understand hereafter" (John 13:7, NASV). Peter then permitted Jesus to wash his feet.

3. *Escalating Assertion.* Escalating assertion comes into focus when one person fails to respond to the minimal assertion of another and does not acknowledge the individual's rights. The speaker gradually escalates the assertion and thereby becomes increasingly firmer.

May cites Jesus' response to temptation in the desert as a perfect Biblical example of this.

> Man shall not live on bread alone, but on every word that proceeds out of the mouth of God (Matthew 4:4, NASV).

When this was not effective and Satan reappeared the second time, Jesus' assertion became more personal and succinct:

> You shall not tempt the Lord your God (Matthew 4:7, NASV).

Finally, after Satan insisted on procuring Jesus' fall, Jesus made an emphatic assertion.

> Be gone, Satan! For it is written, You shall worship the Lord your God, and serve Him only (Matthew 4:10, NASV).

When Satan continued to pressure Jesus, he escalated his assertion until Satan left.

4. *Confrontive Assertion.* This type of assertion is relevant when a person fails to do that which he said he would do. Jesus masterfully demonstrated this assertive type in his confrontation with the Pharisees on several occasions (Matthew 12:10ff.; Matthew 15:1-20; John 8:3-7). There was a contradiction between the Pharisees' allegiance to God and their continual rejection of Jesus' teachings.

Paul also provided an example of confrontive assertion when he confronted Peter with his contradictory behavior in refusing to eat with Gentile Christians.

> When Peter came to Antioch, I opposed him to his face, because he was in the wrong. Before certain men came from James, he used to eat with the Gentiles. But when they arrived, he began to draw back and separate himself from the Gentiles because he was afraid of those who belonged to the circumcision group. The other Jews joined him in his hypocrisy, so that by their hypocrisy even Barnabas was led astray.
>
> When I saw that they were not acting in line with the truth of the gospel, I said to Peter in front of them all, "You are a Jew, yet you live like a Gentile and not like a Jew. How is it, then, that you force Gentiles to follow Jewish customs? (Galatians 2:11-14, NIV).

5. *Language.* This approach is similar to the empathetic approach except it stresses "I" statements and is used to convey negative feelings. Examples of this approach may be found in Paul's trial with Agrippa (Acts 26:2-23). Paul acknowledges Agrippa's position and his knowledge prior to making his defense.

It is clear that assertiveness was used in the New Testament. In like manner, assertiveness is called for in our times.

Assertiveness enables a Christian to present his needs and to have a procedure that enables him to deal with his angry feelings without unduly hurting another person and without swallowing his anger and becoming depressed. Still another reason for the Christian to be assertive involves his role as a Christian and as a worker in the church.

Christians are called to action and firmness. An example of assertiveness is found in Peter as he bravely asserted, "We cannot stop speaking what we have seen and heard" (Acts 4:20). May contends that the Peter on this occasion is a radically changed man from the one who denied his Lord three times.

In the area of assertiveness many Christians desperately need to make some radical changes for the cause of the Kingdom they represent and for their own personal mental health. The firmness that assertiveness recommends encourages appropriate action, and it also encourages appropriate resistance. Learning to say no is a lesson many Christians need. Of course, this is particularly relevant in the face of temptations. A lack of assertiveness can deter our leadership abilities in the Lord's work. Assertiveness encourages us to use the creativeness and wisdom that God provides through practical experience and direction in the Word of God. The non-assertive person, in a role of leadership, will fail to present the benefits of his unique council.

Conclusion

Our discussion of the negative effects of anger has touched upon aggressive acts of violence and inappropriate verbal outbursts. Anger that is held in may result in depression or in psychosomatic disorders. The connection of anger to physical problems can be observed in such expressions as "he is a pain in the neck," "he makes me sick to my stomach," "a blinding rage" or "itching to get our hands on someone." As a matter of fact we have a choice. We can deal with the source of the pain in our neck or literally have a pain in the neck. The energy that builds up in our system can harm our body as well as influence our emotions. Leo Madow describes the changes that take place inside of us when we get angry.

> More sugar pours into our system so we have more energy. More blood, containing needed nourishment, is circulated by increasing the blood pressure and making the heart beat faster. More adrenalin is secreted, to dilate the pupils of the eyes and make us see better, and to help mobilize other such needed activities. If there is no discharge of this build-up, as is usually the case, we remain in a chronic state of preparedness, with heart beating rapidly, blood pressure up, and chemical changes in the blood, and eventually this condition can harm us physically.[11]

By applying the insights and procedures in this chapter, you should find help in channeling this energy in a more productive manner.

DISCUSSION QUESTIONS: *Coping With Anger*

1. Name and describe four explanations for anger.
2. What did Jesus say about the origin of violence in Matthew 5:21-22 and also in Matthew 5:23-26?
3. Relate Ephesians 4:26-27 to the above passages.
4. When was Jesus angry? How were His feelings different from ours when we are angry?

---

11. *Ibid.*, p. 73.

5. How can we apply Paul's injunction, "be angry and sin not" (Ephesians 4:26, 27) to our lives? How does Jesus help us deal with anger in Matthew 5:43, 44? How does Paul's imperative in Romans 12:20, 21 help us?

6. Describe the three approaches in vogue today to control anger. Explain each. Which one is best and why?

7. Describe the three different temperaments. Which one best describes yourself?

8. Describe the four step procedure found in Leo Madow's book, *Anger, How to Recognize and Cope With It?*

9. What is assertiveness? Is there a place for this in the Christian's life? Explain your answer from a Biblical perspective.

Chapter Thirteen

MAXIMIZING MARRIAGE AND FAMILY LIFE

Chasing Rainbows

Every person searches for the supreme marital and family relationship. The childhood fairy tales, the romantic movies, the stories with the happy endings begin early in life to set an individual's heart on a long path strewn with many happy daydreams. Starry-eyed, most young adolescents envision in their idealism that their marriage is going to be the perfect marriage. Of course, they will also be perfect parents and naturally have perfect children who will live happily ever after.

Childhood and young adolescent dreams are grounded in much more fantasy than reality. In later adolescence many are hurt enough in the nitty gritty encounters with the opposite sex to deflate that perfect bubble of perfection. Slowly, those visions of the beautiful maiden and the knight in shining armor begin to fade in the light of grim reality. That first teenage romance was exhilarating but the pain excruciating.

The concept that the ideal man or woman awaits somewhere over the rainbow begins to fade. Life is not quite as simple as imagined in youth. The bitter blends with the sweet, the pain with the pleasure.

Life will always bring showers with the sunshine, some sickness with health, death with life. Most young couples contemplate little about the sickness and too much of an illusion of health and happiness.

What is needed for marital and family life is protection for sickness and sorrow. Few adults are naive enough to assume they will not come; most couples hope to survive the bad times as well as the good and even to grow because of them.

Purpose in Life

If an individual has a purpose he can handle the bad times. If a couple shares a common purpose they can survive any blow. For the Christian that purpose should never be in doubt. God has a purpose for every individual on the face of the earth. This purpose is made clear from the account of the creation of the first persons.

> Then God said, "Let us make man in our image, in our likeness, and let them rule over the fish of the sea and the birds of the air, over the livestock, over all the earth, and over all the creatures that move along the ground."
>
> So God created man in his own image, in the image of God he created him; male and female he created them.
>
> God blessed them and said to them, "Be fruitful and increase in number; fill the earth and subdue it. Rule over the fish of the sea and the birds of the air and over every living creature that moves on the ground.
>
> Then God said, "I give you every seed-bearing plant on the face of the whole earth and every tree that has fruit with seed in it. They will be yours for food. And to all the beasts of the earth and all the birds of the air and all the creatures that move on the ground—everything that has the breath of life in it—I give every green plant for food." And it was so.
>
> God saw all that he had made, and it was very good. And there was evening, and there was morning—the sixth day (Genesis 1:26-31, NIV).

Men and women are created by God. "God formed man from the dust of the ground" (Genesis 2:7a, NIV). Man's body is the result of God's workmanship. In light of this workmanship man should neither indulge in inordinate pride nor on the other hand unduly depreciate his body. Some people suffer from a poor self concept. They are severely critical of their bodies. This is evidenced in everything from the diet craze to the cosmetic boom. Society has become enamored with the outward appearance. The Christian has ample rationale for both appreciation of the body he or she has received from God and recognition of the value of his spiritual endowment. The Scriptural phrase "in the image of God" applies to those internal qualities. When God "breathed into his nostrils the breath of life, man became a living being" (Genesis 2:7b, NIV). Man's body is to be prized but he is more than mere physical organization. God breathed into his body and generated a living soul. Within man is the seat of thought, emotion and immortality. God has given men and women their bodies to be revered and respected but most of all he has given us the priceless gift of a soul. With these gifts comes a grave responsibility to administer them in keeping with His divine teaching.

Our body is a magnificent piece of work. Men and women ought to continually praise God for their bodies.

The Maximal Source of Help

Since the Lord Himself created man and woman and ordained the first marriage, it stands to reason that He should have the last word on the subject. In this age people expect so much of marriage and few really seek insight from the ultimate source of knowledge on marriage and family life. This is one explanation for the spiraling divorce rate.

The Lord God said, "It is not good for the man to be alone. I will make a helper suitable for him" (Genesis 2:18, NIV).

229

Scriptural Lessons from Genesis 1:26-31 and 2:18

1. *Marriage is an answer to loneliness.* To catch the full impact of this passage one ought to imagine what it must have been like prior to the creation of Eve. Imagine what it would be like if you were the last person in the world. Your every need would be provided. Food, clothing and shelter would be available. Every luxury is accessible—only one aspect is missing—another human companion. In all probability, once you got over the initial shock, you would plunge into the depths of despair. Even if all the wealth and splendor imaginable were yours, if you had no one to share it with, what good would it do? So it was with Adam. The glories of creation were his to enjoy but there was no one with whom he could share on his own level. Obviously, he had the Lord and he had animals but each were in another realm. God was in a sphere above him while his intelligence was far superior to the animal kingdom. The Lord recognized his need and created a woman who could meet his need. (Perhaps it was far more traumatic for Adam than it would be for the last person on the earth.)

2. *Marriage provides occasion for companionship.* No element provides a deeper need. Sexual desire waxes and wanes in the course of the years but the desire for a companion fills the depths of humanity. Companionship stimulates intellectual growth. Apart from contact with others, one would be out of touch with all meaningful knowledge. By constant contact with one's mate, thoughts are sharpened, ideas are tested, inquiry is kept alive and one's mental growth is assured. Most couples tend to be attracted to and to marry a person of equal intelligence; thus, they are able to share with each other the intellectual interests and growth perspectives with their mate. Often, a couple complements

230

each other's capacities and thereby enriches and stretches each other in various aspects of cognitive development.

So often as a counselor I hear women complain that after taking care of a two-year old, they long for adult conversation. This is a serious need. A child does not provide an even relationship and cannot converse on the same level or meet adult emotional needs. Sometimes this can be met by a trade-off. The husband is given time to unwind: take his shower, read the newspaper, debrief from his overinvolvement with people's demands on his energy. Then he must acknowledge his wife's companionship needs by listening and sharing a part of his world with her.

3. *Marriage provides an occasion to join each other in worship.* In the course of life, many joys will be shared as well as many of life's sorrows. Each is to minister to each other's pain and celebrate one another's joys. Adam and Eve were the recipients of God's blessings and the fellowship of His presence. As the progenitors of humanity they had a unique place and a most fulfilling relationship with their God. Today, a husband and wife are to contribute to each other's religious life through common prayer and worship for that can enhance their daily existence. The body and soul of man comes directly from God. Therefore, life must be lived in appreciation for these gifts. These gifts are to be employed in the pursuit of communion with the Author and Giver of life.

4. *God has ordained that human beings have dominion over all living things.* This dominion clearly demonstrates man's potential. God has given gifts which make this rule over all other life and all the resources of the universe possible. Man's enormous ability to channel these resources to his advantage is not accidental; it is God-ordained. Man's

231

capacities appropriately serve his own interest but this must never be at the exclusion of the giver of this potential.

5. *God has created a beautiful world for man's enjoyment.* In times of despair nothing is more effective to my mind than a walk through the woods. God made a beautiful world. When He looked out upon His handiwork, He exclaimed that it was very good. Few pleasures are more fulfilling than a romp through the woods, or a walk in the moonlight. The Psalmist considered the glory of the universe that inspires the spirit and he wrote:

> When I consider your heavens, the work of your fingers, the moon and the stars, which you have set in place (Psalm 8:3, NIV).

To watch the sun rise or to gaze at the star-studded canopy is an awe-inspiring experience for anyone. Frequently in counseling a couple, I suggest they share these simple and yet profound experiences together. It awakens them to good that is everywhere to be enjoyed. It inspires closeness to the Creator at the same time as they share an event of majestic beauty. These are the kind of moments that help to make a marriage. Another aspect I often encourage is bird-watching. This is a hobby we share at our house. Capturing a glimpse of God's handiwork is a great way to begin a day. One can never cease to be amazed and to appreciate these amazing creatures. To observe birds, to know their markings, to mark their comings and goings in the spring, and to recognize their songs is a fantastic and intriguing pursuit. Other animals, great and small, provide an endless array of interesting and commanding camaraderie. As children we loved to trace the habits of squirrels and pheasants and rabbits. Squirrels and birds played on our porch and the roof of our house. Some of my fondest boyhood memories surround these experiences.

Beauty in nature and animal life is everywhere. Man has always had a certain affinity for animal life. Animals, especially dogs, cats, horses, and birds give companionship to countless numbers of children and adults around the world. Even some of the most feared beasts such as lions, tigers, bears and reptiles have become pets for man. A missionary friend of mine, Don Baughman, has an unusual hobby—snakes. Many of the hobbies known to people in this country are inaccessible to him. Snakes are plentiful and he sincerely cares for them as most of us would a dog or cat. This interest in and training of many of these animals give evidence to the truth of man's "dominion over every beast of the earth."

6. *God who created us in His image longs to recreate constant renewal.* God gives man the opportunity for many beginnings. Some noteworthy chances to begin may be found as one relects upon the past year and contemplates the year that stretches before. Crises in life severely test the Christian but these trials often challenge individuals to renew their strength and to channel their energies in life-propelling activities. To the repentant sinner, the Lord forgives and covers with the pure white snow of forgiveness. Incessantly, every person succumbs to temptation just as the first man and woman. However, the Lord covers all the tracks of past sins with the unblemished covering of salvation. "Though your sins be as scarlet, they shall be as white as snow" (Isaiah 1:18, KJV).

As a child, I remember asking people if they would like to live their lives over again. Most people fantasize how they would rectify their mistakes if they had a second chance. Unfortunately one life is all that anyone has. However, during the course of life many opportunities are presented for renewal of faith.

One of the largest problems among people on the job is that which has been labeled "burn out." Burn out strikes doctors, lawyers, teachers, and even ministers. Every individual needs ways to continually find renewal. Everyone must replenish their energy level through a change of pace, new activities, pleasurable non-pressured activities and plenty of rest and relaxation. The individual who successfully accomplishes this will survive these occasions when he is bogged down, depressed, tired, and suffers psychosomatic stresses. The wise person learns to read the messages his body and mind give him and to back off from the treadmill that threatens one's mental balance. By the same token a couple is wise who seeks a retreat, who cultivates variety in their schedules and in their lovemaking. Many great opportunities can be found that will challenge any couple toward renewal. Some of these opportunities may be found in marriage and family retreats, marriage enrichment and marriage encounter experience.

Jesus Himself found solace in the midst of His hectic ministry. He used these times of retreat to renew His tired body and share important truths and give support to His Apostles. Undoubtedly, Jesus helped His disciples cope with the death of John the Baptist at this time also.

So he immediately sent an executioner with orders to bring John's head. The man went, beheaded John in the prison, and brought back his head on a platter. He presented it to the girl, and she gave it to her mother. On hearing of this, John's disciples came and took his body and laid it in a tomb.

The apostles gathered around Jesus and reported to him all they had done and taught. Then, because so many people were coming and going that they did not even have a chance to eat, he said to them, "Come with me by yourselves to a quiet place and get some rest."

So they went away by themselves in a boat to a solitary place (Mark 6:27-32, NIV).

Indispensable Lessons for Marital and Family Life

In the first wedding service God sets forth basic principles vital to every marital relationship and family unit. These three lessons involve leaving and "cleaving" and the concept of one flesh. Attention now turns to exploration of each of these vital insights so crucial to marital and family existence.

For this reason a man will leave his father and mother and be united to his wife, and they will become one flesh (Genesis 2:24, NIV).

Leaving father and mother. This phrase conjures up immediate pictures of a literal leaving of father and mother. This is usually a wise decision. Few couples find adequate space in the parents' home to establish their own lives as a couple. Outside of emergency situations for a short period of time this would probably be unwise. Close proximity of any people requires additional adjustments.

A married couple needs to depend upon each other and to look to one another for their basic sustenance emotionally. Young people are in the process of achieving differentiation from parents in their individual lives. Adolescence is a time to begin the process of separation. This movement from parental dependence is never completed for many people

It is probably unlikely it will be achieved unless some deliberate work is done to secure the termination of a parent-child relationship. Here the focus is upon emotional distance —not physical. Whether the child is 20 or 55 years of age, the relationship basically evolves around a parent-child transaction. Much of the work that family therapists do involves difficulties regarding the failure to terminate this hierarchial boundary between adults and their older parents.

This issue is usually suppressed for most individuals for a number of reasons. The fear of rejection by the parents intimidates the child from initiating the process. The fear of parental vulnerability may block the process. The achievement of ultimate leaving of father and mother may only be realized when there finally exists a peer relationship between the older and younger generation.[1] This does not mean that the older generation may not be wiser than the younger. (Although it does suggest that the younger may have some knowledge that the older generation does not possess.) It does suggest that neither is any longer responsible for the other. Each can offer support to the other spontaneously out of intimacy, tenderness, or gratitude. Trouble brews when, for example, the first generation assumes they are responsible for the happiness of their children and intervenes in ways that are usually resented. Later these same children, who resent the interference of their parents, will turn around and assume it is their duty to take over the responsibility of deciding what to do with their parents as they get older and decisions concerning a rest home may

---

1. Donald S. Williamson, "Personal Authority via Termination of the Intergenerational Hierarchical Boundary: A New Stage In The Family Life Cycle," *Journal of Marital and Family Therapy*, 1981 7(4), pp. 441-451.

emerge. Children sometimes assume that at a certain point they have the obligation to reverse the roles and intervene into their parents' lives. It is as if they suddenly become the parents to their parents.

Indication that this termination is not complete is evidenced in the following situations.

1. *When the parents continue to control the children even after they move away.* They exercise the power in the organization. Children continue to look to them for permission in decision making. Instead of the two adults possessing equal significance, the older generation tips the balance of power in favor of its decisions. If the adult child (a contradiction in itself) attempts to appease the older generation, this indicates a failure to get in touch with one's own authority as an adult. This is not to say that they may not consult each other out of respect to their wisdom and concern but when there is a permission-giving appeasement and a power play this certainly connotes far more than an equal relationship.

2. *When children rebel against their parents and never resolve their differences.* This often indicates that their relationship has become stagnated in an adolescent-parent stage. This may be illustrated by the child going home for two days during which both the parents and the child continue to bicker and jockey for control. The grown child is threatened as if his status as an adult will be jerked out from under him. He must make a stand for himself and make it perfectly clear he is an adult. The older parent grapples with the issues of control believing he is still responsible for straightening out his son's ways. They seem to be locked into perpetual conflict. One or the other must work through the issue of authority. If, for example, the child is able to

get in touch with his own sense of autonomy he would no longer be threatened and thus be able to affirm himself but not be embroiled in emotional confrontation. The internal tension is no longer present so he is able to disengage himself appropriately since he no longer sees the encounter as a testing ground for his adulthood. If this autonomy is proven to his own satisfaction, he no longer has to prove it to his parents.

3. *When children continue to yearn for validation from their parents concerning such areas as "appearance, job, marriage, children, values, and life-style."*[2] When the goals of parents, such as professional expectations, no longer restrict life, this is a positive indication. If an unspoken expectation, such as carrying on a family tradition in medicine, law or ministry, carries strong emotional ties to a family script, this may indicate a lack of freedom to leave the family expectation.

4. *When expectation transmitted from parents affects the marital relationships.* The basic model a husband or wife has for marriage comes from their family of origin. Negative habits and life-style affect a marriage. Some of the negative factors are rather obvious, child abuse and excessive drinking to name a few. Other less obvious legacies such as habits of socialization involving comfort with touching and various levels of emotional intimacy are a part of the background each partner brings to marriage. The ability to mesh the differences by understanding tolerance and change affects the outcome of every marriage. The capacity to stretch one's horizons beyond the policies of one's parents' ways of handling money, disciplining children, and treating others

---

2. *Ibid.*, p. 445.

is vital to a growing relationship. The maximum marriage will depend upon each couple's willingness to capitalize on the strengths of their family background and to minimize the faults. The more a couple can share what they bring to a relationship, the more each will be prepared to understand the other in these problem areas and the richer will be the individual, marital and family life.

Not only negative aspects impact upon marital relationships, but also the positive aspects as well. What husband has not lived under the shadow of his bride's father who was the perfect fix-it man, or great financial provider? What wife has not lived in perpetual frustration to measure up to mom's cooking or her ability to keep house? There is much leaving that needs to be done. The ideology of parents strongly affects marital relationships. It provides ideals that are often unattainable. Some negotiation and elimination of the ghosts of the past is vital to any relationship.

In mentioning "leaving" it must be acknowledged that the ideals of former long friends must also be left. There is sometimes a tendency to deify in one's mind the "old flame." It is obviously destructive for a partner in marriage to compete with a past lover in memory and fantasy as well as in flesh and blood.

Some people never leave home emotionally. They never leave father and mother and old acquaintances. The extent to which these factors are unresolved will continue to impede the capacity to achieve intimacy in any relationship between a husband and wife.

Cleaving to the other. It is unreasonable to assume an individual can achieve differentiation before he has a new home, a place where his needs can be met, where intimacy may be achieved and marital and family responsibilities can be expected. Young people prior to marriage may be very frustrated in attempting to achieve this termination. They may touch the project but not complete it. One has to become a self before joining with another in marriage. Some would disagree with Erikson as to how much of one's identity can be achieved prior to marriage. It stands to reason that the more one has worked through the issues of his own identity, the more available he will be for Erikson's next stage of intimacy.

One flesh. This phrase symbolizes a relationship that involves an identification of one personality with the other in a community of interests and pursuits, and a union consummated in intercourse. This unity suggests a process. In Western civilization, a couple dates. They become more and more acquainted with each other over a period of time. They share in each other's dreams and aspirations. They find mutual support in each other. When there exists a lack of compatibility in their interests and goals in life this would suggest an absence of oneness. When a woman cannot be a helpmeet to the man and he cannot love her as his own flesh then this relationship should not be consummated in the marital act of one flesh—sexual intercourse. If they are compatible, then marriage and the subsequent act of intercourse is appropriate. One flesh does not mean that a couple must always act in unison. Friction is inevitable in any relationship of two free persons. Marriages that are built on a system whereby the man or woman feels compelled to placate the other's unreasonable demands provides an unsettling contract for a lasting marriage. The clash of minds and wills is inevitable. Unity must be worked on and will increasingly solidify, but will never be finally completed. The common interests and goals and companionship and the pleasures of sexual relations serve to deepen the marriage and provide the energy to work on differences. The more familiar a couple is with their moods, their habits and their possible points of collusion, the more prepared they will be to enter marriage as a process of growing intimacy in spite of possible conflicts. Any couple who enters marriage should become familiar with procedures to resolve conflict because confrontation is inevitable.

Premarital counseling can be extremely helpful in conflict resolution. Especially is this critical when conflict is apparent throughout the courtship period. A trained counselor can help the couple evaluate their differences in temperament, understand each other better and learn various techniques helpful in resolving conflict. Learning how to achieve the Biblical advice of "not letting the sun go down on your wrath" is very much needed.

The Scripture does stress the monogamous relationship. Especially is this clarified in New Testament passages. This commitment is basic. An engaged couple should make a covenant to live together until death separates them.

> And he answered and said unto them, Have ye not read, that he which made them at the beginning male and female, And said, For this cause shall a man leave father and mother, and shall cleave to his wife; and they twain shall be one flesh? Wherefore they are no more twain, but one flesh. What therefore God hath joined together, let not man put asunder. They say unto him, Why did Moses then command to give a writing of divorcement, and to put her away? He saith unto them, Moses because of the hardness of your hearts suffered you to put away your wives: but from the beginning it was not so (Matthew 19:4-8, KJV).

Although God permitted divorce due to the hardness of their hearts, divorce was not in God's design (Matthew 19:8).

241

When a commitment is made for life, more energy can be directed toward resolution of conflicts rather than how to get out of the relationship. If a couple is committed to marriage as a lifelong adventure, they are going to be more inclined to accurately assess the strengths of their relationship if they feel involved in a permanent rather than a temporal one.

A permanent relationship also assures a more stable environment for rearing children. This admonition regarding children comes also in the context of the creation account.

> So God created man in his own image, in the image of God he created him; male and female he created them. God blessed them and said to them, "Be fruitful and increase in number" (Genesis 1:27-28, NIV).

Be fruitful and increase in numbers. A monogamous permanent relationship provides a stable context for rearing children.

If this stable setting also is truly intimate in the fullest sense of one flesh, a child finds an ideal context to prosper emotionally. Children need closeness to become healthy physically and emotionally. Frank D. Cox writes:

> To feel close to another, to love and feel loved, to experience comradeship, to care and be cared about are feelings that most of us wish and need to experience. Such feelings can be found in many human relationships. However, it is within the family that such feelings are ideally most easily found and shared—I say "ideally" because it is apparent that there are many families in which such feelings are not found. But families that do not supply much intimacy are usually families in trouble, and often these families disintegrate since members are frustrated in their needs for meaningful intimate relationships to its members.[3]

---

3. Frank Cox, *Human Intimacy: Marriage, the Family and Its Meaning* (St. Paul: West Publishing Company, 1978), p. 12.

An intimate marriage sets the pace for closeness within the family circle.

In focusing on the direction to be fruitful and multiply, it should be stressed that procreation is to be enjoyed as well as to fulfill this need to replenish the earth. Everything God created was good. The world was called "good." He created man and woman and they are good. Some people mistakenly assume that certain parts of the body are not good. At times, people confuse the admonition concerning sex outside of marriage as a statement regarding sexual relationships as evil. God ordained sexual relationships within the context of marriage as good.

If one reads various Scriptures that particularly focus in detail upon the topic of lovemaking, it becomes clear that this is to be celebrated within marriage. Passages in the books of Proverbs and the Song of Solomon especially clarify this concept.

> May your fountain be blessed, and may you rejoice in the wife of your youth. A loving doe, a graceful deer—may her breasts satisfy you always, may you ever be captivated by her love (Proverbs 5:18-19, NIV).

> Your navel is a rounded goblet that never lacks blended wine. Your waist is a mound of wheat encircled by lilies. Your breasts are like two fawns, twins of a gazelle. Your neck is like an ivory tower. Your eyes are the pools of Heshbon by the gate of Bath Rabbim. Your nose is like the tower of Lebanon looking toward Damascus. Your head crowns you like Mount Carmel. Your hair is like royal tapestry; the king is held captive by its tresses (Song of Solomon 7:2-5, NIV).

The many facets of a single relationship and the various needs that are fulfilled in a marital relationship become clear

243

in the following passage. However, one must not miss the truth that though one's mate may at times be like a brother or a student, the caresser in Song of Solomon 7:2-5 vividly describes the embrace of a lover.

In still another passage from the Song of Solomon, the bride distinguishes the groom as the fairest in the land.

> How is your beloved better than others, most beautiful of women? How is your beloved better than others, that you charge us so?
>
> My lover is radiant and ruddy, outstanding among ten thousand. His head is purest gold; his hair is wavy and black as a raven. His eyes are like doves by the water streams, washed in milk, mounted like jewels. His cheeks are like beds of spice yielding perfume. His lips are like lilies dripping with myrrh. His arms are rods of gold set with chrysolite. His body is like polished ivory decorated with sapphires. His legs are pillars of marble set on bases of pure gold. His appearance is like Lebanon, choice as its cedars. His mouth is sweetness itself; he is altogether lovely. This is my lover, this is my friend, O daughters of Jerusalem (Song of Solomon 5:9-16, NIV).

The bride seems exhausted in her attempt to describe his sweet lips, his beautiful eyes, his handsome physique and finally concludes with "he's wonderful!"

The above passages and many more in these books lead a Christian to recognize the beautiful place of sex in marital life.

Frank Cox's definition of family may fit well into this issue on being fruitful and increasing in family size.

> The term family is used here in the broadest sense; it is defined as whatever system a society uses to support and control reproduction and human sexual interaction.[4]

---

4. Kay Halverson, *The Wedded Unmother* (Minneapolis: Augsburg, 1980), p. 9.

The present focus is upon reproduction and human sexual interaction. Control of human reproduction was not a problem in the beginning. Today there is a concern with overpopulation. Many children may benefit some families but in such countries as India the government feels that too many children harm the large society. In western civilization, many people voice concern with overpopulation. The Scripture teaches that children are "a heritage of the Lord" (Psalm 127:3). This admonition to have children is one basic purpose of marriage; to find companionship and to meet sexual needs and to serve the creator God are also purposes of marriage. Children are a blessing and a responsibility that most couples anticipate sharing together. Each couple must come to some agreement as to the number of children they can effectively rear. A mutual decision needs to be made in this regard by both the husband and wife.

Effective birth control methods can best meet the balance between the purpose of procreation, personal pleasure of a continual sex life and responsibility to each child born to the union. If a couple makes a decision to have one child, they are increasing. Although birth control is appropriate to control the size of the family, it would appear that the use of birth control to prevent the birth of any children would be a failure to fulfill one basic purpose God designed for marriage. However, if a couple feels so strongly against having children, the birth of a child to such a union could prove disastrous. Children often have a way of winning even the unwilling parent but a child who will be rejected is tragic to all involved.

In exploring the phrase "be fruitful and multiply" some consideration must be given to countless number of couples who desperately long to bear children but are infertile. The struggles with infertility are difficult to imagine for those who have never experienced that crisis. Kay Halverson's writing of her personal story as she struggled with understanding and accepting infertility, states that she is not alone.

> . . . 10 million of us experience infertility at one time or another in our country. One out of six couples of childbearing age are involuntarily childless.[5]

The long and trying ordeal of pursuing the medical procedures necessary to confirm infertility greatly increase a couple's frustration. In these times adoption is also a laborious procedure that may end in equal frustration.

Any thoughtful treatment of this admonition to have children must acknowledge that some are unable to share in parenthood in the natural way and may experience many serious roadblocks in the process of adoption or other options such as foster care that would help to fulfill the need to become a parent.

Achieving the Ideal

The creation account from Genesis sets forth a definitive model for an ideal marital relationship. This relationship demands an appropriate separation from parents. Solace is found within the marital and family bond where the enriching experience of one flesh helps to insure the emotional and spiritual enrichment of offspring.

This ideal is the way God intended marriage and family life to be. Everyone who searches for guidelines for the ultimate marital and family relationship will do well to implement them.

---

5. Cox, *Human Intimacy: Marriage, the Family and Its Meaning*, p. 17.

DISCUSSION QUESTIONS: *Maximizing Marriage and Family Life*

1. If you are studying in a group, have each person take a few minutes to write up his earliest fantasies about marriage and family life. These will probably include books they have read and movies they have seen that influenced their thinking. Share a range of childhood experiences that effect our concept of the ideal marriage and family life.

2. Continue to share what happened to these ideals in the midst of childhood crushes and the experiences of rejection. How has the concept of the ideal relationship evolved through adolescence to the present? What are the ingredients of the ideal marriage for you now as an adult?

3. How important is a sense of purpose in life? Relate Genesis 1:26-31 to purpose in life for the Christian.

4. What Scriptural lessons from Genesis 2:18 and Genesis 1:26-31 were most helpful to you?

5. What are some suggested ways to find renewal in our personal life, in our marriage? How important is companionship in marriage?

6. What is the significance of the following phrases?
   A. leaving father and mother
   B. cleaving to each other
   C. becoming one flesh
   Indicate theological and personal meaning of each of the above phrases to marriage. What practical insights can you bring to bear upon your own marriage?

7. Explain how the Scripture celebrates sexual relations within marriage?

8. Explore "be fruitful and multiply" for those couples who are not able to have children.

247

Bibliography

INTRODUCTION

Chian, Hung-Min and Abraham, Maslow. *The Healthy Personality.* New York: Van Nostrand Reinhold Co., 1969.
Significant papers are presented by well-known workers in psychology and related fields concerning the problem of psychological health.

Clinebell, Howard J. *Community Mental Health in the Role of Church and Temple.* Nashville: Abingdon Press, 1970.
The significant contribution of the church and temple toward meeting the mental health problems of the community is treated by leaders in the pastoral counseling movement. Guidelines for increasing the effectiveness of the local congregation and its minister's role in promoting mental health.

Collins, Gary R. *The Rebuilding of Psychology.* Wheaton: Tyndale House Publishers, 1977.
Contends that psychology lacks a unifying approach and needs to rebuild on the premise that God exists and is the source of all truth. Critical evaluation of the basic assumptions of the various schools of psychology and a case for the rebuilding of the profession from a Biblical perspective.

Cramer, Raymond L. *The Psychology of Jesus.* Grand Rapids: Zondervan Publishing House, 1959.
Shows how the Sermon on the Mount provides a solid basis for the human personality to move in the direction of growth.

Derlega, Valerian and Janda, Louis H. *Personal Adjustment.* Glenview: Scott, Foresman & Co., 1981.
An introductory college text for classes in Psychology of Adjustment.

249

Grandberg, Lars. *Counseling.* Grand Rapids: Baker Book House, 1967.

Compilation of articles written by counselors addressing several different counseling situations.

Grounds, Vernon. *Emotional Problems and the Gospels.* Grand Rapids: Zondervan Publishing House, 1976.

Combines Biblical and therapeutic observation. Shows resources for healing found in the Gospel.

Guntrip, Henry. *Psychotherapy and Religion.* New York: Harper and Brothers, 1956.

Shows how psychotherapy and religion can come together to help achieve authentic selfhood. Focuses on the constructive use of inner conflict.

Homans, Peter, ed. *The Dialogue Between Theology and Psychology.* Chicago: University of Chicago Press, 1968.

Deals with problems of importance for both theology and psychology. Presupposes some background and interest in the two disciplines. Helpful to serious undergraduate students in psychology and graduate students.

Homans, Peter. *Theology after Freud.* New York: The Bobbs-Merrill Co. Inc., 1970.

Explores the interplay between psychology and theology.

Jung, C. G. *The Undiscovered Self.* Boston: Little, Brown and Co., 1957.

The role of religion in the utilization of a person's unconscious powers as well as the conscious aspects are discussed. A look at both religion and psychiatry in dealing with crisis within individuals and society.

Kelsey, Morton T. *Healing and Christianity.* New York: Harper and Row Publishers, 1973.

Contains an attempt to provide a theological foundation, based on historical and scientific understanding for a ministry of healing today.

Kjell, Rudestam. *Methods of Self-Change.* Monterey: Brooks/Cole Publishing Co., 1980.

Brings together a number of psychotherapeutic techniques amenable to the process of self-change.

Koteskey, Ronald L. *Psychology from a Christian Perspective.* Nashville: Abingdon Press, 1980.

An integration of general psychology into a Christian system. Assumes a knowledge of the various areas that constitute general psychology.

May, Rollo. *Love and Will.* New York: W. W. Norton & Co. Inc., 1969.

An analysis of the real meaning of love and will set forth against the emptiness of a depersonalized technology.

Oates, Wayne. *The Bible in Pastor Care.* Grand Rapids: Baker Book House, 1971.

Specific guidance in the use of the Scripture in particular pastoral care situations. The healing power of Scripture and the potential misuse of the Scripture are treated.

Oates, Wayne E. *When Religion Gets Sick.* Philadelphia: The Westminster Press, 1970.

Dramatically shows how the mentally disturbed can turn religion into a destructive rather than constructive force in their lives. Suggestions for the minister and the church to deal with this pathology.

251

Outer, Albert C. *Psychotherapy and the Christian Message.* New York: Harper and Row Publishers, 1954.

Defines the problems of alliance and conflict between psychotherapeutic thought and the Christian message.

Richardson, Herbert. *New Religious and Mental Health: Understanding the Issues.* New York: The Edwin Mellen Press, 1980.

This book presents a range of issues involved when the government becomes involved in regulating religious practice.

Southard, Samuel. *Christians and Mental Health.* Nashville: Broadman Press, 1972.

An attempt to synthesize mental health and Christianity.

Staton, Knofel. *Check Your Lifestyle.* Cincinnati: Standard Publishing, 1979.

Applies to insights of Proverbs to daily life in a down to earth, straight forward style.

Thorton, Edward. *Professional Education for Ministry.* Nashville: Abingdon Press, 1970.

Traces the history of clinical pastoral education from the 20s, with Cabot and Bosien, to the present time.

Wise, Carroll. *Mental Health and the Bible.* New York: Harper and Row Publishers, 1956.

Relates the insights of the Bible to findings of psychology and medicine. 160 Biblical citations to show the light the Bible casts upon mental health.

CHAPTER ONE: FACING CRISIS

Avelter, Paul. "Crisis—A Short Term Predicament In Huge Proportion." *How to Help a Friend.* Wheaton: Tyndale House Publishers, 1978.

Biblical and therapeutic insights into helping a suicide in crisis.

Barclay, William. "The Letter To The Hebrews." *The Daily Study Bible.* Philadelphia: The Westminster Press, 1955.
A New Testament commentary that seeks to make the Scriptures relevant to life and work today.

Chaplan, Gerald. *Principles of Preventative Psychiatry.* New York: Basic Books Inc., Publishers, 1964.
Basic foundations for crisis counseling theory are found in this book.

Clinebell, Howard J. "Crisis Counseling." *Basic Types Of Pastoral Counseling.* Nashville: Abingdon Press, 1966.
Surveys the help available to minister in meeting crisis situations.

_____, and Clinebell, Charlotte. *Crisis and Growth: Helping Your Troubled Child.* Philadelphia: Fortress Press, 1971.
Attention is given to help recognize disorders, send appropriate professionals if needed and handle family crisis constructively.

Coleman, James C.; Butcher, James N.; and Carson, Robert C. *Abnormal Psychology and Modern Life* (7h ed.) Glenview: Scott, Foresman & Co., 1980.
A popular text for classes in Abnormal Psychology.

Cosgrove, Mark and Mallory, James D., Jr. *Mental Health: A Christian Approach.* Grand Rapids: The Zondervan Corp., 1977.
The central elements of a Christian approach to mental health and psychotherapy are examined.

Dixon, Samuel L. *Working with People in Crisis.* St. Louis: The C. V. Mosby Co., 1979.
A basic guide to the knowledge and techniques of intervention to apply in helping people in crisis.

Erikson, Erik. "The Eight Ages of Man." *Childhood and Society.* New York: W. W. Norton and Co., Inc., 1963.
A foundational chapter upon which much work on developmental psychology rests.

Frankl, Viktor E. *Man's Search for Meaning: An Introduction To Logotherapy.* Boston: Beacon Press, 1962.
Traces the outgrowth of logotherapy beginning with Frankl's prison experience during World War II. Central concepts of logotherapy are presented.

Gleason, John. *Growing up to God — Eight Steps in Religious Development.* Nashville: Abingdon Press, 1975.
Erick Erickson's eight stages of development are surveyed from a religious perspective.

Lindemann, Erich. "Symptomatology and Management of Acute Grief." *Pastoral Psychology.* XIV (September, 1963).
An important article in the development of crisis theory.

Lum, Doman. *Responding To Suicidal Crisis.* Grand Rapids: William B. Eerdmans Publishing Co., 1974.
A practical treatment designed as a guide for both clergymen and laymen. Practical suggestions as well as theological perspectives are treated.

McGarvey, J. W. and Pendleton, Philip Y. *The Fourfold Gospel.* Standard Publishing, n.d.
A commentary and harmony of the Gospels.

Menninger, Karl. *The Vital Balance.* New York: The Viking Press, 1963.
A more hopeful treatment than the older approaches to mental health.

Oates, Wayne E. and Lester, Andrew D., ed. *Pastoral Care in Crucial Human Situations.* Valley Forge: Judson Press, 1969.

Focuses on several crisis situations frequently encountered by the minister.

Parod, Howard J. ed. *Crisis Intervention: Selected Readings.* New York: Family Service Association of America, 1965.

Theoretical formulations, the applied practice are the research in crisis intervention.

Pretzel, Paul. *Understanding and Counseling the Suicidal Person.* Nashville: Abingdon Press, 1972.

Practical and theoretical help in understanding and ministering to the suicidal person.

Rochman, Joan. *A Bibliography Relating to Crisis Theory.* Boston: Harvard Medical School, 1969.

A very extensive bibliography on crisis theory.

Shelly, Judith Allen. *Caring in Crisis: Biblical Studies for Helping People.* Downers Grove: InterVarsity Press, 1979.

Scriptural resources for meeting crisis.

Switzer, David. *The Minister as Crisis Counselor.* Nashville: Abingdon Press, 1974.

Provides a background for understanding crisis theory. Relates how the minister can use available approaches as well as his unique resources as a minister.

CHAPTER TWO: DEALING WITH DEATH

Bane, Donald J.; Kutscher, Austin H.; Neale, Robert E.; Reeves, Robert B. Jr. eds. *Death and Ministry.* New York: The Seabury Press Inc., 1975.

An interdisciplinary collection of papers from professionals in the helping professions. Designed to help ministers understand the psychological and theological needs of the dying and the bereaved.

Bayly, Joseph. *The View from a Hearse.* Elgin: David C. Cook Publishing Co., 1969.

A personal account of grief and the Biblical perspective to cope with it.

Becker, Ernest. *The Denial of Death.* New York: Macmillan Publishing Co, Inc., 1973.

Contends man is innately afraid of death. Probes the psychoanalytic views on the nature of man.

Clerk, N. W. *A Grief Observed.* Connecticut: The Seaburg Press, 1963.

An intimate probe into the depths of one person's grief.

Cullman, Oscar. "Immortality of the Soul or Resurrection of the Dead." *Immortality and Resurrection.* Krister Stendahl ed. New York: Macmillan Publishing Co. Inc., 1965.

Contrasts a Greek approach to immortality with the Christian concept of resurrection.

Cutter, Fred. *Coming to Terms with Death.* Chicago: Nelson-Hall Publishers, 1974.

Help to cope with death personally and in the lives of friends and family members.

Irion, Paul E. *The Funeral and the Mourners.* Nashville: Abingdon Press, 1954.

A study that shows how the funeral service can be a source of strength. Helpful for ministers.

Jackson, Edgar N. *You and Your Grief.* Manhasset: Channel Press, 1961.

Explanation and guidance in caring personal style. Includes religious resources.

Kalish, Richard A. *Death, Grief, and Caring Relationships.* Monterey: Brooks/Cole Publishing Co., 1981.

An introductory college text book that is personal, practical as well as research oriented. Written for classes in death education in a college or university setting.

Kelley, Ron. *Help! I'm Dying.* Lincoln: Lincoln Christian College, n.d.
   Guidelines for the minister and the Christian worker ministering among the dying.

Kubler-Ross, Elisabeth. *On Death and Dying.* New York: Macmillan Publishing Co. Inc., 1969.
   An account of dialogues with dying patients and a formulation of the stages they experience. Sensitive and challenging to face individual mortality and to minister to the dying.

_____. *Death—The Final Stage of Growth.* Englewood Cliffs: Prentice Hall Inc., 1975.
   Contends that the acceptance of finiteness provides the key to growth and meaning in life.

Maddison, David and Agnes, Viola. "The Health in the Year Following Bereavement." *Journal of Psychosomatic Research.* 12(July, 1968).
   The negative impact of bereavement on the physical health in the year following the loss.

Oman, John B. *Group Counseling in the Church.* Minneapolis: Augsburg Publishing House, 1972.
   Guidance in establishing and working with groups in a local congregation.

Parkes, Colin Murray. "The First Year of Bereavement." *Psychiatry.* 33(November, 1970).
   Survey research on the health of the bereaved during the first year following the loss of a loved one.

Pruitt, Carl W. "The Widow's Group." *The Lookout* 93 (September 20, 1981).

Describes a variety of groups established for widows in different locations.

Scherzer, Carl J. *Ministering to the Dying.* Philadelphia: Fortress Press, 1963.

Guidance on ministering to the dying.

Shneidman, Edward S. ed. *Death: Current Perspectives.* Palo Alto: Mayfield Publishing Co., 1980.

A wide selection of recent articles dealing with death and dying. A comprehensive college text.

Stoddard, Sandol. *The Hospice Movement.* New York: Vintage Books, 1978.

A creative program to provide the dying person with care within his home surrounded by his family.

Switzer, David K. *The Dynamics of Grief.* Nashville: Abingdon Press, 1970.

A thorough treatment of the subject of grief. A theoretical approach with some practical application for the student of psychology or pastoral counseling.

Sullender, Scott R. "Saint Paul's Approach to Grief: Clarifying the Ambiguity" *Religion and Health.* 20(Spring, 1981).

Helps to clarify the various passages which focus on the appropriateness of grief and others that set forth the hope of eternal life.

Vanauken, Sheldon. *A Severe Mercy.* San Francisco: Harper and Row Publishers, 1977.

An actual account of a love story that culminates in the death of the lover in the flower of her womanhood. A gripping story of love and grief. Contains works of C. S. Lewis previously unpublished.

Westburg, Granger. *Good Grief.* Philadelphia: Fortress Press, 1962.
　　Describes the stage of the grief reaction in a popular style. Contains Biblical references.

CHAPTER THREE: DEALING WITH DEPRESSION

Agras, A. Steward; Kozdin, Alan E.; and Wilson, Terence. *Behavior Therapy.* San Francisco: W. H. Freeman & Co. Publishers, 1979.
　　Basic concepts, current research and practice of behavorial therapy along with recommendation for future direction.

Berne, Erich. *Games People Play.* New York: Grove Press Inc., 1964.
　　Popularization of Berne's approach to psychotherapy, Transactional Analysis.

_____. *Transactional Analysis in Psychotherapy.* New York: Grove Press Inc., 1961.
　　A basic presentation of Transactional Analysis.

Clinebell, Howard. *Basic Types of Pastoral Counseling.* Nashville: Abingdon Press, 1966.
　　A standard text for use among ministerial students.

_____. *Growth Counseling.* Nashville: Abingdon Press, 1979.
　　The more recent direction of Clinebell's approach to counseling.

Coleman, James C.; Butcher, James N.; and Carson, Robert C. *Abnormal Psychology and Modern Life.* 6th ed. Glenview: Scott, Foresman & Co., 1980.
　　A popular text for advance undergraduate courses or graduate classes in Abnormal Psychology.

Frankl, Viktor E. *From Death-Camp to Existentialism.* Boston: Beacon Press, 1959.
Frankl's prison experiences and the development of logotherapy.

Freud, Sigmund. *The Dynamics of Transference.* Std. ed. Vol. 12. London: Hogarth Press, 1955.
Focuses on this important aspect of psychoanalytic theory.

Freud, Sigmund and Pfister, Oskar. *Sigmund Freud Psycoanalysis and Faith.* ed. Heinrich Meng and Ernst L. Freud. Trans. Eric Mosbacher. New York: Basic Books Inc., Publishers, 1963.
Contains an ongoing dialogue between Freud and a close friend who was a minister.

Glasser, William. *Reality Therapy.* New York: Harper and Row Publishers, 1965.
Sets forth the theory and the practice of Glasser's approach to therapy.

Goldingay, John. *Songs From a Strange Land.* Downers Grove: InterVarsity Press, 1978.
Exposition of the text from Psalm 42-51 with a view to provide practical application.

Harper, Robert A. *Psychoanalysis and Psychotherapy 36 Systems.* New York: Jason Aronson Inc., 1974.
Survey the wide range of approaches employed by therapists today.

Harris, Thomas. *I'm OK, You're OK.* New York: Harper and Row Publishers, 1967.
A popularization of Erick Berne's system of therapy, Transactional Analysis.

Hauck, Paul A. *Reason in Pastoral Counseling.* Philadelphia: The Westminster Press, n.d.

Sets forth the value of Rational Emotive Therapy for Pastoral Counselors.

Menninger, Karl. *Whatever Became of Sin?* New York: Hawthorn Books, Bantam Books, 1978.
A plea to return to responsibility for man's action and a renewal recognition of sin.

Minirth, Frank B. and Meier, Paul D. *Happiness Is a Choice.* Grand Rapids: Baker Book House, 1978.
Help for understanding depression combines clinical experience and Biblical knowledge in a nontechnical resource.

Nietzel, Michael T.; Winett, Richard A.; MacDonald, Marian L.; and Davidson, William S. *Behavioral Approaches to Community Psychology.* New York: Pergamon Press Inc., 1977.
Integrates community psychology with behavioral modification to deal with social problems such as juvenile delinquency, drug addiction, aging, unemployment and environmental protection. Upper level undergraduate courses in psychology and graduate classes in community psychology.

Palmer, James O. *A Primer of Eclectic Psychotherapy.* Monterey: Brooks/Cole Publishing Co., 1980.
An attempt to integrate various methods of psychotherapy into a meaningful and practical approach. For the graduate student or beginning practitioner.

Perls, Frederick. *Gestalt Therapy.* New York: Julian Press, Bantam Books, 1977.
An introductory volume on gestalt psychotherapy.

_____ . *Gestalt Therapy Verbatim.* New York: Real People Press, Bantam Books, 1976.

Verbatims from the work of the originator of Gestalt Therapy. Edited from the audio tapes of intensive weekend sessions.

Rogers, Carl. *Client-Centered Therapy.* Boston: Houghton Mifflin Co., 1951.
An original source for client-centered therapy by the founder of that school of psychotherapy.

Rychlak, Joseph. *Personality and Psychotherapy.* Boston: Houghton Mifflin Co., 1981.
A college text that combines personality theory with psychotherapy.

Sall, Millard J. *Faith, Psychology and Christian Maturity.* Grand Rapids: Zondervan Publishing House, 1975.
Integrates therapeutic psychology and the Christian faith. Introductory text for college students and laymen in the field.

Seligman, Martin E. P. *Helplessness, on Depression, Development and Death.* San Francisco: W. H. Freeman & Co. Publishers, 1975.
Insights from experimental psychology on the causes and cures of depression.

Spence, H. D. And Exell, Joseph S. ed. *The Pulpit Commentary.* Grand Rapids: Wm. B. Eerdmans Publishing Co., 1950. *The Psalms* by G. Rawlingson, E. R. Conder and W. Clarkson.
A commentary that includes practical application for sermonizing.

Stedman, Ray C. *Folk Psalms of Faith.* Glendale: Regal G/L Publications, 1973.
An exposition of selected psalms with an emphasis on practical application for today.

Sundel, Martin and Sundel, Sandra Stone. *Behavior Modification in the Human Services*. New York: John Wiley & Sons Inc., 1975.
    Application of behavior modification to mental health problems. College text book.

Tweedie, Donald F. *Logotherapy*. Grand Rapids: Baker Book House, 1961.
    Provides an evaluation of Frankl's existential approach to psychotherapy from a Christian perspective.

Ward, Waylong O. *The Bible in Counseling*. Chicago: Moody Press, 1977.
    Relates psychological and Biblical insights to personal problems. Shows how the Bible relates to everyday problems.

CHAPTER FOUR: COPING WITH ANXIETY

Branch, C. H. Hardin. *Aspects Of Anxiety*. Philadelphia: J. B. Lippincott Co., 1965.
    A text originally designed for physicians that shows the relationship of anger to various physical problems. Contains technical language.

Coleman, James; Butcher, James N.; and Carson, Robert C. *Abnormal Psychology*. Glenview: Scott, Foresman & Co., 1980.
    A standard text in Abnormal Psychology that includes a good treatment of anxiety as well as wide range of other problems. Used in upper level courses in psychology.

Cramer, Raymond L. *The Psychology Of Jesus*. Grand Rapids: Zondervan Publishing House, 1980.

The Sermon on the Mount provides the focal point for meeting various problems including anxiety, fear and depression.

Kelly, Desmond. *Anxiety and Emotions.* Springfield: Charles C. Thomas Publisher, 1980.

Traces the physiological basis and treatment of anxiety. Access to a body of scientific literature is provided for those in helping professions. Detailed and technical.

Jess, John D. *Coping With Anxiety.* Grand Rapids: Baker Book House, 1973.

A series of radio sermons on the subject of anxiety and related themes.

Narramore, Clyde M. *How to Win over Nervousness.* Grand Rapids: Zondervan Publishing House, 1969.

A brief booklet that describes anxiety and provides suggestions to deal with the problem in light of Scripture.

Nelson, Marion H. *Why Christians Crack Up.* Chicago: Moody Press, 1960.

Discusses discouragements Christians often face and how they attribute these problems to personal spiritual failure. The author maintains that Christians and non Christians must abide by God's natural law.

Pike, James A. *Beyond Anxiety.* New York: Charles Scribner's Sons, 1953.

The Christian faith is presented as the supplier of answers to the basic questions that disturb people.

Sue, David; Sue, Derald Wing; and Sue, Stanley. *Abnormal Behavior.* Boston: Houghton Mifflin Co., 1981.

Wood, John T. *What Are You Afraid Of?* New Jersey: Prentice-Hall Inc., 1976.

The relationship of fear to anxiety and phobias and other emotions is treated.

CHAPTER FIVE: CHILDREN OF BROKEN HOMES

Barclay, William. *The Letters of James and Peter. The Daily Study Bible Series.* Philadelphia: The Westminster Press, 1960.

A commentary that stresses the background material to New Testament studies and a practical application to daily life.

Boeckman, Charles. *Surviving Your Parent's Divorce.* New York: Franklin Watts Inc., 1980.

Guidelines that parents can give their children to help prevent excessive pain and permanent damage as a result of divorce.

Dobson, James. *Hide or Seek.* Old Tappan: Fleming H. Revell Co., 1974.

Help for parents in increasing the self-image of their children.

Grollman, Earl A. *Explaining Divorce To Children.* Boston: Beacon Press, 1969.

Suggested approaches to telling children about their parents' divorce.

Hamachek, Don E. *Encounters With The Self.* New York: Holt, Rinehart & Winston, 1975.

A college text dealing with self concept.

Hudson, Lofton R. *'Til Divorce Do Us Part.* Nashville: Thomas Nelson Inc., 1974.

A Christian approach to dealing with divorce.

Oates, Wayne E. *The Bible In Pastoral Care.* Grand Rapids: Baker Book House, 1971.

Specific guidance in the use of the Scripture in pastoral care encounters. The healing potential as well as the possible misuse of the Scripture is stressed.

Meier, Paul D. *Christian Child-Rearing And Personality Development.* Grand Rapids: Baker Book House, 1977.
Principles of child-rearing from a Christian perspective.

Petri, Darlene. *The Hurt And Healing Of Divorce.* Elgin: David C. Cook Publishing Co., 1976.
Personal advice from a divorced mother of three children on how to cope with divorce. Written from a Christian view.

Roosevelt, Ruth and Lofas, Jeannette. *Living In Step.* New York: McGraw-Hill Inc., 1976.
Defines the problems and offers direction to many of the unique problems confronting step parents.

Smoke, Jim. *Growing Through Divorce.* Irvine: Harvest House Publishers Inc., 1976.
Practical guidance to help people struggling through divorce. Authored by the singles minister of the Garden Grove Community Church in California.

Staton, Knofel. *Divorce — The Divider.* Cincinnati: Standard Publishing, 1979.
A booklet, from a series of articles in the *Lookout*, that deals with what the Bible has to say about divorce.

Trobisch, Walter. *Love Yourself.* Downers Grove: Inter-Varsity Press, 1976.
Scriptural and psychological verification for a positive self concept.

Visher, Emily B. and Visher, John S. *Step-Families: A Guide to Working with Stepparents and Stepchildren.* New York: Brunner/Mazel Inc., 1979.
An important contribution to the recent clinical interest in the stepfamily written by a husband and wife team who are both professional psychotherapists and stepparents.

Wallerstein, Judith S. and Kelly, Joan Berlin. *Surviving the Breakup*. New York: Basic Books Inc. Publishers, 1980.

Insights for surviving divorce gathered from extensive research. Intended for professionals in various fields as well as those experiencing divorce or desiring to help others in the midst of the failure of a marriage.

Watts, Virginia. *The Single Parent*. New Jersey: Fleming H. Revell Co., 1976.

Practical advice for single parents from one who faced the task of rearing children alone.

CHAPTER SIX: THE STRUGGLE FOR MEANINGFUL MATURITY

Allport, Gordon. *Becoming*. New Haven: Yale University Press, 1955.

The growth of the human personality is presented with a strong apologetic for the dignity and growth potential of the individual. Assesses relevance to religion in a positive manner.

Binstock, Louis. *The Power of Maturity*. New York: Hawthorn Books Inc., 1969.

Explores the keys to maturity and encourages continual checking on the maturity level.

Birren, James E.; Kinney, Dennis K.; Schaie, K. Warner; and Woodruff, Diana S. *Developmental Psychology*. Boston: Houghton Mifflin Co., 1981.

A standard text book for courses in college that cover developmental psychology from a life-span perspective.

Blacker, M. M. and Wekstein, D. R., ed. *Your Health after 60*. New York: E. P. Dutton, 1979.

This book contains advice on dealing with a variety of physical problems faced in the later years of life. The chapters in the book are the outgrowth of lectures sponsored by the Sanderson-Research Center at the University of Kentucky for the older citizens of Lexington, Kentucky.

Collins, Gary R. *Man In Transition.* Carol Stream: Creation House, 1971.

Shows how psychology applies to development from infancy through adulthood. Indicates characteristics of each stage of development and how the Christian worker can minister to people encountering stress throughout life.

Cottrell, Jack. *Being Good Enough Isn't Good Enough.* Cincinnati: Standard Publishing, 1976.

Helps to clear up confusion over basic theological issues that may impede spiritual maturity. Helpful for individuals and Bible study groups.

Erikson, Erick H. "Eight Ages of Man" in *Childhood and Society.* New York: W. W. Norton & Co. Inc., 1963.

This chapter sets forth Erikson's approach to his life scope, psychosocial stages of development which have greatly influenced psychology. He sees growth as a life long experience involving a series of crisis at various stages of life. The book itself is of help to anyone seriously interested in the study of children or the fields of psychology.

_____. *Young Man Luther.* New York: W. W. Norton & Co. Inc., 1958.

The life of Martin Luther is presented from a perspective of ego psychology. An interest in history and psychoanalysis is helpful. Appropriate for courses in adolescent psychology.

Gillespie, Bailey V. *Religious Conversion and Personal Identity.* Birmingham: Religious Education Press, 1979.
A psychological examination of religious conversion.

Gleason, John. *Growing up to God.* Nashville: Abingdon Press, 1975.
A religious overlay to Erik Erikson's approach to developmental psychology based on eight stages in the life cycle.

Levinson, Daniel J. *The Seasons of a Man's Life.* New York: Alfred A. Knopf Inc., 1979.
Research evidence regarding the nature of adult development.

Sherrill, Lewis Joseph. *The Struggle of the Soul.* New York: Macmillan Inc., 1951.
The entire life span is treated in its religious aspects. Helpful for courses in developmental psychology and crisis counseling from a theological perspective.

Staton, Knofel. *You Don't Have to Stay the Way You Are.* Cincinnati: Standard Publishing, 1976.
Foundational reading for spiritual growth.

Tournier, Paul. *Learn to Grow Old.* New York: Harper and Row Publishers, 1972.
The relationship of Christian faith to the process of aging in today's society.

_____. *The Seasons Of Life.* Richmond: John Knox Press, 1968.
Tournier contends that life can be continually renewed like the seasons of the year. A Biblical basis for renewal is presented.

Vaillant, George E. *Adaptation To Life.* Boston: Little, Brown & Co., 1977.

A book based upon a long term study of adult male development. Focus is on ways men alter themselves to adapt to life.

CHAPTER SEVEN: THE TWO-CAREER MARRIAGE

Bird, Caroline. *The Two Paycheck Marriage.* New York: Rawson, Wade Publishers, 1979.

Research on two paycheck marriages to understand the impact upon the country, upon individual families and the options available to these couples.

Bolles, Richard Nelson. *What Color Is Your Parachute? A Practical Manual For Job-Hunters and Career-Changers.* Berkeley: Ten Speed Press, 1981.

Basic principles of job-hunting gathered from interviews with those who have successfully dealt with this potential problem. Revised annually since 1970.

Bryson, Jeff R. and Bryson, Rebecca. *Dual Career Couples.* New York: Human Science Press Inc., 1978.

A special issue on the Psychology of Women Quarterly. Scholarly research over two and one half years. Contains some of the necessary adjustments to sustain dual-career couples.

Darley, Susan A. "Big-Time Careers for the Little Woman: A Dual-Role Dilemma" in *The Changing Family,* Jerald Savells and Lawrence J. Cross eds. New York: Holt, Rinehart & Winston, 1978.

The difficulties women face in dealing with the role of homemaker-parent and a career outside the home.

Driver, S. R.; Plummer, A.; and Briggs, C. A. *International Critical Commentary.* Edinburgh: T. and T. Clark, 1899.

"A Critical and Exegetical Commentary on the Book of Proverbs" by Crawford H. Toy.

A scholarly commentary on the Old Testament. Emphasis upon the original language.

Erikson, Erik. "Eight Ages of Man" in *Childhood and Society*. New York: W. W. Norton & Co. Inc., 1950.
Provides the basic outline of Erikson's psychosocial stage of development. Treats the entire life scope.

_____. *Identity and the Life Cycle*. New York: International Universities Press Inc., 1959.
One of Erikson's works that focuses on the adolescent identity struggle.

Gleason, John. *Growing up to God*. Nashville: Abingdon Press, 1975.
Provides a theological over-lay to Erich Erickson's psychosocial stages of development.

Heaton, E. W. *Everyday Life in Old Testament Times*. London: B. T. Batsford LTD, 1956.
Helpful in understanding customs and everyday practices in Old Testament times.

Hovde, Howard. *The Neo-Married*. Valley Forge: Judson Press, 1968.
Helpful suggestions for working with a group of newly married couples.

Lederer, William and Jackson, Don D. *The Mirages of Marriage*. New York: W. W. Norton & Co. Inc., 1968.
Crushes destructive misconceptions held about marriages today and offers provocative remedies to improve the marital relationship. Written by leaders in the field of marital therapy.

Mace, David. "Simple Living in Today's World." *Marriage and Family Life*. February, 1981.
A testimony to a life that is both simple in style but rich in the basic care of what makes life meaningful. A tribute to a simple lifestyle.

Miller, Sherod; Nunnally, Elam W.; and Wackman, Daniel B. *Alive and Aware*. Minneapolis: Interpersonal Communication Programs, 1975.
A set of detailed instruction to increase communication skills. Foundation for the couple communication programs.

Napier, Augustus Y. and Whitaker, Carl A. *The Family Crucible*. New York: Harper and Row Publishers, 1978.
Vivid descriptions of what actually happens in family therapy.

Oates, Wayne. *Confessions of a Workaholic*. Nashville: Abingdon Press, 1978.
A humorous and yet very disturbing description of a common problem. Contains suggestions for changing destructive patterns of over-work.

Rapaport, Robert and Rhona. ed. *Working Couples*. New York: Harper and Row Publishers, 1978.
The issues and methods employed by working couples to deal with them.

Phillips, Bob. *How Can I Be Sure?* Irvine: Harvest House Publishers Inc., 1978.
Resources for evaluating basic issues in marriage. A pre-marital inventory.

Robert, Wes. and Wright, H. Norman. *Before You Say "I Do."* Irving: Harvest House Publishers Inc., 1979.
Practical help prior to marriage.

Rowatt, Wade and Mary. *The Two Career Marriage*. Philadelphia: The Westminster Press, 1980.
Practical advice for coping with the stresses that arise when both husband and wife work. Written from a Christian perspective.

Sheehy, Gail. *Passages*. New York: E. P. Dutton, 1976.

A popular detailed study gathered from extensive research among adults. Personal and thorough presentation.

Sherrill, Lewis Joseph. *Struggles Of The Soul.* New York: Macmillan Co. Inc., 1955.
Surveys the life-scope from a Biblical and psychological view.

Spence, H. D. M. and Excell, Joseph S., eds. *The Pulpit Commentary.* Grand Rapids: Wm. B. Eerdmans Publishing Co., 1950. *Ecclesiastes-Song of Solomon,* by W. J. Deans and S. T. Taylor-Taswell.
A commentary with practical application of the text.

Staton, Julia. *What The Bible Says About Women.* Joplin: College Press Publishing Company, 1980.
A thorough presentation of the women in the Bible and what the Bible has to say about them.

CHAPTER EIGHT: WHEN YOUR KIDS GROW UP

Bart, Pauline. "Depression in Middle Aged Women." in *Female Psychology: The Emerging Self,* pp. 349-67. Edited Sue Cox. Chicago: Science Research Association, 1976.
An article which stresses that the empty nest syndrome is a vital issue that depressive women particularly struggle with in middle age.

Bocknek, Gene. *The Young Adult.* Belmont: Wadsworth, 1980.
The liberating aspect of children leaving home is stressed as the responsibility shifts from sustaining others to maintaining oneself.

Collins, Gary. *Man In Transition.* Carol Stream: Creation House, 1971.

Recommends a new appraisal of life's goals as an adjustment to the "empty nest." The role of the church accented.

Haley, J. *Leaving Home*. New York: McGraw-Hill Book Co., 1980.

A book for the professional therapist to help him in his work with families when children are leaving home.

Harkins, Elizabeth Bates. "Effects of Empty Nest Transition on Self-Report of Psychological and Physical Well-Being." *Journal of Marriage and the Family*. 40 (August, 1978): 549-56.

According to this research the empty nest effects were slight and disappeared two years following the event.

Hulme, William E. *Mid-Life Crisis*. Philadelphia: The Westminster Press, 1980.

The many struggles of mid-life that surround the occasion of the children leaving home are treated from a Biblical perspective.

Hurlock, Elizabeth. *Developmental Psychology*. 5th ed. New York: McGraw-Hill Book Co., 1980.

Surveys positive and negative factors revealed in research on the impact of the empty nest. Apart from the divorced or widowed the ending of parental responsibilities appears to be positive for most couples if they can endure the relatively brief transition.

Rubin, Lillian B. "The Empty Nest: Beginning or Ending?" in *Women of a Certain Age*. New York: Harper and Row Publishers, 1979.

Contends society's system of social roles has assumed depression in women is linked to the empty nest. This transition should be approached not as an ending but a beginning to be confronted as the next stage in life.

Sheehy, Gail. *Passages*. New York: E. P. Dutton, 1974.
Compares and contrasts the empty nest for father and mother. She sees women as transcending dependency through self-declaration as they refocus on their own needs. Men on the other hand struggle with replenishing mid-life through nurturing and serving others.

Thielicke, Helmut. *The Waiting Father*. Translated by John W. Doberstein. New York: Harper and Row Publishers, 1959.
This is a sermon in Thielicke's book by the same title. The sermon book treats several of the parables of Jesus.

CHAPTER NINE: UNDERSTANDING AND MINISTERING AMONG AGING

Binstock, Robert H. and Shanas, Ethel. *Handbook of Aging and the Social Sciences*. New York: Van Nostrand Reinhold Co., 1976.
The issues of aging are presented from various professional disciplines. Basically most relevant for students entering the field of gerontology.

Birren, James E. and Schoie, K. Warner. *Handbook of The Psychology of Aging*. New York: Van Nostrand Reinhold Co., 1976.
A reference source of the literature on the psychological aspects of aging. The book is intended for advance students, researchers and professionals in need of a definitive work.

Blacker, M. M. and Wekstein, D. R., ed. *Your Health after 60*. New York: E. P. Dutton, 1979.
This book contains expert advice on dealing with a variety of physical problems faced in the later years of life. The chapters in this book are the outgrowth of lectures sponsored by the Sander Research Center at the University of Kentucky for the older citizens of Lexington Kentucky.

Brown, Paul J. *Counseling with Senior Citizens*. Philadelphia: Fortress Press, 1964.

One of the earliest practical guides to a ministry among the aging.

Clements, William M. ed. *Ministry with the Aging*. San Francisco: Harper and Row Publishers, 1981.

Deals with aging from a Biblical and Theological perspective as well as the psychological and sociological dimension. Provides a solid theoretical base for a practical ministry with the elderly.

Curtin, Sharon R. *Nobody Ever Died of Old Age*. Boston: Little, Brown & Co., 1973.

A compassionate presentation of the plight of the elderly in America. Contains moving portraitures of the elderly in a vigorous writing style.

Gray, Robert M. and Moberg, David O. *The Church and the Older Person*. Grand Rapids: Wm. B. Eerdmans Publishing Co., 1962.

This represents an early effort to understand the role of religion in the lives of older people.

Hulicka, Irene. *Empirical Studies in the Psychology and Sociology of Aging*. ed. B. R. Bugelski. New York: Thomas Y. Crowell Co., Publishers, 1977.

A representative selection of articles to introduce the psychological and social problems relevant to the study of aging.

Lester, Andrew and Lester, Judith L. *Understanding Aging Parents*. ed. Wayne Oates. Philadelphia: The Westminster Press, 1980.

Practical advice on coping with problems of aging. Aid for dealing with one's feelings and the feelings of aging parents.

Madden, Myron C. and Madden, Mary. *For Grandparents, Wonders and Worries.* ed. Wayne Oates. Philadelphia: The Westminster Press, 1980.

A practical and personal look at grandparents by a couple who are themselves grandparents.

McClellan, Robert W. *Claiming A Frontier: Ministry and Older People.* Los Angeles: University of Southern California Press, 1977.

A practical guide for ministry among older persons in the church, synagogue and community. Resources and references.

McGarvey, J. W. and Pendleton, Philip Y. *The Fourfold Gospel.* Cincinnati: Standard Publishing, n.d.

An older commentary that provides a harmony of the Gospels.

McKenzie, Sheila. *Aging and Old Age.* Glenview: Scott, Foresman & Co., 1980.

An introductory test for courses in psychology of aging.

Morley, David. *Half Way Up The Mountain.* New Jersey: Fleming H. Revell Co., 1979.

Provides religious perspectives for mid-life.

Ragan, Pauline K., *Aging Parents.* Los Angeles: The University of Southern California Press, 1979.

A monograph published from Parents Conference in 1978 at the Andrus Gerontology Center at the University of Southern California. Expertise from a wide range of discipline and approaches.

Schmidt, Donna. "A Ministry of Calling." *The Lookout,* 92(September 28, 1980):4.

How an older couple used their retirement as an opportunity to build a significant hospital ministry.

Tilberg, Cedric W., ed. *The Fullness of Life*. New York: Division for Missions in North America: Lutheran Church in America, 1980.

Insight into the aging process. Stimulates a positive image of aging while advocating justice toward the aging.

Williamson, Dale. "Not too Old to Serve," *Christian Standard*, 116(August 23, 1981):12.

Describes creative ways older people can serve in the church.

CHAPTER TEN: MINISTERING WITH THE WIDOWED

Carter, Hugh and Glick, Paul. *Marriage and Divorce: A Social and Economic Study*. Cambridge: Harvard University Press, 1970.

Sociological research on marriage and divorce.

Coleman, James C.; Butcher, James N.; and Carson, Robert C. *Abnormal Psychology and Modern Life*. 6th ed., Glenview: Scott, Foresman & Co., 1980.

A standard text in Abnormal Psychology for college classes.

Hansen, Robert P. "In the Company of Heaven." *The Lutheran Standard*. 13(November, 1973):5.

The personal account of a minister who lost his wife through death.

Harvey, Carol D. and Bahr, Howard M. "Widowhood, Morale, and Affiliation." *Journal of Marriage and the Family* 36(1974):99.

Low morale among the widowed appears to be a result of their poorer economic condition. Includes research among widows in five countries.

Lopata, Helena. *Women as Widows*. New York: Elsevier, 1979.

Results of eight years of research on widows in the Chicago area. Emphases is placed upon the support systems involving this segment of American society.

Marris, Peter. *Widows and Their Families*. London: Routledge and Kagan Paul, 1958.

This book relates extensive research among London widows.

Morris, Sarah. *Grief And How To Live With It*. New York: Gossert & Dunlap Inc., 1972.

A personal account of the grief experienced by a widow.

Pruitt, Carl W. "The Ministry of a Widow's Group" *Christian Standard*. 89(April 17, 1977):3-6.

Answers questions frequently asked concerning a widow's group.

_____. *Ministering With Widows Through Small Groups In The Local Church*. An unpublished dissertation submitted to Lutheran Theological Seminary, Columbus, Ohio. May, 1974.

Provides sociological, psychological and theological perspectives of working with widows and traces the ministry among widows in one congregation.

_____. "The Widow's Group" *Lookout*. 93(September 20, 1981):7.

A description of the formation and work of five widow's groups started within five different local congregations.

Toffler, Alvin. *Future Shock*. New York: Random House Inc., 1970.

Startling insights into the impact of modern life upon the population as well as predictions concerning the future trends.

U. S., Department of Commerce. Bureau Of The Census. *Statistical Abstracts Of The United States,* 1971.
Statistical data from census reports.

CHAPTER ELEVEN: DEVELOPING DISCIPLINE IN CHILDREN

Buttrick, George Arthur, ed. *The Interpreter's Bible Commentary.* Nashville: Abingdon-Cokesbury Press, 1953. Vol. 2: I Samuel, by George B. Caird.
This commentary has both an exegesis of the text and an exposition of the Scripture.

Dobson, James. *Dare to Discipline.* Wheaton: Tyndale House Publishers, 1970.
Approaches to discipline based on psychological insight and Biblical principles.

Fancher, Raymond E. *Pioneers In Psychology.* New York: W. W. Norton & Co., 1979.
Biographical data on the founders of contemporary psychology.

Gardner, Judith, ed. *Readings In Developmental Psychology.* Boston: Little, Brown & Co., 1978.
"Baby In A Box," by B. F. Skinner.
Standard text for a class in developmental psychology in college or university.

Gardner, Howard. *Developmental Psychology.* Boston: Little, Brown & Co., 1978.
A life scope approach to developmental psychology. A text for college or university with references to parenting styles.

Gordon, Thomas. *P. E. T.: Parent Effectiveness Training.* New York: Peter H. Wyden, 1974.
An approach to parenting that stresses listening skills.

Heidebrecht, Paul and Rohrbach, Jerry. *Fathering A Son.* Chicago: Moody Press, 1979.
    Help for fathers in understanding their sons and dealing with discipline and other aspects of parenting.

Hof, Larry, and Miller, William R. *Marriage Enrichment: Philosophy, Process, and Program.* Bowie: Prentice-Hall Inc., 1981.
    Overview of the movement and suggestions for establishing a Marriage and Family Enrichment Program.

Hunt, Gladys M. *Focus On Family Life.* Grand Rapids: Baker Book House, 1970.
    Designed for adult discussion groups interested in exploring family life. Includes a treatment of discipline.

Jersild, Arthur J.; Brook, Judith S.; and Brook, David W. *The Psychology of Adolescence.* New York: Macmillan Inc., 1978.
    A text book for adolescent psychology that contains references to parenting styles.

MacDonald, Gordon. *The Effective Father.* Wheaton: Tyndale House Publishers, 1977.
    Biblical and practical principles on parenting. Action Guide for Effective Fathers is a workbook for individual study to stimulate interaction and discussion of material in The Effective Father.

Matthews, Charles. *The Christian Home.* Cincinnati: Standard Publishing, n.d.
    Various aspects of family life are treated from a Christian perspective. Helpful for study groups. Includes section on discipline.

Narramore, Bruce. *A Guide To Child Rearing.* Grand Rapids: Zondervan Publishing House, 1972.
    Psychological and theological bases for child-rearing in a workbook format.

_____ . *Help! I'm A Parent.* Grand Rapids: Zondervan Publishing House, 1971.

Combines the practical insights of psychology with the truths of the Bible to help parents with present day problems. Includes specific techniques for guiding a child's behavior.

Papalia, Diane E. and Olds, Sally Wendkos. *Human Development.* New York: McGraw-Hill Book Co., 1981.

A developmental psychology text for college or university that contains references to parenting styles.

Patterson, Gerald R. *Families.* Champaign: Research Press, 1971.

A behavioral approach to parenting.

CHAPTER TWELVE: COPING WITH ANGER

Adams, Jay. *The Use Of The Scriptures In Counseling.* Grand Rapids: Baker Book House, 1975.

An approach to the use of Scripture in dealing with personal problems. Specific Scriptures provided for meeting anxiety, depression, fear and other problems.

Aronson, Elliot. "Human Aggression" in *The Social Animal.* San Francisco: W. H. Freeman & Co., 1980.

Explanations of aggression and discussion of the reduction of violence is found in this chapter of this Social Psychology text book.

Baron, Robert A.; Byrne, Ronn and Kantowitz, Bany. "Aggression and Violence" in *Psychology: Understanding Behavior.* Philadelphia: W. B. Saunders Co., 1979.

The roots of aggression as well as its prevention and control are discussed in this introductory psychology text.

Bowie, Walter Russel. "The Book Of Genesis" in *The Interpreter's Bible*. Paul Scherer, ed. Nashville: Abingdon-Cokesburg Press, 1952.

An exegesis and practical application of the Scriptures.

Burwick, Ray. *Anger: Defusing The Bomb*. Wheaton: Tyndale House Publishers, 1981.

Suggestions for dealing with anger from a psychological and Scriptural perspective.

Dobson, James. *Emotions: Can You Trust Them*. Ventura: Regal Books, 1980.

"Anger" is included among the emotions treated in this psychological or Biblically oriented book.

Grounds, Vernon. "The Bible and Anger" in *Emotional Problems and the Gospel*. Grand Rapids: Zondervan Publishing House, 1976.

Biblical insights for dealing with anger.

Madow, Leo. *Anger: How To Recognize And Cope With It*. New York: Charles Scribner's Sons, 1972.

Medical and psychological explanations of the effects of anger as well as practical help in dealing more effectively with it.

CHAPTER THIRTEEN: MAXIMIZING MARRIAGE AND FAMILY LIFE

Ackerman, Nathan W. *The Psychodynamics of Family Life*. New York: Basic Books Inc., Publishers, 1958.

Approaches to the treatment of the disturbed family by a leader in the field.

Butler, Robert N. and Lewis, Myrna I. *Sex After Sixty*. New York: Harper and Row Publishers, 1976.

Clinical guidelines on medical aspects of sex after age sixty.

Cox, Frank. *Human Intimacy: Marriage, The Family and Its Meaning.* St. Paul: West Publishing Company, 1978.
A standard text for university or college on family life.

Dahl, Gerald L. *Why Christian Marriages Are Breaking Up.* Wheaton: Tyndale House Publishers, 1979.
Courses for Christian marriage failures and suggestions to work toward cure are provided.

Dillow, Jospeh. *Solomon on Sex.* New York: Thomas Nelson Inc., 1977.
Approaches the Song of Solomon as a love song with divine instructions on sex. Application of present marital problems. An appendix dealing with specific sexual problems is included.

Drakeford, John W. *Made for Each Other.* Nashville: Broadman Press, 1973.
A Christian approach to human sexuality. Practical advice and Biblical references.

Foley, Vincent. *An Introduction to Family Therapy.* New York: Grune & Stratton Inc., 1974.
Insights on marital therapy gleaned from the innovators in the field. Provides a theoretical base for understanding family therapy.

Glickman, Craig S. *A Song for Lovers.* Downers Grove: InterVarsity Press, 1976.
Frank discussion of love, sex and marriage based on the Song of Solomon.

Halverson, Kay. *The Wedded Unmother.* Minneapolis: Augsburg Publishing House, 1980.
Insights into the struggles involved in infertility.

Harnick, Bernard. *Risk and Chance In Marriage.* Waco: Word Inc., 1972.

A presentation of lessons derived from psychology and personal faith.

Hyde, Janet Shibley. *Human Sexuality.* New York: McGraw-Hill Book Co., 1982.

A textbook on human sexuality for college and university use. Contains a section on ethics, religion and sexuality.

Kilgore, James E. *Try Marriage Before Divorce.* Waco: Word Inc., 1978.

Descriptions of what often goes wrong in marriages and some practical guidelines for renewal.

Lamb, Michael E., ed. *The Role of the Father in Child Development.* New York: John Wiley & Sons Inc., 1976.

Analyzes critically the contribution made by fathers from a psychological and social research perspective.

LeBar, Lois. *Family Devotions with School-Age Children.* New Jersey: Fleming H. Revell Co., 1973.

Creative guidelines for implementing family devotions.

Mace, David and Mace, Vera. *How to Have a Happy Marriage.* Nashville: Abingdon Press, 1977.

Designed as a six week work book approach to improving a marriage. Helpful to ministers and marriage counselors to help couples work on their relationship.

McDonald, Cleveland. *Creating a Successful Christian Marriage.* Grand Rapids: Baker Book House, 1975.

A text book for Christian institutions covering a wide range of practical areas necessary for a happy marital adjustment.

Monfalcone, Wesley R. *Coping with Abuse in the Family.* Philadelphia: The Westminster Press, 1980.
From mild and subtle abuse to violent abuse is treated. Written for the Christian family.

Okun, Barbara E. and Rappaport, Louis J. *Working with Families.* North Scituate: Duxbury Press, 1980.
An introductory text for college and university classes in Marital and Family Therapy. A manual to accompany the text is also available, *Exercises For Working With Families,* which helps to personalize the material.

Samuel, Dorothy T. *Fun and Games in Marriage.* Waco: Word Inc., 1973.
Directions in how to turn little things into a creative force. Stimulating sensuality defusing negative moods and learning to play together. Advice on how to make the most of marriage.

Satire, Virginia. *Conjoint Family Therapy.* Palo Alto: Science and Behavior Books, 1956.
A manual for therapist containing the approach and technique of family therapy by one of the leaders in the field.

Taylor, R. Robert. *Christ in the Home.* Grand Rapids: Baker Book House, 1973.
The importance of placing Christ at the center of the family is stressed. A Biblical perspective to family problems.

Wheat, Ed and Wheat, Gayle. *Intended for Pleasure.* New Jersey: Fleming H. Revell Co., 1976.
Biblical and psychological insights to enhance sexual pleasure. Some direction to help with sexual dysfunction. Frank discussion of details of human sexuality.

_____. *Love Life*. Grand Rapids: Zondervan Publishing House, 1981.

Assistance in building intimacy in marriage and family life through practical Biblical counsel.

Williamson, Donald S. "Personal Authority via Termination of the Intergenerational Hierarchical Boundary: A New Stage in the Family Life Cycle" *Journal of Marital And Family Therapy,* 1981.

Treats the importance of movement toward a peer relationship between parents and their offspring.

Wright, Norman H. *The Pillars of Marriage*. Glendale: Regal Books Division, G/L Publications, 1980.

Help in enhancing key areas of a marital relationship.

Index of Scriptures

289

GOD'S ANSWERS TO PERSONAL PROBLEMS

TOPICAL INDEX FOR *WHAT THE BIBLE SAYS ABOUT GOD'S ANSWERS TO PERSONAL PROBLEMS*

As arranged in *Monser's Topical Index and Digest of the Bible* edited by Harold E. Monser with A. T. Robertson, D. R. Dungan and Others.

AGE. John 9:21, 23. **Full.**—Job 5: 26; Heb. 5:14.

Old age a blessing.—Promised to Abraham—Gen. 15:15; Job 30:2; Ps. 91:16. Bestowed—Gen. 25:8.

People of old age.—Called: Elders—Job 12:20. Gray-haired—Job 15: 10. Aged—Job 29:8.

Instances of.—Abraham and Sarah—Gen. 18:11-13; 21:2, 7. Lot—Gen. 19:31. Isaac—Gen. 27:2; Jacob—Gen. 37:3; 44:20. Moses—Deut. 34:7. Joshua—Josh. 13:1; 23:1, 2; Gideon—Ju. 8:32. Man at Gibeah—Ju. 19:16, 17. Naomi—Ruth 4:15. Eli—I Sam. 4:18. Samuel—I Sam. 12:2. Barzillai—II Sam. 19:32, 35. David—I Ki. 1:1, 15; I Chr. 23:1; 29:28; Ps. 37:25. Solomon—I Ki. 11:4. Prophet at Bethel—I Ki. 13: 11, 25, 29. Ahijah—I Ki. 14:4. Asa —I Ki. 15:23. Shunammite's husband—II Ki. 4:14. Jehoiada—II Chr. 24:15. Job—Job 32:6; 42:17. Elisabeth—Lu. 1:7, 36. Zacharias—Lu. 1:7. Anna—Lu. 2:36. Paul—Philemon 9.

Counsel with old men.—I Ki. 12:6, 8, 13; II Chr. 10:6, 8, 13.

Proverbs concerning.—Pr. 17:6; 20: 29; 22:6; 23:22.

Duties of the aged.—Titus 2:3.

Appeal to.—I John 2:13f.

Prophecies concerning.—I Sam. 2: 31; Job 5:26; Ps. 92:14; Is. 46:4; 65:20; Jer. 6:11; 31:13; Joel 1:2; 2:28; Zech. 8:4; Acts 2:17.

Miscellaneous.—Men of Sodom—Gen. 19:4. No compassion on—II Chr. 36:17. Jews—Esth. 3:13. Prayer of an old man—Ps. 71:9, 18. King —Eccl. 4:13. Vanity of, unless filled with good—Eccl. 6:3; 12:1.

Figurative.—Lam. 2:21.

The title "elder" originally had reference to old age.—Ex. 3:16; Josh. 24:31; I Ki. 20:8.

Attainment of old age a special blessing.—Job 5:26; Zech. 8:4.

Wisdom of the aged proverbial.—Job 12:12; 32:7.

Reverence to be shown the aged.—Lev. 19:32; Pr. 23:22.

Failure of reverence an evil.—Deut. 28:50; I Ki. 12:8; Is. 47:6.

Past.—Heb. 11:11.

ANGER. God provoked to anger—I Ki. 21:22; Ezra 5:12; Neh. 4:5; Hos. 12:14; Zech. 8:14. Because of idolatry—Deut. 9:7, 8, 18; 31: 16, 17; 32:21; Ju. 2:12-15; I Ki. 14:9, 15; 16:2-4, 7, 13, 26, 33; II Ki. 17:9-18; 21:1-15; 22:16, 17; 23:19, 26, 27; II Chron. 28:25; 33: 1-11; 34:24, 25; Ps. 78:58; 106: 28, 29; Is. 65:2-7; Jer. 7:18-20; 8: 19; 11:17; 25:7-11; 32:26-35; 44: 3, 7-30; Ez. 7:8.

His anger invoked.—Ps. 56:7; 59:13; 69:24; 79:6, 7; 138:7; Jer. 18:23. Prophesied—Deut. 4:25, 26; 11:13 17, 18; 29:18-28; 31:16, 17, 29; Josh. 23:16; 9:20.

Results of God's anger.—Num. 11:1; 12:9; 25:5, 9; 32:10-15; Deut. 32: 22; Ju. 2:14, 20, 21; 3:8; 10:7; II Sam. 6:7; II Ki. 13:3; Job 9:5; 21: 17; Is. 42:24, 25; Ez. 16:26, 27.

293

Anger turned aside.—Prayer for: Judah to Joseph—Gen. 44:18. Aaron to Moses—Ex. 32:22. To God: By Moses—Ex. 32:12. Gideon—Ju. 6:39. Solomon—I Ki. 8:46; Ezra 9:14; Ps. 74:1; 80:4; 85:4, 5; 89: 46, 47. Turned: Joseph—Gen. 45: 4, 5, 7, 8. Gods—Ex. 32:14; Nah. 25:10; Josh. 7:26; Ezra 10:14; II Chr. 12:7, 12; Ps. 85:3; 106:23; Is. 12:1; Ez. 16:42; Hos. 14:4; Jonah 3:9, 10.

The wrath of the Lamb.—Ps. 2:5, 9, 12; Is. 63:3, 6; Mk. 3:5; Lu. 14:21; Rev. 6:16, 17.

Justifiable.—Jacob—Gen. 30:2; 31: 36. Sons of Jacob—Gen. 34:7. Moses—Ex. 11:8; 32:19; Lev. 10: 16; Num. 16:15. Ephraim—Ju. 8: 3. Samson—Ju. 14:19. Saul—I Sam. 11:6. Jonathan—I Sam. 20:34. David—II Sam. 12:5. Nehemiah— Neh. 5:6; 13:17, 25. Ahasuerus— Esth. 7:7, 10; Job 18:4. Elihu—Job 32:2, 3, 5. Jeremiah—Jer. 15:17. Jesus—Mk. 3:5. Paul—Acts 17:16; 23:3. Corinthians—II Cor. 7:11.

Wicked anger.—Cain—Gen. 4:5, 6, 8. Esau—Gen. 27:41, 45. Potiphar —Gen. 39:19. Jacob's sons—Gen. 49:5-7. Moses—Num. 20:10, 11. Balaam—Num. 22:27. Balak—Num. 24:10. Zebul—Ju. 9:30. Eliab—I Sam. 17:28. Saul—I Sam. 20:30. Nabal—I Sam. 25:17. Army—II Chr. 25:10. Sanballat—Neh. 4:1. King —Esth. 1:12; 2:1. Haman—Esth. 3:5; 5:9. Nebuchadrezzar—Dan. 2:12; Jonah 4:1, 4, 9. Ten Apostles —Mt. 20:24. Judas—Mk. 14:4; John 12:4, 5. Nazarenes—Lu. 4:28. Ruler —Lu. 13:14. Elder brother—Lu. 15:28. Jews—John 7:27. Saddu- cees—Acts 5:17. Mob—Acts 7:54; 21:35, 36. The Devil—Rev. 12:12, 17.

Laws against.—Provoking God to anger—Deut. 6:14, 15; 7:1-4. Being angry—Num. 18:5; Ps. 37:8; Mt. 5:22; Rom. 12:19; Gal. 5:19; Eph. 4:26, 31; 6:4; Col. 3:8; Titus 1:7; Jas. 1:19, 20.

Proverbs concerning.—Pr. 11:4, 23; 14:35; 15:1, 18; 16:14, 32; 19:19; 21:14, 19; 25:23; 27:4; Eccl. 7:9.

CHASTEN. Job 33:19; Heb. 12:11; Rev. 3:19. Children—Deut. 8:5; 21:18; Pr. 13:24; 19:18. God, By —Deut. 8:5; Job 5:17; Ps. 94:12; 118:18; Pr. 3:11; I Cor. 11:32; Eph. 6:4; Heb. 12:5, 7. Rod, With—II Sam. 7:14. Self—Ps. 69:10; Dan. 10:12.

CHILDREN: The chosen type of the kingdom.—Mt. 18:2-5; 19:14; Mk. 10:14, 15; Lu. 18:17; I Cor. 14:20; I Pet. 2:2.

Promised as an inducement to right- eousness.—Gen. 15:5; 22:17; Ex. 32:13; Lev. 26:9; Deut. 7:12-14; 13:17; 30:5; Job 5:24, 25; Ps. 45: 16, 17; 128:1-6; Is. 44:3, 4; 48:18, 19; Jer. 33:22; Rom. 4:18.

Come from God.—Gen. 4:1, 25; 17: 20; 29:31-35; 30:2, 6, 17-20; 33:5; 48:9; Deut. 7:13; Ruth 4:13; I Sam. 1:19, 20; Ps. 107:41; 113: 9; 127:3-5; 128:1-6.

Children a blessing.—Gen. 5:29; Ps. 113:9; 127:3-5; Pr. 10:1; 15:20; 17:6; 23:24; 27:11; 29:3.

Childlessness an affliction.—Gen. 15:2, 3; 30:1; I Sam. 1:6, 7; Jer. 20:30; 22:30; Lu. 1:25.

Given in answer to prayer.—Gen. 15:2-5; 25:21; I Sam. 1:10-20, 27; Lu. 1:13.

By special appointment.—Isaac— Gen. 15:2-6; 17:16; 21:1-3. Jacob and Esau—Gen. 15:21-26. Samuel —I Sam. 1:11, 19, 20. John the Baptist—Lu. 1:13-25, 57-80; Lu. 1:26-42. Jesus—Mt. 1:18-23; Lu. 1:26-28.

Children taken away in punishment.
—Ex. 12:29, 30; Deut. 28:32, 41;
II Sam. 12:14, 15; Job 27:14, 15;
Ps. 21:10, 11; Hos. 9:12.

Covenant of circumcision.—Gen. 17:
10-14; Lev. 12:3; Phil. 3:5.

Named.—Gen. 21:3; 30:6, 8, 10, 13,
18, 20, 21, 24; 41:51, 52; Ex. 2:
22. Ruth 4:17; I Sam. 4:21. At
circumcision—Lu. 1:59; 2:21. After
relatives—Lu. 1:59, 61. From remarkable events—Gen. 21:3, 6; 18:
13; Ex. 2:10; 18:3, 4. From circumstances connected with their birth—
Gen. 25:25, 26; 35:18; I Chr. 4:9.
Named by God—Is. 8:3; Hos. 1:4,
6, 9; Lu. 1:31.

Treatment at birth.—Ez. 16:4-6; Lu.
2:7, 12.

**Brought early to the house of the
Lord.**—I Sam. 1:24.

Weaning of.—Gen. 21:8; I Sam. 1:
22-24; I Ki. 11:20; Ps. 131:2; Is.
11:8; 28:9.

Nurses of.—Gen. 24:59; Ex. 2:7, 9;
Ruth 4:16; II Sam. 4:4; II Ki. 11:2.

Adopted.—Gen. 48:5, 6; Ex. 2:10.

Education of.—Gen. 18:19; Ex. 10:
2; 13:8-10; Deut. 4:9; 11:19; 31:
12, 13; Ps. 78:3-8; Pr. 4:1-22; 13:
1, 24; 22:6, 15; Is. 28:9, 10; Lu.
2:46; II Tim. 3:14, 15.

Training of.—Pr. 22:6, 15; 29:17;
Eph. 6:4.

Parental authority.—Gen. 9:24, 25;
18:19; 21:14; 38:24; Pr. 13:1, 24.

Parental indulgence.—Gen. 27:6-17,
42-45; 37:3, 4. Indulgence forbidden
—Deut. 21:15-17.

Parental example.—Gen. 18:19; II
Tim. 1:5.

Duties of children to parents.—Ex.
20:12; 21:15, 17; Lev. 19:3; 20:
9; Deut. 5:16; 27:16; Pr. 1:8; 6:20;
15:5; 23:22; 24:21; Is. 45:10; Eph.
6:2, 3; Col. 3:20; I Tim. 5:4; I Pet.
5:5.

Penalty for disobedience.—Deut. 21:
18-21; Pr. 30:17.

**Prosperity of, greatly depended on
obedience of parents.**—Deut. 4:
40; 12:25, 28; Ps. 128:1-3.

Amusements.—Job 21:11; Zech. 8:
5; Mt. 11:16, 17; Lu. 7:31, 32.

Fellowship with parents.—Gen. 6:
18; 13:15-16; Lev. 26:45.

Children sacrificed to idols.—Lev.
18:21; 20:2-5; Deut. 12:29-31; 18:
10; II Ki. 17:31; II Chr. 28:3; 33:
6; Ez. 16:20, 21.

Prayers for.—Gen. 17:18; I Chr. 29:
19.

Discriminations: Male.—Redeemed
as belonging to God—Ex. 13:13-
15. Under care of tutors—II Ki. 10:
1; Acts 22:3; Gal. 4:1, 2. Inherited
possessions of their fathers—Deut.
21:16, 17; Lu. 12:13, 14. Received
paternal blessing—Gen. 27:1-4; 48:
15; 49:1-33.

Female.—Drawers of water—Gen. 24:
13; Ex. 2:16. Inheritors of property
in default of sons—Num. 27:1-8;
Josh. 17:1-16. Were given in marriage by father, eldest preferred—
Gen. 29:16-29. Being debarred from
marriage a reproach—Jer. 11:37;
Is. 4:1.

Illegitimate.—Disregarded by father—
Heb. 12:8. Despised by brothers—
Ju. 11:2. Excluded from congrega-
tion—Deut. 23:2. Exiled from family
—Gen. 21:14; 25:6. Had no inheri-
tance—Gen. 21:10-14; Gal. 4:30.

Good children.—Obey parents—Gen.
28:7; 47:29-31; Ex. 20:12; Pr. 10:
1; 13:1; Col. 3:20. Observe the law
of God—Ps. 119:9, 99; Pr. 28:7.
Submit to discipline—Pr. 8:32-36;
Heb. 12:9. Honor and care for parents—Gen. 45:9-11; 46:29; 47:12;
Pr. 10:1; 29:17. Respect the aged
—Lev. 19:32.

Examples of.—Shem and Japheth—Gen. 9:23. Isaac—Gen. 22:6. Judah—Gen. 4:32. Joseph—Gen. 37:13; 46:29. Jacob's sons—Gen. 50:12. Jephthah's daughter—Ju. 11:36. Samuel—I Sam. 3:19; 22:6. David—I Sam. 17:20; Ps. 71:5. Solomon—II Ki. 2:19. Josiah—II Chr. 34:3. Esther—Esth. 2:20. The Rechabites—Jer. 35:5-10. Daniel—Dan. 1:6. Jesus—Lu. 2:51. Timothy—II Tim. 3:15.

Wicked children.—To their parents—Gen. 26:34, 35; Deut. 27:16; I Sam. 2:25; II Sam. 15:10-15; I Ki. 1:5-10; Pr. 15:5, 20; 19:26; 28:24; 29:15; 30:11; Ez. 22:7. To their leaders—II Ki. 2:23, 24; Job 19:18. Not restrained by parents—I Sam. 3:11-14. Sons of Belial—I Sam. 2:12-17, 22-25; 8:1-3.

Punishment of.—Ex. 21:15; Deut. 21:18, 21; 27:16; II Ki. 2:23; Pr. 28:24; 30:17; Mk. 7:10.

Fondness and care of mothers for.—Ex. 2:2-10; I Sam. 2:19; I Ki. 3:27; Is. 49:15; I Thess. 2:7, 8.

Grief occasioned by loss of.—Gen. 37:35; 44:27-29; II Sam. 13:37; Jer. 6:26: 31:15.

Consequences of sin entailed on children in this world.—Ex. 20:5; 34:7; Lev. 26:39, 40; Num. 14:33; Deut. 5:9; I Ki. 14:9-10; Job 5:3-7; Ps. 21:10; 37:28; Is. 1:4; 13:16; 14:20-22; Jer. 32:18; Lam. 5:7; Mt. 23:32-36; John 9:2, 3, 34.

Children not punished for sins of parents.—Deut. 24:16; II Ki. 14:6; II Chr. 25:4; Jer. 31:29, 30; 32:18; Ez. 18:2-4, 20; Mt. 19:13, 14; Mk. 10:13-15; Lu. 18:15-17.

Children of God.—Heb. 12:5-9; I Pet. 1:14.

Children of light.—Lu. 16:8; John 12:36; Eph. 5:8; I Thess. 5:5.

CORRECT. Acts 24:2; II Tim. 2:25; 3:16. Child—Pr. 22:15; 23:13; 29:17. God, By—Job 5:17; 37:13; Ps. 39:11; 94:10; Pr. 3:1; Jer. 2:30; 5:3; 10:24; 30:11; 46:28; Hab. 1:12. Wickedness—Jer. 2:19.

DEATH.—Metaphorical equivalents of the term death: "Returning to dust"—Gen. 3:19; Ps. 104:29; Eccl. 3:20; 12:7. Going "to the fathers"—Gen. 15:15. "Gathered to his people"—Gen. 25:8; 49:29. "Giving up the ghost"—Gen. 25:8; 35:29. "To sleep with thy fathers"—Deut. 31:16. "Crushed like the moth"—Job 4:19. "Tent cord pulled up"—Job 4:21. "An exhaled breath"—Job 7:7. "Not to be"—Job 7:8, 21; 27:19. "Cut down like a flower"—Job 14:2. "Not to be found"—Job 20:7, 9; cf. Gen. 5:24; Heb. 11:5. "Brought to the king of terrors"—Job 18:14. Devoured by a divine fire—Job 20:26. Lying down in the dust—Job 7:21; 21:26. The spirit going upward—Eccl. 3:21. The spirit returning to God—Eccl. 12:7. Going to his everlasting home—Eccl. 12:5. Sleeping in the dust of the earth—Dan. 12:2. A sleep—Mt. 9:24. Fallen asleep—John 11:11; Acts 7:60; 13:36; I Cor. 15:18, 51; I Thess. 4:14. Clothed with the house not made with hands—II Cor. 5:2. Swallowed up of life—II Cor. 5:4. Absence from the body—II Cor. 5:8. A journey—Phil. 1:23; II Pet. 1:15, marg. "Putting off the tabernacle"—II Pet. 1:14; cf. John 1:14, marg.

Result of sin.—Pr. 2:18; 5:5; 7:27; 8:36; 11:19; 13:13, 14; 14:12; 15:10; 16:25; 21:6; 24:11; Ez. 18:32; 31:14; 33:11; John 5:14; Rom. 5:12-21; 6:16-23; 7:5-8; 8:2-6; I Cor. 15:21; II Cor. 7:10; Jas. 1:15; I John 3:14.

Penalty for sin.—Gen. 2:17; Ex. 10: 17; 11:5; Num. 14:35; 16:31-35; 35:30, 31; Deut. 30:15; I Ki. 1:52; II Chr. 24:24; Ezra 7:26; Pr. 10:21; Jer. 9:21; 15:2; 21:8; 31:30; 43: 11; Ez. 18:4; Amos 9:10; Mt. 15: 4; Mk. 7:10; John 19:7; Rev. 18:8.

Mysterious and terrible.—II Sam. 22: 5, 6; Job 3:5; 10:21; 12:22; 16:16; 18:4; 24:17; 28:3; 34:22; 38:17; Ps. 13:3; 23:4; 44:19; 55:4; 107: 10-14; Is. 9:2; Jer. 2:6; 13:16; Amos 5:8; Mt. 4:16; Lu. 1:79; Heb. 2:15.

End of earthly things.—Ruth 1:17; Job 7:9, 10; 14:12; Ps. 6:5; Eccl. 9:5-10; 12:5-7; Is. 38:18; Rom. 7: 2; I Cor. 7:39; Gal. 2:19; Heb. 9: 15-27.

Robs of our possessions.—Job 1:21; Ps. 49:17; Lu. 12:16-20.

To be braved in line of duty.—Ju. 5: 18; Is. 53:12; Mt. 10:28, 39; 26: 35; Mk. 14:31; Lu. 11:50, 51; 12: 32, 33; 18:32, 33; 21:16; 22:33; Acts 20:24; 21:13; 25:11; Rom. 5:7; I Cor. 15:31; II Cor. 4:11, 12; 7:3; Phil. 2:8, 30; 3:10, 11; Heb. 2:9-15; 11:35-38; 12:2-4; I Pet. 2: 24; Rev. 2:10; 12:11.

Figurative.—As a state of sin—John 5:24, 40; 6:50; 8:21, 24; Rom. 7: 9-11; Eph. 2:1, 5; Col. 2:13; I John 3:14; Rev. 3:1. It includes lack of knowledge of God and His Christ— John 17:3. Absence of faith—John 8:21, 24; Heb. 11:5, 6. Dwelling in darkness—Mt. 4:16; John 1:4, 9; 3:19, 20.

Alienation from God and Christ.— Ez. 18:4; John 15:5, 6; Rom. 8:6; Eph. 2:12, 13; 4:18.

Death is not annihilation.—Eccl. 12: 5, 7; Mt. 17:3; 22:32; Mk. 9:4; Lu. 9:30, 31; 23:43; Acts 7:55, 56, 59; II Cor. 5:1-8; Phil. 1:20-26; II Tim. 1:10; 4:6-8; II Pet. 1:13-15; Rev. 6:9, 10.

Christ saves by His death.—Is. 53:5, 6; Mt. 20:28; 26:26, 28; Mk. 10: 45; 14:22-24; Lu. 22:19, 20; 24: 46, 47; John 3:14; 12:32; Acts 3: 18; 4:12; Rom. 5:10; 6:3-5; I Cor. 1:22-24; Eph. 2:16; Col. 1:20-22; I Tim. 2:6; Heb. 2:9-15; I Pet. 2: 24.

Jesus conquered death.—Mt. 9:23-25; 11:5; 28:1-10; Mk. 5:40-42; 16:1-7; Lu. 7:11-15; 8:49-55; 24: 1-6; John 2:19; 10:18; 11:43, 44; 20:1-17; Acts 2:24; 9:36-40; 20:9, 10; Rom. 1:4; 6:23; 7:24, 25; 8:6-10; I Cor. 15:4, 20-22, 55-57; Eph. 4:8-10; Col. 2:12; 3:1; II Tim. 1: 10; Heb. 2:14, 15.

Death of the wicked.—A judgment —Num. 16:29, 30; I Sam. 25:38; Is. 14:9; Lu. 12:20; Heb. 9:27. Sudden—Job 21:13, 23; Pr. 10:25, 27; 29:1; Is. 17:14; Acts 5:3-10. Feared —Job 18:11-15; 27:19-21. In sin —Ez. 3:19; John 8:21. Illustrated —Lu. 16:23-26.

Death of the righteous.—Release from toil and care—I Ki. 19:4; Job 3:21; 7:15; 14:13; I Cor. 9:15. From evil —II Ki. 22:20; Is. 57:1, 2. To a crown—II Tim. 4:8; Rev. 2:10. To rest—Job 3:13; II Thess. 1:7. To glory—Ps. 73:24-26. To Christ and gain—Phil. 1:21, 23. To new body —II Cor. 5:1, 2. Precious to God— Ps. 116:15; Rev. 14:13.

Entrance upon new state.—Pr. 14: 32; Is. 25:8; Mt. 17:2, 3; 22:32; Mk. 12:27; Lu. 16:19-31; 20:35-38; 23:43; John 5:28, 29; 12:24; I Cor. 3:22; II Cor. 5:6-8; Phil. 1: 21-23; II Tim. 4:8; Heb. 9:27; Rev. 14:13.

Death chosen.—Num. 23:10; Jer. 8:3; Rev. 9:6.

For the believer.—Christ has abolished death—John 6:47, 50, 51; 8:51, 52; 11:26; Heb. 2:9, 14; II Tim. 1: 10.

Death is a separation from the source of life and joy.—(1) Physical: A branch separated from the vine dies —John 15:6. A fish taken from water dies—Is. 50:2. Man cut off from air dies—II Ki. 8:15. (2) Spiritual: Fools die from lack of wisdom—Pr. 10: 21. Sin kills—Rom. 7:10, 11, 24. Separates from life and peace—Rom. 8:6. From church and God—5:17, 18; Eph. 2:12; I Tim. 5:6. (3) Eternal, or the second death of the soul is banishment, under a curse, from the kingdom, into the eternal fire and company of wicked angels—Mt. 25: 41, 46; II Thess. 1:9. Undying worm —Mk. 9:43-48. A lake of fire—Rev. 2:11; 19:20; 20:6; 21:8.

Death penalty for crime.—Murder— Gen. 9:5, 6; Num. 35:16-21. Adultery—Lev. 20:10; Deut. 22:24. Incest—Lev. 20:11, 12, 14. Sodomy —Lev. 18:22; 20:13. Perjury—Zech. 5:4. Kidnapping—Ex. 21:16. Witchcraft—Ex. 22:18. Abusing parents —Ex. 21:15, 17. Blasphemy—Lev. 24:23. Sabbath-breaking—Ex. 35: 2; Num. 15:32-36. False teaching —Deut. 13:1-10. Sacrificing to false gods—Ex. 22:20.

Death a penalty inflicted only on testimony of two or more witnesses.— Num. 35:30; Deut. 17:6.

Exemplified.—Korah. Num. 16:32. Absalom—II Sam. 18:9, 10.

EXAMPLE: Christ an example.— John 13:15; Acts 20:35; I Pet. 2: 21, 22; I John 2:6; 3:3.

Christians admonished to be.—Mt. 5:48; II Cor. 4:10; Eph. 3:19; Phil. 2:5; 3:17; I Thess. 1:6, 7; II Thess.

3:9; Heb. 7:26; 12:3-5; I Pet. 1:15, 16; I John 2:6; 3:3. To youth—I Tim. 4:12. Paul as an example as far as he imitated Christ—I Cor. 11:1; I Tim. 1:16.

Like prophets.—Jas. 5:10.

Elders.—I Pet. 5:3.

Examples of disobedience.—I Cor. 10:6, 11; Heb. 4:11; II Pet. 2:6; Jude 7.

Miscellaneous.—Example to Moses —Heb. 8:5. Many may not be public example—Mt. 1:19.

FAITH. *Pisteuo,* to believe. A union of assurance and conviction—Heb. 11:1. See Hab. 2:4; Mt. 6:25-34; Lu. 12:22-31; 18:8; Heb. 13:7.

Given by God.—Lu. 17:5, 6; Rom. 12:3; I Cor. 2:4, 5; 12:8, 9.

Comes by hearing the Word of God. —Acts 15:7; Rom. 10:13-17; I Cor. 1:21; Gal. 3:1, 2; I Thess. 2:13.

Distinction between Old Testament and New Testament faith. In Old Testament: In God.—II Chr. 20: 20; Ps. 3:3-6; 4:3, 8; 7:1, 10; 9:9, 10; 13:5; 23:1-6; 32:10; 33:18-22; 36:7-9; 40:3, 4; 55:22; 56:3, 4; 62: 8; 84:5, 12; 91:2; 115:9-18; 116: 10; 118:8, 9; 125:1; 143:8; Pr. 3: 5, 6, 24-26; 16:20; 29:25; Eccl. 11: 1; 12:2; Is. 26:3, 4; 41:10-14; 43: 1-5; 49:15; 50:10; 51:12, 13; Jer. 17:7, 8.

In the New Testament: Faith is usually in Christ.—John 1:12; 3:14-18, 36; 6:29, 40; 7:38; 8:12, 21-32; 9: 35-38; 10:25-28; 12:36, 46; 14:1; 20:31; Acts 2:36-41; 8:37 *marg.*; 10:43; 13:38, 39; 14:22; 15:11; 16:29-34; 18:8; 19:4, 5; 20:21; 26: 18; Rom. 1:16, 17; 3:21-26; 5:1, 2; 10:1-10; I Cor. 1:21-24; 3:10, 11; Gal. 2:20; 3:22; Eph. 1:12-14; 2:19-22; 3:11, 12; Phil. 1:27-29; 3:9-11; Col. 2:12; I Tim. 1:13, 14;

II Tim. 1:12; Philemon 5; I John 5: 1, 10, 13; Heb. 12:1, 2; Jas. 2:1.
In God.—Lu. 1:38-55; Acts 27:25; Heb. 6:1; I Pet. 1:21; 4:19; I John 3:21.
Facts produce feeling.—Mt. 23:37-38; 27:3-5, 54; Lu. 15:4-10, 16-20; John 11:8, 16, 32-33; 21:15-17; Acts 2:22-24, 37; 5:27-28; 7:51-54; II Cor. 5:14-15.
Testimony produces faith.—John 1:7; 3:11-12; Acts 2:40-42; 8:4-8; 10:39-43; 26:16-18; Rom. 10:13-17; I John 1:1-3; 5:8-10.
The assurance of faith.—John 1:12; 3:16; 5:24; 6:35, 47; 11:26; Rom. 8:1; Eph. 1:13; 2:6-8; Phil. 1:6; II Tim. 1:12; Heb. 6:12; I Pet. 1:8; I John 2:23-25; 5:5, 10.
Great faith.—Mt. 8:10, 13; 9:2, 22, 29; 15:28; Mk. 2:5; 5:34; 10:53; Lu. 5:20; 7:9, 50; 8:48; 17:19; 18:42; II Cor. 8:7.
Apostolic faith weak.—Mt. 6:26-34; 8:24-27; 14:23-33; 16:5-12, 21-23; 17:7; 19:23-29; Mk. 6:47-52; 8:14-21; Lu. 5:9-11; 12:22-34; 24:19-27; John 6:16-21; 14:7-13.
Faith an active principle.—Leads to utterance—II Cor. 4:13. Grows exceedingly—II Thess. 1:3. Obtains a fulness—Heb. 10:22. The work of God—John 6:9. Works through love—Gal. 5:6. Purifies the heart—Acts 15:9. Brings salvation—Acts 16:31. Assures life—John 3:14-16, 36; 5:24; 6:47; 11:25, 26; Rom. 1:17; Gal. 3:11; Heb. 10:38, 39. Enables us to stand—Rom. 11:20; I Cor. 16:13; II Cor. 1:24; Col. 1:23. Enables us to walk—II Cor. 5:7. To fight—II Cor. 4:7, 8; I Tim. 6:11-17. Helps to overcome—I John 2:14; 5:4. Is the means of justification—Rom. 3:25-28. Awards the sonship

to us—Gal. 3:26. Makes us heirs and joint heirs—Rom. 8:17. Gives us access to God—Rom. 5:2; Eph. 3:12. Secures peace with God—Rom. 5:1. Enables us to please God—Heb. 11:6. Leads to sanctification—John 17:17; Acts 26:18; Col. 1:23, 24.
Objects of faith.—God—Num. 20:12; Deut. 1:32; 9:23; II Ki. 17:14; I Chr. 5:20; II Chr. 20:20; Ps. 78:22, 32; 118:8, 9; Is. 26:3; 43:10, 12; Dan. 3:17, 18; 6:23; Mt. 6:25-34. The prophets—II Chr. 20:20; Lu. 24:44-45; Acts 26:27. The word of God—Deut. 32:1-3; Ps. 119:15, 16, 24, 35, 40, 97, 98, 99, 105, 111. The Gospel—Mt. 13:18-23; Mk. 4:14; 16:15-16; Lu. 8:11-15; John 8:31-32; 20:31; Rom. 1:16-17; II Thess. 2:12; II Tim. 3:15; Heb. 4:2; I Pet. 1:22-23.
The power of faith.—Mt. 21:21; Mk. 9:23; 11:23; Lu. 17:5, 6; John 14:12. Curing the blind—Mt. 9:27-30. Child possessed with evil spirit—Mk. 9:17-29.
Unity of faith.—John 17:17-21; I Cor. 1:10-13; 12:13-20; Eph. 2:19-21; 4:1-6, 15, 16, 25.
Faith as a grain of mustard seed.—Mt. 17:19, 20; Lu. 17:5, 6. Faith of Abraham—Rom. 4:18-22. In quenching fiery darts—Eph. 6:16. The prayer of faith—Jas. 5:15.
The aim of faith.—To grow in the knowledge of the truth—Ps. 119:97-105, 129-131; John 8:31-32; II Tim. 2:15; Heb. 6:4-6; I John 2:5, 14. To grow into the favor of God—Acts 2:46-47; Rom. 4:4-5; 5:2; I Cor. 15:10; Eph. 4:15; Heb. 4:16. To attain unto a perfect manhood—Eph. 2:20-22; 4:1-3, 11-13, 15-16. To be transformed into the image of Christ—Rom. 8:29; I Cor. 15:49; II Cor. 3:18; 4:3-6. To be

kept in constant security—Rom. 6:
12-14; 11:20; I Cor. 9:27; 15:1-
2; Phil. 4:7; II Thess. 3:3; II Tim.
4:7-8; I Pet. 1:3-5; I John 1:9. To
be joyful on earth—Rom. 5:2-5, 11;
15:13; Phil. 1:18-19; 2:17-18.

The obedience of faith.—Mt. 28:19-
20; Acts 6:7; Rom. 6:8-14; 8:1-11;
Phil. 2:1-16; 3:8-16. Not works of
law—Rom. 3:27-28; 4:1-8. The
work tells—Mt. 3:8; John 6:29; Rom.
6:16-18; 16:19; II Cor. 10:5-6; II
Thess. 1:8; I Tim. 1:5; Heb. 5:8-
9; Jas. 2:14-18, 26; 3:13; I Pet. 3:
1-2.

Works of faith.—Gal. 5:6; I Thess.
1:3; 2:13; II Thess. 1:11; Jas. 1:3.

Righteousness of faith.—Rom. 1:17;
3:21-30; 4:3, 11; 9:31-33; 10:4-
11; Gal. 2:16; Phil. 3:9; Heb. 11:7.

The testing of faith.—I Pet. 1:5-9, 21;
4:19; Abraham's offering—Gen. 22:
15-18. Caleb's courage—Num. 13:
30. Joshua's renunciation—Josh.
24:14-15. Job's patience—Job 19:
25-27. Daniel's refusal—Dan. 1:8.
Shadrach, etc.—Dan. 3:16-18.
Martha's trustfulness—John 11:21-
22. Jesus in Gethsemane—Mt. 26:
36-46; Mk. 14:32-42; Lu. 22:40-
46. Peter and John—Acts 4:19-20.
Stephen—Acts Ch. 7. Paul's afflictions—Rom. 8:28, 35-39; II Cor.
4:8-18; 6:3-10; 11:23-29; Phil. 1:
21; I Tim. 1:15-17. Trials in life—
Jas. 1:3; I Pet. 1:7.

The fruits of faith.—Remission of
sins—Lu. 24:47; John 20:22-23;
Acts 2:38-39; 3:19; 10:43. The in-
dwelling of Christ—Eph. 3:17-19.
The sealing of the spirit—Gal. 3:14.
The father's love—John 16:27;
Rom. 8:35-39. Heavenly mansions
—John 14:2. The crown of life—
Rev. 2:10. Eternal life—John 10:
28; I Tim. 4:10; I Pet. 1:9.

Failing faith is fatal.—Mt. 14:30-31;
Lu. 22:31-32; John 20:25-29; I Cor.
15:12-19; I Tim. 6:10-11; II Tim.
4:3-4; Heb. 3:14-19; I Pet. 5:8-9;
II Pet. 1:5-9.

What faith is proof of: Unworthiness
—Mt. 8:8; Lu. 15:18-19. Teach-
ableness—Mt. 13:23; Lu. 8:15; Jas.
1:21, 25. Adoption—John 1:12-
13; Rom. 8:14-16; Gal. 3:26-27.
Entrance into rest—Heb. 4:1-3.

Prayer without faith is vain.—Pr. 28:
9; Mt. 21:22; Acts 10:31-33; Eph.
6:16-18; Heb. 10:21, 22; 11:6; Jas.
1:5-7; 5:15-18.

The denial of faith.—Josh. 24:27; Pr.
30:8-9; Mt. 10:33; 26:34; Mk. 14:
30; 16:16; Lu. 12:9; I Cor. 15:12-
14; I Tim. 5:8; II Tim. 3:5; II Pet.
2:1; I John 2:22-23; Jude 3; Rev.
2:13; 3:8.

Whatsoever is not of faith is sin.—
Rom. 14:22, 23.

Unfeigned faith.—II Tim. 1:5.

**Through the spirit by faith wait for
the hope of righteousness.**—Gal.
5:5-7.

Breastplate of faith.—I Thess. 5:8.

Shield of faith.—Eph. 6:16.

Examples in the Old Testament.—
Abel—Heb. 11:4. Abraham—Gen.
12:1-7; 15:4-18; 22:1-10; 24:7,
40; John 8:56; Rom. 4:18-21; Heb.
11:8-19. Caleb—Num. 13:30; Josh.
14:6, 12. Daniel—Dan. 6:4-23.
David—I Sam. 17:45-49; 30:6; I
Chr. 27:23; Acts 2:25-31; Heb. 11:
32. Elijah—I Ki. 17:13-16; 18:21-
39. Enoch—Heb. 11:5. Gideon—
Ju. 6:14-18, 36-40; Heb. 11:32,
33, 39. Habakkuk—Hab. 2:4; 3:
17-19. Hagar—Gen. 16:13. Hezekiah—II Ki. 18:5, 19. Isaac—Heb.
11:20. Isaiah—II Ki. 19:6, 7; 20:8-
11. Jacob—Gen. 48:8-21; 49:1-
27; Heb. 11:21. Jahaziel—II Chr.

20:15-17. Jehoshaphat—II Chr. 20: 20. Job—Job 1:21, 22; 2:9, 10; 5: 6-27; 13:15, 16; 14:14, 15; 16:19; 19:25-27; 23:6. Jonah—Jonah 2:2; 3:1-4. Joseph—Gen. 50:20, 24; Heb. 11:22. Joshua—Num. 14:6-9; Josh. 1:11-15; 10:25. Manoah, Wife of; Mother of Samson—Ju. 13: 23. Micah—Mic. 7:7-9, 18-20. Moses —Ex. 14:13-31; 15:1-19; 17:15; Num. 16:28, 29; Deut. 1:20, 21, 29-31; 3:2, 22; 7:1-24; 8:2; 20:1; 31:8, 23; Heb. 11:24-29. *Lack of faith*—Ex. 3:11, 12; 4:10-16. Nehemiah—Neh. 4:20; 8:22. Ninevites —Jonah 3:5. Noah—Gen. 6:14-22; 7:1-24; Heb. 11:7. Rahab—Josh. 2:9-21; Heb. 11:31. Shadrach, Meshach and Abed-nego—Dan. 3:8-30. Widow of Zarephath with cruise of oil and a handful of meal—I Ki. 17:18-24.

In the New Testament: Anna the prophetess—Lu. 2:36-38. Antioch, People of—Acts 11:21-24. Barnabas—Acts 11:24. Blind men—Mt. 9: 27-31; 20:30-33; Mk. 10:46-52; Lu. 18:35-42; John 9:1-38. Canaanitish woman—Mt. 15:21-28. Colossians —Mk. 7:24-30; Col. 1:2-4. Cripple at Lystra—Acts 14:8-10. Crispus and Corinthians—Acts 18:8; I Cor. 1:14; 15:11. Disciples—John 2:11, 22; 16:30, 31; 17:7, 8, 20. Elisabeth—Lu. 1:25. Ephesians—Eph. 1:15. Ethiopian eunuch—Acts 8: 26-39. Eunice, Lois and Timothy—Acts 16:1; II Tim. 1:5. Father of epileptic boy—Mt. 17:14-19; Mk. 9:17-24; Lu. 9:38-42. Five thousand—Acts 4:4. Gentiles—Acts 11: 19-21; 13:48; 15:7. Jailer, Philippian—Acts 16:25-34. Jews at Jerusalem—John 2:23; 8:30; 11:45; 12:11. Jews at Rome—Acts 28:24.

John—John 20:8. Joppa, People of—Acts 9:42. Joseph, Husband of Mary—Mt. 1:18-25; 2:13, 14. Lepers, Ten—Lu. 17:11-19. Lydda and Sharon, People of—Acts 9:35. Lydia—Acts 16:14. Martha—John 11:27. Mary (Martha's sister)—Lu. 10:39, 42; John 11:32. Mary, Mother of Jesus—Lu. 1:38-55. Multitudes—Acts 5:14. Nathaniel—John 1:49. Nobleman—John 4:50-53. Paralytic, Friends of—Mk. 2:4, 5. Paul—Acts 9:29; 27:23-25; II Tim. 4:7. Peter—Mt. 16:15-20; Lu. 5:8; Acts 3:16. Philemon—Philemon 1, 5. Philip John 1:45, 46. Priests—Acts 6:7. Ruler—Mt. 9:18, 19, 23-25; Mk. 5:22-24, 35-42; Lu. 8:41, 42, 49-56. Samaritans—John 4: 39-42; Acts 8:12. Sergius Paulus—Acts 13:12. Sick of Gennesaret—Mt. 14:34-36; Mk. 6:54-56. Simeon —Lu. 2:23-25. Simon the sorcerer —Acts 8:13. Stephen—Acts 6:8. Thessalonians—I Thess. 1:6; 3:6-8; II Thess. 1:3, 4. Thomas—John 20:28. Three thousand at Pentecost —Acts 2:41. Timothy—I Tim. 6:12. Unclean spirit, Man with—Mk. 1: 24; Lu. 4:34. Woman with issue of blood—Mt. 9:20-22; Mk. 5:25-34; Lu. 8:43-48.

FATHER (*Heb.* Ab; *Chald.* abba. Ancestor, source. Ab, when a prefix to a name, signifies "father of").

As an ancestor.—Gen. 2:24; 9:18, 22; 10:21; 11:28, 29; 22:7, 21; 26: 3, 15, 18, 24; 31:3; 47:3, 9, 30; 48:15; 49:29; Ex. 8:13; 10:6; 13: 5; Deut. 1:8, 11; Josh. 24:6; Ju. 2:10; I Sam. 12:6, 8, 15; II Sam. 7:12; I Ki. 11:12; 13:22; II Ki. 8: 24; I Chr. 29:18; II Chr. 9:31; Ezra 7:27; Neh. 9:2, 9; Ps. 22:4; 49:19; 106:7; Jer. 7:7; 11:10; Ez. 18:2;

Zech. 1:4; 23:10; Mk. 11:10; Lu. 1:32, 73; 6:23, 26; John 7:22; Acts 7:2.

As chief or ruler.—Priest—Ju. 17:10; 18:19; Acts 22:1. Prophet—II Ki. 2:12; 6:21; 13:14. King—Josh. 15: 13; I Ki. 15:24. Apostle—I Cor. 4: 15. Syrian general—II Ki. 5:13.

Father of nations or tribes.—Gen. 17:4, 5; 19:37, 38; 36:9, 43; 45: 18; Num. 3:30; Josh. 17:1; I Chr. Chs. 2, 4; 9:19. (In Num. Ch. 17, *house* is used for *tribe*.)

Father, as related to household.—Gen. 12:1; 20:13; 24:7, 23, 38, 40; 28:21; 31:14; 38:11; 41:51; 46: 31; 50:8, 22; Lev. 22:13; Num. 2: 2; 18:1; Deut. 22:21; Josh. 2:12; Ju. 6:15; 9:5, 18; 11:2, 7; I Sam. 2:31; 9:20; 18:2; 22:1, 11, 16, 22; II Sam. 3:29; 14:9; I Ki. 18:18; I Chr. 7:2; II Chr. 21:13; Neh. 1:6; Is. 7: 17; 22:23, 24; Lu. 2:49; 16:27; Acts 7:20.

Father as source or inventor of.—Gen. 4:21; Job 17:14; 38:28; John 8:44; Rom. 4:11, 12; 9:5; I Cor. 4:15; II Cor. 1:3.

As an object of respect.—II Ki. 2:12; 5:13; 6:21; Jer. 2:27; Acts 7:2; 22:1.

In earliest times his jurisdiction was supreme.—Gen. 22:31, 32; 38: 24; 42:37.

In later times jurisdiction was distributed.—Court of judges determine —Ex. 21:22, 15, 17; Lev. 20:9; Deut. 21:18-21. Power to sacrifice children, still his—II Ki. 16:3; Jer. 7:31; 19:5; Ez. 16:20; 20:26. Done in violation of law—Lev. 18:21; 20: 1-5; Deut. 12:31; 18:10.

Children treated by fathers as slaves or chattels.—Arbitrary marriages —Gen. 38:6; Ju. 12:9; Ezra 9:2. Children pledged or sold—II Ki. 4: 1; Is. 50:1. Harlotry of daughters forbidden—Lev. 19:29. Bonds of daughters disallowed—Num. 30:5. Wives divorced at pleasure—Gen. 21:9-10.

Blessing of father.—Gen. 27:4-38; 48:9-22; 49:1-28.

Malediction of father.—Gen. 9:25-27; 27:27-40; 48:17-19; 49:1-28. (In which blessing and curse mingle.)

Qualities of a father: To command —Gen. 18:19; 49:33; Deut. 32:46. To provide—Ju. 1:14-15; Mt. 7:9-11; Lu. 11:11-13; 12:32; 15:12. To renounce—Gen. 22:2-3; Hos. 11:8; Lu. 15:11-12. To pity—Ps. 103:13. To grieve—Gen. 21:11-12; 37:34-35; 42:38; 44:29; II Sam. 18:33. To love—Gen. 25:28; 37:3; II Sam. 2:32. To protect—Job 29: 16; Ps. 27:10; 68:5; Deut. 32:6. To correct—Pr. 3:12; 23:13; 29: 17; Heb. 12:9.

Duties of children to fathers: To obey —Gen. 27:8, 13, 43; Deut. 21:18-21; Jer. 35:14; Eph. 6:1; Col. 3: 20. To honor—Ex. 20:12; Lev. 19: 3; Mt. 15:4; 19:19. To love—Gen. 45:9-11; 46:29; 47:12, 29-30. To gladden—Pr. 10:1; 17:21; Phil. 2: 22.

Influence of fathers upon posterity: Evil influence—Ex. 20:5; 34:7; Lev. 26:39; Num. 14:18; Deut. 5:9; 8: 3; I Ki. 15:12; II Ki. 17:14, 41; II Chr. 30:7, 8; Neh. 9:2, 16; Ps. 78:57; 106:6; Is. 14:21; 65:7; Jer. 2:5-9; 6:21; 7:26; 9:16; 13:14; 14: 20; 16:12; 19:4; 44:9; Lam. 5:7; Ez. 20:30-32; Dan. 9:16. Amos 2: 4; Zech. 1:4-6; Mal. 2:10; Mt. 23: 29-32; Lu. 11:47-48; Acts 7:51-53. Good influence—Gen. 15:15; 47:9; I Ki. 2:10; 15:11, 12, 23, 24; II Chr. 14:2-6; 32:32-33; Heb. 12:9.

Children not to suffer for sins of fathers.—Deut. 24:16; II Ki. 14:6; II Chr.

25:4; Jer. 31:29-30; Ez. Ch. 18.

Fatherless.—Abuse of—Ex. 22:22; Job 6:27; 22:9; 24:9; Ps. 94:6; 109:10-12; Is. 10:2; Jer. 7:6; 22: 3; Ez. 22:7; Zech. 7:10. To be cared for—Deut. 14:29; 16:11, 14; II Sam. 9:3; II Ki. 11:1-2; Job 31:17-18; Ps. 68:5; 146:9; Jer. 49:11; Jas. 1:27.

Father-in-law.—Gen. 38:13; Ex. 2: 18; 3:1; 18:1-27; Num. 10:29; Ju. 1:16; 4:11; 19:4, 7, 9; I Sam. 4: 19, 21.

New Testament references.—Whose son asks for a loaf—Mt. 7:9-11. To bury my father—Mt. 8:21; Lu. 9:59. He that loveth father more—Mt. 10:37. Father give me the portion —Lu. 15:12. Devil is father of lies —John 8:34. Father of all that believe—Rom. 4:11, 17. As a child serveth father—Phil. 2:22. Father of our flesh—Heb. 12:9. Your father tried me—Heb. 3:9.

GRIEF. Eccl. 1:18; 2:23; Lam. 3:32; Heb. 13:17; I Pet. 1:6; 2:19. Children cause—Gen. 26:35; Pr. 17: 25. David, Of—Ps. 6:7; 31:9. Day of—Is. 17:11. Jeremiah, Of—Jer. 10:19. Jesus, Of—Is. 53:3, 4, 10. Job—Job 2:13; 15:5, 6.

HOPE. What is it? A union of desire and expectation.—Rom. 8:25.
A reasonable act.—I Pet. 3:15.
One of the three graces.—I Cor. 13: 13.
A triumphant fact.—Rom. 8:38, 39.
Its basis.—Job 4:6; I Pet. 1:3; Acts 26:6-8.
Objects of.—Ps. 39:7; 130:6; 131:3; Jer. 17:7, 13; Lam. 3:24; Joel 3: 16; Rom. 15:13; I Pet. 1:21. The Christ—I Cor. 15:19; I Tim. 1:1. The promises—Acts 26:6, 7; Tit. 1:2. The word—Ps. 119:81; 130:5. Righteousness—Gal. 5:5. Gladness —Pr. 10:28.

HUSBAND: Laws concerning.—Ex. 21:22; Lev. 19:20; 21:3, 7; Num. 30:6-16; Deut. 22:22, 23; 24:5; 25: 11; 28:56; Ez. 44:25. Jealousy— Nu. 5:13, 19, 29-31. Marriage of captive women—Deut. 21:13. Bishops—I Tim. 3:2. Elders—Tit. 1:6. Divorce—Deut. 24:3, 4; Mt. 5:31, 32; 19:3-9; Mk. 10:12; Lu. 16:18; Rom. 7:2, 3.

Duties of.—Deut. 24:5; Pr. 5:18; I Cor. 7:2-4, 10, 16, 34, 39; Eph. 5:23-33; Col. 3:19; I Tim. 5:8; I Pet. 3:7.

Exhortation to.—Eccl. 9:9; Eph. 5: 23-33; Col. 3:19; I Tim. 5:8; I Pet. 3:7.

Making husbands contemptible.— Esth. 1:17.

Prophecy concerning.—Jer. 6:11.

Figurative.—Is. 54:5; Jer. 31:32; II Cor. 11:2; Gal. 4:27. Christ the husband of His people—Eph. 5:25-32; Rev. 19:7f.

Illustrative.—Jer. 3:1; Ez. 16:32, 45; Hos. 2:2, 7; Joel 1:8; Rev. 21:2.

Mention of.—Adam to Eve—Gen. 2: 18, 23, 24; 3:6, 16. Abraham to Sarai—Gen. 16:3. Isaac to Rebekah —Gen. 24:67. Jacob to Leah—Gen. 29:32, 34; 30:15, 18, 20. Manoah —Ju. 13:6, 9, 10. Samson to Philistine woman—Ju. 14:15. Elimelech to Naomi—Ruth 1:3, 5, 12. Of Ruth 1:9, 12; 2:11. Of Orpah—Ruth 1: 9, 12. Elkanah to Hannah—I Sam. 1:8, 22, 23; 2:19-21. Phinehas as —I Sam. 4:19, 21. Nabal to Abigail —I Sam. 25:19. Paltiel to Michal— II Sam. 3:15, 16. Uriah to Bathsheba —II Sam. 11:26. To woman of Tekoa—II Sam. 14:5, 7. To the Shunammite woman—II Ki. 4:9, 14, 22, 26. Sons of prophets were —II Ki. 4:1. Of a worthy woman—

303

Pr. 12:4; 31:11, 23, 28. To Samaritan—John 4:16-18. Zacharias to Elizabeth—Lu. 1:5, 13, 39, 40. Joseph to Mary—Mt. 1:16, 19. To Anna—Lu. 2:36. Ananias to Sapphira—Acts 5:9, 10. Aquila to Priscilla—Acts 18:24-28; I Cor. 16:19.

Husband head of the house.—Esth. 1:22; Eph. 5:23; Col. 3:18.

INSTRUCTION, or, **TEACHING,** and **TEACHERS: Importance.**—Valued as one's life—Pr. 4:13; 6:23. Die without—Job 4:21; 36:12; Pr. 5:23. Gives freedom—John 8:32. Better than gold—Pr. 8:10; I Cor. 14:6. Wisdom is knowledge of God and the way of life—Ps. 34:11-14; Pr. 1:7; 8:32-35; 23:15-18; John 7:17; 17:3; 20:31.

Who instruct?—God—Deut. 4:36; Job 35:11; 36:22; Ps. 71:17; 90:12; 94:10, 12. He taught Moses—Ex. 4:12, 15. Ordinances—Ps. 119:108. Statutes—Ps. 119:93, 102, 171. The good way—I Ki. 8:36; II Chr. 6:27; Ps. 25:8, 12; 27:11; 32:8; 86:11; Is. 2:3; 8:11; 48:17; Mic. 4:2. War—II Sam. 22:35; Ps. 18:34; 144:1. How to live—Tit. 2:12.

The Holy Spirit.—Neh. 9:20; Is. 44:3, 4; Joel 2:28, 29; Zech. 12:10; Mt. 10:19, 20; Lu. 12:12; John 14:26; 16:13; Acts 2:4, 11, 17, 18, 33, 36; 4:8; 6:10; 10:19, 20; I John 2:27.

Jesus called teacher.—Mt. 8:19; 9:11; 10:24, 25; 12:38; 17:24; 19:16; 22:16, 24, 36; 26:18; Mk. 4:38; 5:35; 9:17, 38; 10:17, 20, 35; 12:14, 19, 32; 13:1; 14:14; Lu. 3:12; 6:40; 7:40; 8:49; 9:38; 10:25; 11:45; 12:13; 18:18; 19:39; 20:21, 28, 39; 21:7; 22:11; John 1:38; 3:2; 8:4; 11:28; 13:13, 14; 20:16. He taught with authority—Mt. 7:29; Mk. 1:38, 39; Lu. 4:32. Sitting

down—Mt. 5:1; Lu. 5:3; John 4:6. Claims to teach God's words only—John 3:11-13; 5:19; 8:28. By apostles—Acts 4:2, 18; 5:21, 25, 28, 42; Eph. 4:20, 21; II John 9, 10. Still teaching—Acts 1:1.

Parents.—Abraham—Gen. 18:19. Jonadab—Jer. 35:6, 8, 18. The law—Ex. 12:26, 27; 13:8, 14, 15; Deut. 4:9, 10; 6:7, 20-25; 11:19; Pr. 1:8; 4:1-4, 11; 6:20; 13:1; 30:17; 31:1; Song of Sol. 8:2; Joel 1:3; II Tim. 3:14; Tit. 2:3.

Doctors called rabbis.—Mt. 23:7, 8; Lu. 2:46; 5:17; John 1:38, 49; 3:2, 26; 6:25.

Moses.—Ex. 18:20; 24:12; Deut. 4:1, 5, 14; 5:31.

Priests.—Lev. 10:11; Deut. 24:8; 33:10; II Chr. 35:3; Ezra 7:10, 25.

Princes.—II Chr. 17:7, 9.

Judges.—Deut. 17:10, 11; I Sam. 12:23.

Sages.—Job 4:3; Dan. 11:33.

Scribes.—Ezra 7:6, 10; Neh. 8:1-3; Mt. 7:29; 13:52; 23:22; Mk. 1:22; 9:11; 12:35.

Apostles.—Their commission.—Mt. 28:20. Their practice—Acts 2:42; 4:2; 5:21, 28, 42; 11:26; 15:35; 18:11; 20:20; I Cor. 4:17; Col. 1:28; 3:16.

Pharisees.—Jews—Mt. 16:6, 11, 12; 23:2, 3; Mk. 8:15-21; Lu. 12:1.

Christians.—Acts 15:1, 5.

Evangelists.—I Tim. 4:11; 6:2; II Tim. 4:2.

Figurative.—Beasts—Job 12:7. Old age—Job 32:7. Former age—Job 8:8. Thy right hand—Ps. 45:4. Heart—Pr. 16:23. Earth—Job 12:8. Idols cannot teach—Jer. 10:8; Hab. 2:19.

False teaching.—Prophets—I Ki. 13:11-18; 22:5, 6, 10-12, 19-23; Jer.

14:13-16; 23:31, 32; 28:8, 9, 21-
23; Zech. 10:2. Idolaters taught
abomination—Deut. 20:18. Teachers
—I Tim. 1:7; II Tim. 2:7, 8; 4:3, 4;
Tit. 1:9, 10. For money—Mic. 3:
11; Tit. 1:11. Judaizes—II Cor. 11:
13-15; Gal. 1:6-9.

What was taught.—Arts—Gen. 4:
21, 22; Ez. 17:17; Deut. 31:19, 22;
II Sam. 1:18; I Chr. 25:7, 8; Dan.
1:4. Jehovah is the one God and is
to be loved—Deut. 6:4-7; Ps. 25:4,
5, 9; 34:11. The law—Deut. 6:1;
31:9-13; Josh. 8:32-35; II Ki. 23:
2; Ezra 7:10; Neh. 8:1-3, 8, 9; Ps.
119:12, 26, 64, 68, 124, 135; I Tim.
1:7. Jesus Christ or the gospel—Acts
4:2; 5:20, 21, 28, 40-42; 14:21;
15:35; 18:11; 20:24; 28:23; I Cor.
4:17; I Tim. 1:10; 2:7; II Tim. 1:11;
Tit. 1:9; 2:7, 12; Heb. 5:12; 8:11;
I John 2:27; II John 9:10.

Who were taught?—All Israel—Ex.
4:12; Lev. 10:11; Deut. 17:11; 24:
8; 33:10; I Ki. 8:36; II Chr. 6:27;
Jer. 6:8; Ez. 44:23. Children—Ex.
12:26, 27; 13:8, 14; Deut. 4:10;
Rom. 2:20. All nations—Is. 2:3, 4;
42:4; 60:3; Mic. 4:2; Zech. 2:10,
11; Mt. 28:19, 20. Christians—Lu.
1:3, 4; Acts 2:42; 18:25, 26; I Cor.
14:26; Col. 1:28; 2:7; 3:16.

Methods of instruction.—Miracle. Parable. Precept—Neh. 9:14; Ps. 119:
4, 15, 27, 40, 45, 56, 63, 69, 78,
87, 93, 94, 100, 104, 110, 128,
134, 141, 159, 168, 173; Is. 28:
10, 13; 29:13; Jer. 35:18; Dan. 9:
5; Mk. 10:5; Heb. 9:19. Prophecy.
Proverbs—Ez. 12:22. Revelation—
Deut. 29:29; I Sam. 3:7, 19-21; Is.
22:14; Dan. 2:19, 22, 28, 29, 30,
47; Mt. 11:25, 27; 16:17; Lu. 10:
21, 22; I Cor. 2:10; 14:6, 26, 30;
II Cor. 12:1, 7; Gal. 1:12; 2:2; 3:
23; Eph. 1:17; 3:3, 5; I Pet. 1:12;
Rev. 1:1.

LOVE. Song of Sol. 8:6, 7; Lu. 7:42,
47; I Cor. 8:1; 13:1-13; 16:14; Eph.
5:2; Phil. 1:9; Col. 3:12-14; I Thess.
5:8; I Tim. 1:5.

Source is in God.—I John 4:16.

Love of God.—For men—Ex. 20:6;
Deut. 5:10; 7:9; 10:18; II Sam. 12:
24; Job 7:17; Ps. 91:14; 103:13,
14; Pr. 8:17; Mt. 5:43-45; 10:29-
31; 18:1-14; Lu. 6:35; 12:6, 7; John
14:21, 23; 16:27; 17:23, 26; II Cor.
9:7; 13:19; II Thess. 2:16; I Tim.
2:3, 4; II Pet. 3:9, 15; I John 3:1;
Jude 21.

He manifests His love for man—Ps.
31:19, 21; 90:1; Pr. 3:12; Is. 38:
17; 56:6, 7; Jer. 32:18; Mal. 3:16-
18; Mt. 5:45; I Cor. 2:9; Heb. 11:
16; 12:6.

By sending His Son—John 3:16; 14:
21, 23; 15:13; 17:26; Rom. 5:6-8;
8:31, 32, 38, 39; II Cor. 5:14-19;
Gal. 2:20; Eph. 1:3-14; 2:4-7; 3:1-
6; Col. 1:19, 20; Tit. 3:4-6; I John
4:7-19. For Israel—Ex. 6:7, 8; Deut.
4:37; 7:7, 8, 12, 13; 13:17; 23:5;
Is. 43:3, 4; 63:9; Zeph. 3:17; Mal.
1:1-5; Rom. 11:28, 29.

His love manifested—Ex. 6:7, 8; 19:
4; Lev. 25:42; 26:12; Deut. 28:9;
32:9-14; Is. 5:1-4; 49:14-23; 54:5-
17; Jer. 31:1-14; Hos. 11:4.

For Christ—Mt. 3:17; 12:18; 17:5;
Mk. 9:7; Lu. 9:35; John 3:35; 5:
20; 15:9; 17:23, 24, 26.

Love for God.—Deut. 7:9; 10:12; 11:
1, 22; 19:9; 30:6, 16, 20; Josh. 23:
11; Ju. 5:31; Ps. 5:11; 18:1; 31:
23; 37:4; 63:5, 6; 69:36; 73:25,
26; 97:10; Pr. 23:26; Lu. 11:42;
8:28; I Cor. 8:3; II Thess. 3:5; I
John 5:2-5.

With all the heart—Deut. 6:5; 11:13;
13:3; 30:6; Josh. 22:5; Mt. 22:37;
Mk. 12:30; Lu. 10:27.

Love of Christ.—Passeth knowledge —Eph. 3:17-19. Constraining—II Cor. 5:14. To the Father—John 14: 31. For the lost—Is. 40:11; Mt. 23: 37; Mk. 3:5; 10:21; Lu. 19:10. For His church—Eph. 5:2, 25, 29. For John the apostle—John 13:23; 19: 26; 20:2; 21:7, 20. For Peter—Lu. 22:31-32.

For His disciples—John 14:21; 15:9-15; Rom. 8:35-39; Gal. 2:20; II Thess. 2:13; I John 4:19; Rev. 1:5; 3:9, 10. For Lazarus, Mary, and Martha—John 11:5, 33-36.

Love for Christ.—Mt. 10:37-39; 26: 35; Mk. 16:10; Lu. 7:37-50; 23: 27, 55, 56; 24:1-10; John 8:42; 10: 17; 11:16; 13:37; 14:21-24; 19: 38-42; 20:1-18; 21:15-17; II Cor. 8:8, 9; Jas. 1:12; I Pet. 1:8.

For brethren.—Ps. 33:1-3; Mal. 2: 10; John 13:14, 15, 34, 35; 15:12, 13, 17; Acts 21:13; 28:15; Rom. 12:14-16; 13:8; 14:19, 21; 15:1-7; I Cor. 10:24; 16:22; Gal. 5:13-15; 6:1, 2, 10; Eph. 4:2, 32; Phil. 2:2; I Thess. 3:12; 4:9, 10, 18; Col. 2:2; Philemon 6; Heb. 13:1; I Pet. 1:22; 2:17; 3:8; 4:8; 3:10-19, 23; 4:7-11, 20, 21; 5:2.

For neighbors.—Ex. 20:17; Job 31: 16-22; 42:11; Pr. 17:9; Mt. 7:12.

As thyself—Lev. 19:18; Mt. 19:19; 22:39, 40; Mk. 12:31, 33; Lu. 10: 25-37; Rom. 13:8-10; Gal. 5:14, 15; Jas. 2:8.

For friends.—Ex. 32:31, 32; I Sam. 16:21; 18:1, 16; 20:16, 17; II Sam. 1:26; I Ki. 5:1; 18:4; Neh. 5:17-19; Pr. 17:17; 18:24; 27:10, 17; Lu. 7:2-10; John 11:11; 15:13-15.

Love for enemies.—Ex. 23:4, 5; Pr. 24:17; Mt. 5:43, 44, 46; Lu. 6:27, 32, 35; Acts 7:60; 26:29; Rom. 12: 20; I Cor. 13:5.

For sojourners.—Ex. 22:21; Lev. 19: 34; 25:35; Deut. 10:18, 19; II Ki. 6:21-23; Jer. 2:25.

Love for children.—Gen. 22:2; 30: 1; 44:20; II Sam. 1:23; 18:33; Ps. 127:3-5; Is. 2:17-18; Mk. 10:13-16; Lu. 18:15-17; Tit. 2:4.

Man's love for his fellow-man.—Ps. 133:1-3; Mt. 25:34-40; Mk. 9:41; Lu. 6:31-35; I Cor. 10:24; Gal. 6: 1, 2, 10; Eph. 4:2, 32; Phil. 2:2; I Thess. 5:8, 13, 14; Jas. 1:12.

Love of man and woman.—Gen. 24: 67; 29:18-20, 30, 32; 34:3, 12; Ju. 16:4; Ruth Chs. 2-4; I Sam. 1:5; II Sam. 13:1; I Ki. 11:1; II Chr. 11: 21; Esth. 2:17; Song of Sol. 1:4, 7; 2:4-8; 3:2; 4:1, 7-10; 5:1, 9, 16; Hos. 3:1; John 11:5, 36; Eph. 5: 25, 28-31; Col. 3:19; Tit. 2:4.

Love for God cannot exist with: Love of the world—I John 2:15; Jas. 4:4. Love of mammon—Mt. 6:24; Lu. 16:13. Love of self—Mt. 10: 39; 16:25-26; Mk. 8:35-36; Lu. 9: 24-25; John 12:25-26. Love of Satan—Ps. 97:10; Mt. 4:10; Lu. 4:8; John 12:31; 14:30. Sinful fear—II Tim. 1:7; I John 4:18. Hatred of a brother—Mt. 5:22; I John 3:10-16; 4:20-21. Love's antagonism with sin—Gen. 18:23-33; Ex. 20:5; Deut. 7:10-11; 10:17-18; Ps. 27: 5; 97:10; Is. 63:1-4; Hos. 3:1; Mt. 23:37-39; 26:48-50; 27:3-5; Lu. 15:11-32; John 13:21-27; I Cor. 4:21; Heb. 12:6; Rev. 2:2-6; 2:9-10; 2:13-16; 2:19-28; 3:1-5; 3:8-12; 3:15-21.

Love as an active principle.—John 14:15; Gal. 2:19-20; Heb. 13:1-2; Jude 21; I John 2:5; 3:17; 4:8; II John 6.

An evidence of the new life.—John 13:35; 14:23-24; Gal. 2:19-20; Col.

306

1:4-8; I Thess. 1:3; II Tim. 1:7; I John 3:14-17; 4:12-13.

Love is the fulfilling of the law.—Mt. 22:40; Mk. 12:23; Lu. 10:28; Rom. 13:10; I Cor. 13:1-7; I Tim. 1:5.

Love is the fruit of the Spirit.—Mt. 7:16-20; Rom. 5:3-5; 6:21-22; I Cor. 13:4-7; Gal. 5:22; Eph. 5:8-11; Col. 3:12-14.

True love is without hypocrisy.—Mt. 7:3-5; 22:16-22; Rom. 12:9; Eph. 6:24; I Pet. 1:22; II Pet. 2:15.

The measure of love.—Mk. 12:33; John 3:16; 13:34; 15:13; Rom. 8:35-39; I Cor. 2:2; II Tim. 4:8; I John 4:10-11.

Love constrains to unselfish service.—I Cor. 4:9-13; 9:16-23; II Cor. 4:8-12; 5:14; Gal. 4:15; Phil. 4:12-13; Heb. 10:24; I Pet. 3:10.

Love at its topmost height.—Mt. 26:6-13; John 13:34-35; 15:12; I Cor. 16:14; Gal. 2:20; 6:14; Phil. 2:12-18; II Tim. 4:6-8.

The characteristics of love.—Precious —Pr. 15:17. Unquenchable—Pr. 17:17; Song of Sol. 8:7. Covereth sins—Pr. 10:12; I Pet. 4:8. Strong as death—Song of Sol. 8:6. Worketh no ill—Rom. 13:10. Casteth out fear —I John 4:18.

Is without hypocrisy.—Rom. 12:9. Is tenderly affectionate—Rom. 12:10.

In honor prefers another.—Rom. 2:10. Accords with others—Phil. 2:2.

The Christian "in love," in twelve particulars: Before God in love— Eph. 1:4. Rooted and grounded in love—Eph. 3:17. Forbears one another in love—Eph. 4:2. Speaks the truth in love—Eph. 4:15. Edifies body in love—Eph. 4:16. Walks in love—Eph. 5:2. Knit together in love—Col. 2:2. Does all his acts in love—I Cor. 16:14. Is unfeigned in

love—II Cor. 6:6. Is truthful in love —I John 3:18. Keeps himself in love with God—Jude 21. Increases in love—I Thess. 3:12.

Forsaken love.—Mt. 26:14-16; John 5:42; 6:66-67; Gal. 3:1-3; II Tim. 4:10; Rev. 2:4; 3:1-2.

Loving chief seats.—Mt. 23:6; Lu. 11:43; 20:46.

Loving darkness rather than light. —John 3:19.

Love to stand praying.—Mt. 6:5.

MARRIAGE: Ordained of God.— Gen. 2:18, 24; Mt. 19:5, 6; Mk. 10:7, 8; I Cor. 6:16; 11:11, 12; Eph. 5:31; Heb. 13:4.

Expressed by.—Joining together—Mt. 19:6; Mk. 10:9. Making affinity— I Ki. 3:1; 7:8; 9:16; II Chr. 8:11. Taking to wife—Ex. 2:1; Ruth 4:13. Giving daughters to sons, and sons to daughters—Deut. 7:2; Ezra 9:12.

Commended.—Pr. 18:22; 31:10-12; Jer. 29:6; I Tim. 5:14, 15.

For this life only.—Mt. 22:30; Mk. 12:23; Lu. 20:27-36.

Marriage of near relatives.—Abraham and Sarai were half brother and sister—Gen. 20:12. The mother of Moses and Aaron was the aunt of her husband—Ex. 6:20. Of cousins —Gen. 24:50-67; 28:2; Num. 36:1-12.

Marriages contracted by parents.— Gen. 21:21; 24:1-67; 34:4-10; 38:6; Ex. 21:7; 22:17; Ju. 1:12; 14:2, 3; I Sam. 17:25; 18:17-27.

Father gave daughters in marriage. —Ex. 22:17; Deut. 7:3; Josh. 15:16, 17; Ju. 14:20; 15:1-6; I Sam. 18:17-21; 25:44. Eldest daughter usually given first—Gen. 29:26. A dowry given to woman's parents before marriage—Gen. 24:53; 29:18; 34:12; Deut. 22:29; I Sam. 18:25-28; Hos. 3:2.

Consent of parties necessary.—Gen. 24:57, 58; I Sam. 18:20, 21; 25: 40, 41.

Marriage contract made at gate of city.—Ruth 4:1-11.

Marriage laws of the Jews: Concerning near relatives.—Lev. 18:6-18, 24; 20:11-21; Deut. 22:30; 27:20-23; Mk. 6:17-19. **After seduction.**—Deut. 22:28, 29; Ex. 22:16.

Levirate marriage.—In case a man died without an heir—Brother or near kinsman to marry widow—Gen. 38:8-11; Deut. 25:5-10; Ruth 2:1, 10-13; 3:2-18; 4:1-13; Mt. 22:24-28; Mk. 12:19-23; Lu. 20:28-33.

Marriages were to be between members of the same tribe.—Ex. 2:1; Num. 36:6-12.

Marriages of priests.—Lev. 21:7, 13, 14; Ez. 44:22.

Marriages with Gentiles forbidden because of idolatry.—Gen. 24:3-6; 27:46; 28:1, 2, 6-9; 34:13, 14; Ex. 34:13-16; Deut. 7:3, 4; Num. 25:6-15; Josh. 23:12, 13; I Ki. 11: 2; 16:31; Ezra 9:11, 12; Neh. 10: 30; 13:23-30.

Marriages made with Gentiles.—Jer. 14:1-5; I Ki. 11:1; Neh. 13:23-30.

Marriage of captives.—Deut. 21:10-14.

Married man exempted from going to war for one year after marriage.—Deut. 20:7; 24:5.

Infidelity of those contracted in marriage same as if married.—Deut. 22:23, 24; Mt. 1:19. Tokens of virginity—Deut. 22:13-21.

Not to be married considered a calamity.—Ju. 11:37, 38; Ps. 78:63.

Weddings.—Celebrated with feasting—Gen. 29:22; Ju. 14:10-12; Esther 2:18; Jer. 16:8, 9; 33:11; John 2: 1-10. Feasting lasted seven days—Gen. 29:27; Ju. 14:12. Garments provided for guests at the wedding—Mt. 22:12. Christ attends the wedding feast in Cana—John 2:1-10.

The bride.—The bath and anointing—Ruth 3:3. Receives presents—Gen. 24:53. Given a handmaid—Gen. 24:59; 29:24, 29. Adorned—Ps. 45:13, 14; Is. 49:18; Jer. 2:32; Rev. 19:7, 8. *With jewels*—Is. 61: 10. Attended by bridesmaids—Ps. 45:9. Stood on right hand of bridegroom—Ps. 45:9. Receives benediction—Gen. 24:60; Ruth 4:11, 12. Must forget father's house and people—Ruth 1:8-17; Ps. 45:10.

Bridegroom.—Specially clothed—Is. 61:10. Attended by many friends—Ju. 14:11; John 3:29. Crowned with garlands—Song of Sol. 3:11; Is. 61:10. Rejoices over bride—Ps. 19:5; Is. 62:5. Returns with bride to his house at night—Mt. 25:1-6.

Paul's teaching concerning—Advises marriage.—I Tim. 5:14, 15. For the sake of chastity—I Cor. 7:1-6, 9. Lawful in all—I Cor. 7:8-40; 9: 5. Rebukes those who advise against marriage—I Tim. 4:3. Elders or bishops and deacons to be husbands of one wife—I Tim. 3:2, 12.

Should be only in the Lord.—I Cor. 7:39. Honorable in all.—Heb. 13:4.

Seems to think that to remain unmarried and virtuous is better, because of persecution of that time.—I Cor. 7:8, 17, 25-40.

Be not unequally yoked with unbelievers.—II Cor. 6:14, 17.

Marriage of widows.—Rom. 7:1-3; I Cor. 7:39, 40.

Monogamy taught in the Bible.—Wife singular number—Mt. 19:5. God gave Adam one wife—Gen. 2: 18-24. Each man had one wife in the ark—Gen. 7:13. Gen. 2:24; Mal. 2:15; Mt. 19:5, 7; Mk. 10:7, 8; I Cor. 11:11, 12; Eph. 5:31; I Tim. 3:2, 12.

Polygamy and concubinage practiced. Lamech the first polygamist— Gen. 4:19. Abraham—Gen. 12:5; 16:1-6: 25:1, 6. Jacob—Gen. 29: 25-30. Esau—Gen. 36:2, 3. Gideon the judge—Ju. 8:30, 31. Elkanah the father of Samuel—I Sam. 1: 2. Saul—II Sam. 3:7. David—I Sam. 27:3; II Sam. 5:13; I Chr. 14:3. Solomon—I Ki. 11:1-3; Song of Sol. 6:8. Rehoboam—II Chr. 11:21.

Marriage figurative.—Symbolizes: Idolatry—Mal. 2:11. God's union with the Jews—Is. 54:5; Jer. 3:14; Hos. 2:19, 20. Christ's union with the church—Mt. 22:1-14; 25:1-10; Rom. 7:4; Eph. 5:23, 24, 32; Rev. 19:7.

MOTHER. Must honor her—Ex. 20: 12; Deut. 5:16; Pr. 1:8; 23:22; Mt. 15:4; 19:19; Mk. 7:10; 10:19; Lu. 18:20; Eph. 6:2. Eve, the mother of all—Gen. 3:20. Love of mothers contrasted with God's—Is. 49:15. Sarah a mother of nations—Gen. 17: 16. Punishment for maltreatment of—Ex. 21:15, 17; Lev. 18:7; 20: 9; Pr. 30:11; 30:17. Foolish son heaviness of—Pr. 10:1. Despise not, when old—Pr. 23:22. He that loveth, more than Me—Mt. 10:37. Mother of Lord come to Me—Lu. 1:43. Mother of Jesus was there—John 2:1. Peter's wife's mother—Mt. 8: 14; Lu. 4:38. Who is my mother? —Mt. 12:48; Mk. 3:34. Mary, Mother of Jesus, steadfast—Acts 1: 14. Can a man enter second time, etc. —John 3:4. Entreat elderly women as mothers—I Tim. 5:2.

PARENTS: The father.—Father was the priest of the family group—Gen.

31:53; 32:9; I Sam. 20:6. As such, Reverence due him—Ex. 21:15, 17; Mt. 15:4-6; Mk. 7:10-13.

House.—Fathers constituted elders of Hebrew communities—Ex. 3:16, 18; 4:29; 12:21; 17:5; 18:12; 24: 1, 9. Ruled the household—Gen. 18:19; Pr. 3:12; 13:24; I Tim. 3: 4, 5, 12; Tit. 1:6; Heb. 12:7. Decided on marriages of children— Gen. 24:4; 28:2; Ju. 14:2. Sold daughters to bridegrooms—Ex. 21: 7; Neh. 5:5.

Wives and mothers.—Wives were bought and paid for; thus legally property of husband—Gen. 29:18- 30; 31:41; Ex. 20:17. Wife not a mere chattel. Wife largely the provider—Pr. 31:10-29. Superior to concubine in that her children were preferred—Gen. 17:18-21. Law sympathetic to wife—Ex. 21:2, 12; Deut. 21:14.

Mother.—To be childless a disgrace —Gen. 30:1; I Sam. 1:5-7; Is. 4:1. To possess children a great joy— Gen. Ch. 30. Mother to be honored —Ex. 20:12; 21:15; Lev. 19:3; Mt. 15:4; 19:19; Eph. 6:2. Beloved by children—Pr. 31:28. Comforts her children—Is. 66:13.

Parents: Responsibilities of.—To maintain children—Pr. 19:14; II Cor. 12: 14. To educate—Gen. 18:19; Ex. 12:26, 27; 13:8; Deut. 6:6, 7; Eph. 6:4. Sons depend on fathers after passing from mother's control—Pr. 1:8; 3:12; 4:1; 13:1.

Further duties of parents.—To love— Tit. 2:4. To train children up for God —Deut. 4:9; 11:19; Pr. 22:6; Is. 38:19; Eph. 6:4. To command obedience to God—Deut. 32:46; I Chr. 28:9. To teach them God's power —Ex. 10:2; Ps. 78:4. His judgments —Joel 1:3, 4. To pity them—Ps. 103:

13. To bless them—Gen. 48:15; Heb. 11:20. To provide for them—Job 42:15; II Cor. 12:14; I Tim. 5:8. To correct them—Pr. 13:24; 19:18; 23:13; 29:17; Heb. 12:7. Not to provoke them—Eph. 6:4; Col. 3: 21. Not to make unholy connections for them—Gen. 24:1-4; 28:1-2. To impress divine deeds and commands upon them—Deut. 4:9; 6:6; 11:19; 32:46; Ps. 44:2; 78:3-6.

REBELLION OF: Meaning of.—I Sam. 15:23. The heart seat of—Jer. 5:23; Mt. 15:18, 19; Heb. 3:12.

Of nations.—Ez. 2:3. In cities—Ezra 4:19.

Mentioned.—Against house of David —I Ki. 12:19; II Chr. 10:19. Moab against Israel—II Ki. 3:5, 7. Hezekiah against king of Assyria—II Ki. 18:7. Jehoiakim against Nebuchadrezzar—II Ki. 24:1. Zedekiah against Nebuchadrezzar—II Chr. 36: 13.

Of wicked.—Pr. 17:11. Against God —Num. 20:24; 27:14; Deut. 1:26; 9:7, 23, 24; 31:27; Neh. 9:17, 26; Job 34:37; Ps. 5:10; 107:11; Is. 1: 2; 30:9; 63:10; 65:2.

Not against God.—Ps. 105:28; Is. 50:5.

Law concerning rebellious sons.— Deut. 21:18-20. Warning against— Is. 30:1, 9; Ez. 17:12. Punishment for—Jer. 4:17; 28:16; 29:32.

REPROOF: Laws concerning.—Lev. 19:17; Pr. 9:8.

Examples of.—Abraham reproves Abimelech—Gen. 21:25. Rabshakeh reproves God—II Ki. 19:4; Is. 37: 4. God reproves kings—I Chr. 17: 21; Ps. 105:14. Reproved of God —Job 22:4; Ps. 50:8, 21; 141:5; Pr. 30:6. Herod's reproof—Lu. 3: 18. Backsliding a—Jer. 2:19. Snare a—Is. 29:21. Warning a—Hos. 4:4.

Reproof from mouth—Ps. 38:14. Wisdom's—Pr. 1:23, 25, 30; 5:12; 6:23; 19:25; 25:12. Of deceitful friends—Job 6:25, 26. Scoffer reproved—Pr. 15:12; 19:25. Reward of—Pr. 10:17; 12:1; 13:18; 15:5, 10, 32; 29:15. Fear of—John 3:20.

Scripture for.—II Tim. 3:16.

Prophecy concerning.—Ez. 3:26. In Teachings of Paul—Eph. 5:11, 13; II Tim. 4:2.

TRAIN, v. Child—Pr. 22:6. Men— Gen. 14:14; I Chr. 12:8. Young women—Tit. 2:4.

WIDOW. Under God's protection— Deut. 10:18; Ps. 68:5; 146:9; Pr. 15:25; Jer. 49:11. Laws relating to marriage—Deut. 25:5; Lev. 21:14; Ez. 44:22; Mk. 12:19.

Laws respecting: Not to be oppressed —Ex. 22:22; Deut. 27:19; Is. 1:17, 23; 10:2; Jer. 22:3; Zech. 7:10; Mal. 3:5. Creditors not to take raiment—Deut. 24:17. Bound to perform their vows—Num. 30:9. To be allowed to glean in fields—Deut. 24:19. To have a share of triennial tithe—Deut. 14:28-29; 26:12-13. To share in public rejoicings—Deut. 16:11-14.

When childless to be married to husband's nearest kin.—Deut. 25:8-10; Ruth 3:10-13; 4:4-5; Mt. 22: 24-26.

Widows to be cared for by church.— Acts 6:1; I Tim. 5:3-5, 9-16; Jas. 1:27.

WIFE: Laws concerning.—Ex. 20: 17; 21:3-5; 22:16; Lev. 18:8, 11, 14-16, 18, 20; 20:10, 11, 14, 21; 21:7, 13, 14; Num. 5:11-31; 30: 16; 36:8; Deut. 5:21; 13:6; 20:7; 21:11-14; 22:13, 30; 24:5. Divorce —Deut. 24:1, 3, 4; Mt. 5:31, 32; 19:3-10; Mk. 10:2-12; Lu. 16:18; I Cor. 7:32-40.

Proverbs concerning.—Pr. 12:4; 18:
22; 31:10.
Duties of.—Gen. 3:16; Rom. 7:2; I
Cor. 7:2-4, 10, 11, 13, 14, 16;
Eph. 5:22, 24, 33; Col. 3:18; Tit.
2:4, 5; I Pet. 3:1. Honoring hus-
bands—Esth. 1:20.
Illustrative.—Jer. 3:1, 20; Ez. 16:32;
Eph. 5:25-27, 29, 33; Rev. 19:7;
21:9.